W9-CSG-297

Debt Free:

The National Bankruptcy Kit

1st Edition

by Daniel Sitarz
Attorney-at-Law

Nova Publishing Company
Small Business and Legal Publications
Carbondale, Illinois

Editorial and research assistance by Janet Harris Sitarz and Malcolm Wilson.

Cover design by Christine Jacquot of Spectrum Graphics, Murphysboro, IL.

Manufactured in the United States.

ISBN 0-935755-187

Library of Congress Catalog Card Number 95-42082

Library of Congress Cataloging-in-Publication Data
    Sitarz, Dan, 1948-
    Debt Free: The National Bankruptcy Kit/ by Daniel Sitarz - 1st ed.
    256 p. cm. -- (Legal Self-Help Series)
    includes index;
    ISBN 0-935755-187 : $17.95
    1. Bankruptcy--United States--Popular Works. 2. Bankruptcy--United States--States.
    I. Title. II. Series.
    KF 1524.6S48   1995   346.73'078--dc20
    [347.30678]   95-42082 CIP

Nova Publishing Company is dedicated to providing up-to-date and accurate legal information to the public. All Nova publications are periodically revised to contain the latest available legal information.

1st Edition; 1st Printing: October, 1995

This publication is designed to provide accurate and authoritative information in regard to the subject matter covered. It is sold with the understanding that the publisher and author are not engaged in rendering legal, accounting, or other professional services. If legal advice or other expert assistance is required, the services of a competent professional person should be sought.

From a Declaration of Principles jointly adopted by a Committee of the American Bar Association and a Committee of Publishers

DISCLAIMER

Because of possible unanticipated changes in governing statutes and case law relating to the application of any information contained in this book, the author, publisher, and any and all persons or entities involved in any way in the preparation, publication, sale, or distribution of this book disclaim all responsibility for the effects or consequences of any document prepared or action taken in reliance upon information contained in this book. No representations, either express or implied, are made or given regarding the consequences of the use of any information contained in this book. Purchasers and persons intending to use this book for the preparation of any documents are advised to check specifically on the current applicable laws in any jurisdiction in which they intend the documents to be effective. This book is not printed, published, sold, circulated, or distributed with the intention that it be used to procure or aid in the procurement of any effect or consequence in any jurisdiction in which such procurement or aid may be restricted by statute.

Nova Publishing Company
Small Business and Legal Publications
1103 West College Street
Carbondale IL 62901
1(800)748-1175

Distributed to the trade by:
National Book Network
4720 Boston Way
Lanham MD 20706
1(800)462-6420

Table of Contents

CHAPTER 4: Filling Out the Official Bankruptcy Forms 35

Preface

This book is part of Nova Publishing Company's continuing Legal Self-Help series. The various legal guides in this series are prepared by licensed attorneys who feel that public access to the American legal system is long overdue. The books in this series are designed to provide concrete information to consumers to assist them in understanding and using the law with a minimum of outside assistance.

Law in American society is far more pervasive than ever before. There are legal consequences to virtually every public and most private actions in today's world. Leaving knowledge of the law within the hands of only the lawyers in such a society is not only foolish, but dangerous as well. A free society depends, in part, on an informed citizenry. With the proper information, the average person in today's world can easily understand and apply many areas of law. This book is designed to inform the public about the laws regarding personal bankruptcy.

However, in an area as complex as bankruptcy, it is not always prudent to attempt to handle every situation which arises without the aid of a competent professional. Although the information presented in this book will give readers a basic understanding of bankruptcy, it is not intended that this text entirely substitute for experienced professional assistance in all situations. Throughout this book there are references to those particular situations in which the aid of a professional is strongly recommended.

Regardless of whether or not an attorney or other professional is ultimately retained in certain situations, the information in this handbook will enable the reader to understand the framework of bankruptcy and effectively use this knowledge. To try and make that task as easy as possible, technical legal jargon has been eliminated whenever possible and plain English used instead. When it is necessary in this book to use a legal term which may be unfamiliar to most people, the word will be shown in *italics* and defined when first used. A glossary of bankruptcy legal terms most often encountered is included at the end of this book.

Chapter 1

Understanding Bankruptcy

The ability to file for bankruptcy and obtain a fresh start is an important and long-standing part of American law. Your right to file for bankruptcy is guaranteed under federal law and the U.S. Constitution. There are various chapters in the Federal Bankruptcy Code under which you may file for a bankruptcy. Each has certain requirements and each offers certain relief from creditors and debt. This book describes the process for filing for bankruptcy under Chapter 7 of the Federal Bankruptcy Code, which is commonly known as a *personal bankruptcy*. (Information regarding the other types of bankruptcy is included at the end of this chapter.) The culmination of a successful Chapter 7 bankruptcy is the elimination of most of your debts and the prevention of any efforts by creditors to collect on those debts.

An Overview of Chapter 7 Bankruptcy

Chapter 7 bankruptcy is designed for debtors in financial difficulty who do not have the ability to pay their existing debts. By obtaining a personal bankruptcy, individuals are able to restart their economic lives without the burden of their prior debts. There are several effects of filing for a Chapter 7 bankruptcy:

♦ Immediately upon filing for bankruptcy, an *automatic stay* goes into effect. This is a court order which prohibits creditors from harassing you or taking any further action to collect your debts while your bankruptcy is in court.

♦ A bankruptcy court trustee then takes possession of all of your property, except the property that you may claim as *exempt* under state or federal law. Exempt property is that property which the law allows you to keep, even after you are granted a bankruptcy. Much personal property and real estate is exempt from being seized in a bankruptcy. You may also be allowed to keep property that you have purchased which is subject to a security interest (*secured property*).

♦ The trustee then *liquidates* (sells) your non-exempt property and uses the proceeds to pay your creditors according to the priorities of the Bankruptcy Code.

♦ The final result of filing Chapter 7 bankruptcy is to obtain a *discharge* of your existing debts, that is, their total elimination. If, however, you are found to have committed certain kinds of improper conduct described in the Bankruptcy Code, your discharge may be denied by the court, and the purpose for which you filed the bankruptcy petition defeated. If your bankruptcy is granted, however, most of your debts will be wiped clean forever. If you receive a discharge of your debts through bankruptcy, you will not be allowed to file for bankruptcy again for a period of 6 years.

Non-Dischargeable Debts

Even if you receive a discharge in bankruptcy, there are some debts which are not discharged under the law. These are referred to as *non-dischargeable debts*. Therefore, even after a successful bankruptcy, you may still be responsible for the following non-dischargeable debts:

♦ Federal, state, and local income taxes which came due within the last 3 years;

♦ Student loans which became due within the last 7 years;

♦ Court-ordered alimony and child support payments. Also property settlements or other divorce-related debts if your spouse objects to their discharge;

♦ Criminal restitution and court-ordered fines;

♦ Debts for death or personal injury caused while driving while intoxicated from alcohol or drugs;

♦ Debts you incurred to pay off non-dischargeable tax debts;

♦ Debts that you failed to list on your bankruptcy filing papers;

♦ Debts based on fraud or dishonesty. This includes debts which you incurred for cash or luxuries within 60 days of filing for bankruptcy and debts incurred when you knew you couldn't pay.

♦ Certain condominium association fees and charges;

Understanding Chapter 7 Bankruptcy

Chapter 7 bankruptcy is referred also to as a *liquidation* bankruptcy. Chapter 7 requires you, the debtor, to pay the bankruptcy court a $130 filing fee plus a $30 administrative fee upon filing. The filing fee may be paid in installments if you are unable to pay it all upon filing. To file for a bankruptcy of this type, you fill out various official forms which detail your entire recent economic life. These forms will require you to inform the court of the following:

♦ The location and value of all of your real estate. All of your real estate will have to be surrendered to the court unless you claim it as exempt from bankruptcy under a federal or state exemption, or you agree in some manner to keep current on the payments.

♦ The location and value of all of your personal property. All of your personal property will have to be surrendered to the court unless you claim it as exempt from bankruptcy under a federal or state exemption; or you agree to pay the creditor what it is worth (if it was pledged as collateral for a debt); or you agree in some manner to keep current on the payments.

♦ The type of real estate and/or personal property you claim is exempt from being surrendered to the bankruptcy court. You will be allowed to keep all of the property which is exempt. In most states, you will, generally, be allowed to keep much of your property. Every state allows you to use their own state exemptions. In addition, some states also allow you to choose to use federal bankruptcy exemptions instead of the state exemptions. The details of all federal and state bankruptcy exemptions are listed in Appendix B.

♦ The nature of any debts for which you have pledged any type of property as collateral or on which a lien has been created. These are referred to as *secured debts*. Your liability for these debts may be eliminated by a bankruptcy (unless it is a type of debt which is non-dischargeable). However, you may have to surrender the collateral to the creditor.

♦ The nature of any debts which are specified by bankruptcy law as having priority in their repayment. These debts will be repaid first from any money or property which you will surrender to the bankruptcy court. These are referred to as *unsecured priority debts*. If there is insufficient money to pay off these debts, they will also be wiped out by bankruptcy, unless they are non-dischargeable.

♦ The nature of any debts for which you have not pledged any collateral and which are not priority debts. These are referred to as *unsecured non-priority debts*. If there is any money left after paying all other creditors, these debts will be paid off proportionately. Then, they too will be eliminated forever, unless they are considered non-dischargeable.

- The nature of any outstanding contracts or leases. These may also be voided unless the court feels that they can earn you income which can be used to pay off your creditors.

- The identity of any co-signers for any of your debts. If you are successful in obtaining a bankruptcy, your liability on a dischargeable debt will be eliminated. However, anyone who has co-signed or guaranteed a debt will still be held liable for payment on your debt.

- The amount and sources of your current income. Your ability to pay off your debts will be scrutinized by the court.

- The amount and type of expenses that you currently pay. Your spending on monthly expenses will also be carefully examined by the court.

- Any financial transactions within the last 2 years which may have an effect on your ability to pay your current creditors. The bankruptcy court has the ability to void certain transactions that you may have made which might hamper the ability of your creditors to collect on their debts. If you have transferred property to a family member to shelter it from surrender, or if you have paid off one debt to the detriment of other creditors, the court may demand the property or payment back. If you made any transactions with the intention of hiding assets or otherwise tricking creditors, your entire bankruptcy may be denied.

Upon filing the forms containing this information, an automatic stay or court order is put into effect which prevents most creditors from trying to collect on their debts. Then, a bankruptcy trustee, and perhaps your creditors, will meet with you to go over your documents. The trustee will then take possession of your non-exempt property. If necessary, the trustee will sell your non-exempt property and use the proceeds to pay off your creditors as much as possible. Finally, the bankruptcy judge discharges or wipes out all of your current dischargeable debts which have not been paid off.

Other Types of Bankruptcy

There are four chapters of the federal Bankruptcy Code under which you may file a bankruptcy petition. This book describes the Chapter 7 bankruptcy in detail. Each of the other types of bankruptcy is described, in general, as follows:

Chapter 13: This type of bankruptcy is referred to as Repayment of All or Part of the Debts of an Individual with Regular Income. Chapter 13 is designed for individuals with regular income who are temporarily unable to pay their debts, but would like to pay them in installments over a period of time. You are only eligible for Chapter 13 if your debts do not exceed certain dollar amounts set forth in the Bankruptcy Code. Under Chapter 13, you must file a plan with the court stating how you will repay your creditors all or part of the money that you owe them, using your future earnings.

Usually, the period allowed by the court to repay your debts is three years, but no more than five years. Your plan must be approved by the court before it can take effect.

Under Chapter 13, unlike under Chapter 7, you may keep all of your property, both exempt and non-exempt, as long as you continue to make payments under the plan. After completion of payments under your repayment plan, your debts are discharged, except for certain taxes, student loans, alimony and child support payments, criminal restitution, debts for death or personal injury caused while driving while intoxicated from alcohol or drugs, and long-term secured obligations. Chapter 13 bankruptcies are also available to small sole-proprietorship businesses and will allow the business to remain open while paying off burdensome debts over a period of up to 5 years.

A Chapter 13 bankruptcy has advantages over other types of bankruptcies in certain instances. If you are behind in payments on your house, you may file a Chapter 13 plan to keep your house and take 3-5 years to make up your delinquent payments. A Chapter 13 bankruptcy may be the best alternative if you have a large amount of secured debts (debts for which you have pledged some type of collateral). If you have a mortgage on your home, the mortgage debt is a secured debt. Under a Chapter 7 bankruptcy, you may lose your home. Under a Chapter 13 bankruptcy, however, you will be allowed to keep it. If this is your situation and you would like to keep your house, you should consult a competent attorney.

Chapter 11: This type of bankruptcy is referred to as a Reorganization. Chapter 11 is designed primarily for the reorganization of a business, but is also available to consumer debtors. Its provisions are quite complicated, and any decision by an individual to file a Chapter 11 petition should be reviewed with an attorney.

Chapter 12: This bankruptcy is a specialized type of bankruptcy only available to a Family Farmer. Chapter 12 is designed to permit family farmers to repay their debts over a period of time and is, in many ways, similar to Chapter 13. The eligibility requirements are restrictive, however, limiting its use to those whose income arises primarily from a family-owned farm.

As you begin to determine your need for bankruptcy, you should be aware that there are various other alternatives to bankruptcy. You can often personally negotiate with your creditors to obtain relief from your debts, either in terms of making smaller payments, lengthening the time for paying the debt back or actually lowering the amount of the debt. Most creditors will consider these options. You can also just sit tight and forgo payments on your debts until your situation improves. You should also review your entire financial situation and determine how you got in over your head in debt in the first place. This may reveal strategies which you can use to lower you overall debt, for example, by giving up a second car or spending less on entertainment. There are also specific circumstances when a Chapter 7 bankruptcy is not advisable.

When Chapter 7 Isn't the Answer

There are certain situations when a Chapter 7 bankruptcy may not be the best alternative. In those situations, you may need to contact an attorney or other financial professional for advice. A Chapter 7 bankruptcy may not be the answer:

* If you own your own house or have a lot of equity built up on a major investment (such as an expensive car). Under Chapter 7 you may lose your house or car. Negotiation with your creditor or a Chapter 13 bankruptcy may be a better alternative.

* If you have obtained a Chapter 7 bankruptcy within the past 6 years. You will not be allowed to file for bankruptcy again until the 6-year period has elapsed.

* If you filed a prior Chapter 7 bankruptcy petition within the previous 180 days and it was dismissed. Generally, you will not be allowed to file again until after 180 days.

* If you have a co-signer on a debt. A Chapter 7 bankruptcy for you will leave your co-signer or guarantor liable for the entire debt.

* If you're involved in a business partnership or business corporation. You should definitely consult with a lawyer before you file a Chapter 7 bankruptcy.

* If you have been dishonest with your creditors in any manner, including lying on loan applications, concealing assets, or attempting to transfer property to relatives.

* If you have run up large debts in the last few months with no obvious way to repay them. The bankruptcy court will not discharge these type of debts.

* If most of your debts are of the non-dischargeable type (for example, student loans or income taxes). Chapter 7 will offer little relief.

* If you wish to reaffirm a current debt. You may do so under Chapter 7, however, you should seek the assistance of an attorney.

* If you wish to redeem property from the bankruptcy trustee. You may do so under Chapter 7, however, you should seek the assistance of an attorney.

* If you wish to discharge a student loan debt. You may be able to do so under Chapter 7. However, you should seek the assistance of an attorney.

* If you wish to avoid a lien on your property. You may be able to do so under Chapter 7. However, you should seek the assistance of an attorney.

If your situation fits any of the descriptions above, you should consult an attorney. If you have decided that Chapter 7 bankruptcy may be the correct decision for you, the following chapter in this book will explain the entire Chapter 7 bankruptcy process in detail.

Chapter 2

The Chapter 7 Bankruptcy Process

Once you have considered the alternatives and decided that a Chapter 7 bankruptcy may be the answer to your financial problems, you will need an understanding of the entire bankruptcy process. A Chapter 7 bankruptcy can generally be obtained, from start to final discharge, in about 4 months. The process consists, generally, of completing numerous forms to file with the court which detail your financial situation, meeting with the bankruptcy trustee (and perhaps creditors), turning over your non-exempt property to the trustee, and the final elimination of your debts. Within this basic framework, there are various details which must be understood in order for you to emerge from your bankruptcy as financially intact as possible. Throughout the entire process of filing for bankruptcy, you must be entirely honest. All of your documents, your statements, and your dealings with the bankruptcy court will be under close scrutiny. The bankruptcy judges and trustees are extremely adept at detecting fraud or dishonesty. Your efforts to obtain a bankruptcy will be greatly diminished if you feel that you can trick the court or your creditors. Bankruptcy can provide a welcome relief from the burden of excessive debts. However, a bankruptcy court will not grant this relief to a person whom it feels has attempted to trick or defraud the court or creditors in any manner.

There are five basic steps in obtaining your bankruptcy using this book. Filling out a financial questionnaire; filling out the official bankruptcy forms using your questionnaire; filing the completed forms with the bankruptcy court; attending a short meeting with the court-appointed bankruptcy trustee (and perhaps some of your creditors); and obtaining the final discharge of all your debts from the bankruptcy court. These five steps are detailed on the following pages.

Filling Out Your Bankruptcy Questionnaire

The first step in obtaining your Chapter 7 bankruptcy will be to carefully complete the Bankruptcy Questionnaire contained in Chapter 3. On this form you will list all of the property which you own; both real estate and personal property. Every single piece of property which you own or possess must be listed, regardless of how trivial or special it may be to you. You will also list all of the various debts which you currently owe. Again, every debt which you owe must be listed. If you neglect to list a debt, that particular debt may not be wiped out by your bankruptcy. You must be scrupulously honest when filling out this questionnaire and the official bankruptcy forms. If you attempt to hide your assets in any way to prevent them from being lost to bankruptcy, or if you lie on any of the forms or to the court, the bankruptcy judge will most likely deny your bankruptcy. You may also be subject to penalties for fraud and/or perjury, which can be up to $500,000.00 and/or 5 years in prison. On the questionnaire, you will be asked to fill in considerable detail about both your property and your debts. Information regarding ownership, creditor's addresses, account numbers, and various other details will need to be listed. The gathering and recording of this information, however, will constitute the bulk of your efforts in obtaining a bankruptcy. Having the completed questionnaire will greatly assist you in your next step in the bankruptcy process.

Filling Out the Official Bankruptcy Forms

The second step in the process will be to prepare the official court forms for filing for bankruptcy. These consist of a 2-page Voluntary Petition, Schedules A-J, a few additional forms, and a mailing list of your creditor's names and addresses. You will use your Questionnaire to transfer all of the information regarding your assets and debts to the appropriate official bankruptcy schedules. The Voluntary Petition is the form which officially contains your request for bankruptcy. The bankruptcy schedules contain all of the details regarding your current assets, debts, income, and expenses. Schedules A and B contain the details of your real estate and personal property. Schedule C contains a listing of the property which you claim as exempt from bankruptcy by virtue of either state or federal bankruptcy exemption laws. See below under **Determining Your Exemptions** for details.

On Schedules D, E, and F, you will divide your debts into 3 general categories: *secured debts* (those for which you have pledged some type of collateral or against which a lien exists); *unsecured priority debts* (those which are, by law, to be paid off first if you have any money or assets to apply to pay your debts); and *unsecured non-priority debts* (essentially, all of your debts which are not secured or priority debts). For all of your debts, you must also determine if they fit into 4 other sub-categories: a *contingent debt* (a known debt with an uncertain value, such as a claim against you stemming from an auto accident, but which has yet to be resolved by a court); a *disputed debt* (a debt for which you dispute either the amount of the debt or the entire debt itself); a *liquidated debt* (a debt of yours for which a court judgement has been issued); or an *unliquidated debt* (a known undisputed debt which has not been the subject of a court action). The majority of your debts will normally be unliquidated debts.

On Schedule G, you will list any outstanding contracts or unexpired leases. Schedule H will list any co-debtors: either co-signers on a debt or guarantors of a debt. All of your current income will be listed on Schedule I and your current expenditures on Schedule J. You will also complete an official Statement of Financial Affairs on which you will answer various questions regarding your financial situation and most recent transactions. The final forms consist of a summary of all of your schedules; a statement of your intentions regarding your secured debts (if you have any); a mailing list and verification of its accuracy; and a cover sheet for all of your court papers. Sample forms and the details for completing all of these documents are contained in Chapter 4. When you have completed these forms, your work in obtaining a bankruptcy will almost be over.

Determining Your Exemptions

The preparation of Schedule C of your bankruptcy papers is the most important in terms of the property which you will get to keep at the end of your bankruptcy case. It is on this form which you will list all of your property which you claim is totally exempt from bankruptcy. Every state allows certain property to be excluded from being surrendered in bankruptcy. Many states also allow you to choose to use their list of exempt property or choose from the list of federal exemptions. In general, most state's exemption lists allow you to keep household goods; clothing; tools (up to certain limits); health aids (wheelchairs, crutches, etc.); public aid; unemployment; worker's compensation; pensions; and many insurance benefits. In addition, most states also allow you to exempt a certain value for a car and real estate. Most states also allow you to retain 75% of your wages. Some states are very liberal in their exemptions, allowing your residence to be retained regardless of value and other states are far more restrictive. In those states that allow a choice between federal or state exemptions, you will need to carefully determine which set of exemptions will be most beneficial to your in your particular circumstances. A detailed listing of state and federal exemptions is contained in Appendix B. As you fill out your Schedule C, you will need to consult your own state's listing and, possibly, the federal exemption list in Appendix B.

Filing Your Bankruptcy Papers

The filing of the Voluntary Petition is the act which officially begins your bankruptcy. If there is no emergency, you should file all of your completed official bankruptcy forms at the same time. However, if there is an emergency (such as a creditor about to foreclose on your property, or garnish your wages), you may file the Voluntary Petition first and the remaining documents within 15 days. The filing of your Voluntary Petition is your official request to the court for bankruptcy relief. It also creates the automatic stay.

The Automatic Stay

The automatic stay is an official court order which automatically goes into effect upon the filing of your Voluntary Petition. Its effect is to prohibit your creditors from taking any action against you while your bankruptcy is pending. The stay has several effects:

- Lawsuits against you are suspended (with a few exceptions, such as paternity or child support suits).

- Creditors can not repossess any of your property.

- Banks can not foreclose on your home while the stay is in effect.

- Landlords can not evict you.

- Utility companies can not disconnect your utilities. However, this relief only lasts 20 days, at which time a utility company can insist that you furnish a security deposit for future payment of your bills.

- Even the IRS can not collect on your past-due taxes.

- Creditors are blocked by the automatic stay from taking any action to collect or recover any debt. They may not call you; they may not contact your place of employment; and they may not harass or annoy you in any way.

There are a few exceptions to the blanket power of the automatic stay against creditors. Criminal prosecutions are not halted. The IRS can still audit you. Alimony and child support will likely be required to be paid, regardless of the stay. Creditors can also ask that the stay be lifted as to certain debts or property. They may do this, in particular, to protect their collateral on one of your debts. In addition, a Chapter 7 automatic stay does not prevent a creditor from continuing collection procedures against a co-debtor, unless the co-debtor is your spouse and you have filed a joint bankruptcy petition. The automatic stay is a powerful tool to help you as you struggle to get back on your financial feet. If necessary to prevent immediate creditor action, you may decide to file your Voluntary Petition first in order to take advantage of this weapon against creditors. You may then, yourself, send a copy of your filed Voluntary Petition to creditors in order to alert them of the issuance of the automatic stay. In an emergency situation, waiting for the bankruptcy court to sent notice of the automatic stay may take precious weeks.

The Creditors Meeting

About a month after you file your Voluntary Petition, you will be required to attend a short *creditors meeting*. Generally, no creditors will actually be present at this meeting, but they may attend if they seek to challenge some part of your claim to exemptions or dischargeability. Who will attend the meeting, however, is the *bankruptcy trustee*. This is a court-appointed person who will take charge of your property and will pay off your creditors with your assets to the best of his or her ability. All of your property and your right to receive property is together referred to as your *bankruptcy estate*. Upon filing for a personal bankruptcy, the bankruptcy court obtains total control over all of your property: your bankruptcy estate. Until your case is concluded, the court has full authority over your bankruptcy estate. While your bankruptcy case is pending, you must not sell, give away, or dispose of any property without notifying the bankruptcy trustee and obtaining permission.

Your creditors meeting will generally last less than one hour. At the creditors meeting, your bankruptcy trustee will carefully review your documents with you. They will look for any discrepancies, such as undervaluing property or claiming too many expenses. At this time, they will decide if there is any non-exempt property or cash which they feel can be used to pay off your creditors. If they decide that there is certain property that is not exempt and which could be sold to pay off your creditors, they will ask that you surrender it to them. The same goes for any cash or bank accounts. Generally, the trustee will not take any used property with little cash value, even if it isn't exempt. After the meeting, they will then use either the cash or proceeds from a sale of your non-exempt property to pay off your creditors according to a priority list set up by the Bankruptcy Code.

Your Final Discharge

Once the bankruptcy trustee has reviewed your case, collected any non-exempt property, and used the proceeds to pay your creditors, you will be granted a final discharge by the bankruptcy court. This will be the official elimination of the rest of your dischargeable debts. From that moment on, you will cease to have those debts. Your creditors can take no legal action to collect on those discharged debts. All of the exempt property which you were allowed to keep is yours, free and clear from any claims by your previous creditors. You are ready to begin anew.

Up until your final discharge, you may voluntarily ask the court to dismiss your bankruptcy. You may wish to do this if you feel that you have become able to pay off your debts, or if you have reached an agreement with your creditors. If you wish to have your bankruptcy dismissed, you are advised to seek legal assistance.

Instructions for Married Couples

If you are currently married, you must decide how you will file for your bankruptcy. You have several choices. One of you may file individually; both of you may file individually; or you may file jointly. There are several factors which may influence your decision on which way to file for your bankruptcy. In general, there are benefits to jointly filing for bankruptcy. By doing so, all of the dischargeable debts of both you and your spouse, both joint and individual, will be wiped out. If you both file individually, you will incur double filing and administrative fees. In addition, you will each have to complete a separate set of official bankruptcy forms. If you and your spouse have separated and have little or no jointly-owned property or debts, you may wish to file alone. If your spouse individually owns valuable property which could be taken by the court in a joint bankruptcy, you may also wish to file for bankruptcy as an individual. In most cases, however, in which there is little property to be surrendered to the court, you will be safe in filing your bankruptcy petition jointly. Note that the forms have numerous places to indicate if you are filing jointly. If you have any questions regarding the choice on how to file, please consult a competent attorney.

For those married couples who live in community property states (Arizona, California, Idaho, Louisiana, Nevada, New Mexico, Texas, Washington, and Wisconsin) some separate rules apply. If you both file jointly, your situation is similar to married couples in all other states. However, if one of you chooses to file for bankruptcy individually, the community property of the non-filing spouse may be taken by the court to pay off the bills and debts of the spouse who filed for bankruptcy. In addition, however, the community debts of both spouses (generally, those debts incurred during the marriage) will be totally discharged (providing that they are of the dischargeable type).

Checklist of Actions for Obtaining a Chapter 7 Bankruptcy

❑ Carefully read through this entire book.

❑ Gather all of your financial records, bills, deeds, titles, checkbooks, check-stubs, and other paperwork together in one place.

❑ Using your own financial documents, complete the Bankruptcy Question-naire in Chapter 3.

❑ Contact local bankruptcy court clerk for information on local court rules.

❑ Carefully make 2 photo-copies of all of the official bankruptcy forms in Appendix B.

❑ Using your completed Bankruptcy Questionnaire, fill in a first draft of the official bankruptcy forms using a pencil. You will need to refer to either your own state's or federal exemptions as listed in Appendix A in order to complete Schedule C. Use the instructions in Chapter 4.

❑ Once you have a completed draft version of each official bankruptcy form, fill in a final version of each form. You will need to either type or use good handwriting in ink. However, your Mailing List Matrix must be typed.

❑ Sign all official forms where indicated. If you are filing jointly, your spouse must also sign each form where indicated. (See Chapter 4 for instructions).

❑ Make required number of copies of the completed final version of each of the official bankruptcy forms. (See Chapter 5 for instructions).

❑ File the original and required number of copies of your complete set of official forms. Upon filing, you must either pay the required fees in full or fill an application to pay the filing fee in installments. Retain an additional copy for yourself. (See Chapter 5 for instructions).

❑ Attend a creditors meeting and meet with the bankruptcy trustee.

❑ Surrender any non-exempt property to the bankruptcy trustee, if required.

❑ Obtain a final discharge of all dischargeable debts from the bankruptcy court.

Checklist of Schedules, Statements, and Fees for a Chapter 7 Bankruptcy

❑ Filing Fee of $130.00 and Administrative Fee of $30. (If the fee is to paid in installments, the debtor must be an individual and must submit a signed application for court approval on Official Form 2.)

❑ Voluntary Petition (Official Form 1). Names and addresses of all creditors of the debtor MUST be submitted with the petition. This is not required, however, if debtor submits schedules of debts (D-F) with the petition.

❑ Schedules of Assets, Debts, and Exemptions (Schedules A-F). MUST be submitted with the petition or within 15 days.

❑ Schedule of Executory Contracts and Unexpired Leases (Schedule G) and Schedule of Co-Debtors (Schedule H). MUST be submitted with the petition or within 15 days.

❑ Schedule of Current Income and Expenditures (Schedules I and J). MUST be submitted with the petition or within 15 days.

❑ Schedule of Financial Affairs (Official Form 7). MUST be submitted with the petition or within 15 days.

❑ Individual Debtor's Statement of Intentions regarding Secured Property (Official Form 8). Required if the debtor is an individual and Schedule D contains consumer debts which are secured by property of the debtor. If so, this form MUST be submitted within 30 days of filing of the petition or by the date set for the creditors meeting, whichever is earlier.

❑ Statement disclosing compensation paid or to be paid a bankruptcy petition preparer. Only required if you are using a bankruptcy petition preparer. This form is not supplied with this book.

❑ Statement disclosing compensation paid or to be paid an attorney for the debtor. Only required if you are using an attorney. This form is not supplied with this book.

❑ Mailing List Matrix and Verification. Check with court for local rules.

Chapter 3

Gathering Information For Your Bankruptcy

Before you begin to actually prepare your bankruptcy papers, you must have a clear record of what your assets, debts, income, and expenses are. This information regarding your current financial situation will help you understand your overall position. This information will eventually be used on the various bankruptcy forms which you prepare for the court. It is helpful to gather all of the information regarding your personal financial situation together in one place. The following Questionnaire will assist you in that task and should provide you with all of the necessary information to make the actual preparation of your bankruptcy papers a relatively easy task. In addition, the actual process of filling out these questions will force you to think about your current financial situation. You must complete this questionnaire and the related bankruptcy papers with absolute honesty. Any attempts, however minor, to hide your property or trick creditors in any manner may result in the denial of your bankruptcy by the court.

To prepare this Questionnaire, you will need before you all of the paperwork which you have regarding your finances. It will be necessary to consult your bills, payment records, paycheck stubs, mortgages, loan applications, checkbooks, tax returns, and all other financial information in order to complete this Questionnaire. If you are filing jointly, include totals for both spouses. When you have finished completing this Questionnaire, have it before you as you fill in your official bankruptcy forms in Chapter 4. By referring to this Questionnaire, you should be able to quickly and easily fill in all of the necessary legal documents for your bankruptcy.

Bankruptcy Questionnaire
What Are Your Assets?

Real estate

Personal residence
Description _____
Location _____
Market Value: $ _____
How held and percent held? (Joint Tenants, Tenancy in Common, etc?)
_____ / _____ %
Value of your share .... $ _____
Amount of mortgage or other debt .... $ _____

Vacation home
Description _____
Location _____
Market Value: $ _____
How held and percent held? (Joint Tenants, Tenancy in Common, etc?)
_____ / _____ %
Value of your share... $ _____
Amount of mortgage or other debt .... $ _____

Vacant land
Description _____
Location _____
Market Value: $ _____
How held and percent held? (Joint Tenants, Tenancy in Common, etc?)
_____ / _____ %
Value of your share... $ _____
Amount of mortgage or other debt .... $ _____

Other property
Description _____
Location _____
Market Value: $ _____
How held and percent held? (Joint Tenants, Tenancy in Common, etc?)
_____ / _____ %
Value of your share... $ _____
Amount of mortgage or other debt .... $ _____

Total Real Estate_____ $ _____

Personal property

Cash and bank accounts

Cash .... $ _____

Checking Account... $ _____
Bank _____
Address _____
Account # _____
Name(s) on account _____

Savings Account... $ _____
Bank _____
Address _____
Account # _____
Name(s) on account _____

Certificate of Deposit .... $ _____
Held by _____
Address _____
Expiration date _____
Name(s) on account _____

Other Account.. $ _____
Bank _____
Address _____
Account # _____
Name(s) on account _____

Security deposits (held by utilities, landlords, etc.)

Security Deposit... $ _____
Held by _____
Address _____
Reason for deposit _____
Name(s) on account _____

Security Deposit... $ _____
Held by _____
Address _____
Reason for deposit _____
Name(s) on account _____

Miscellaneous household and personal property

Household furnishings .... $ _____
Description _____
Location _____

Audio or video equipment .... $ _____
Description _____
Location _____

Computer equipment .... $ _____
Description _____
Location _____

Books, pictures, or art work .... $ _____
Description _____
Location _____

Stamp, coin, or other collections .... $ _____
Description _____
Location _____

Clothing .... $ _____
Description _____
Location _____

Jewelry and furs .... $ _____
Description _____
Location _____

Firearms and sporting equipment .... $ _____
Description _____
Location _____

Camera and hobby equipment .... $ _____
Description _____
Location _____

Insurance and annuity contracts

Life Insurance (face value) .... Policy Amount $ _____
Company _____Policy # _____
Address _____
Cash Surrender Value .... $ _____

Annuity Contract (face value) .... Policy Amount $ _____
Company _____Policy # _____
Address _____
Cash Surrender Value .... $ _____

IRA, Keogh and or pension/profit-sharing plans

Company or administrator _____
Address _____
Plan type _____
Net Value .... $ _____

Company or administrator _____
Address _____
Plan type _____
Net Value .... $ _____

Stocks and mutual funds

Company _____
CUSIP or Certificate # _____
and Type of shares _____
Value .... $ _____

Company _____
CUSIP or Certificate # _____
and Type of shares _____
Value .... $ _____

Business interests

Sole Proprietorship
Name _____
Location _____
Type of business _____
Your net value .... $ _____

Interest in Partnership
Name _____
Location _____
Type of business _____
Gross value $_____
Your share held _____
Your net value .... $ _____

Corporation Interest
Name _____
Location _____
Type of business _____
Gross value $_____
Percentage shares held _____
Your net value .... $ _____

Joint Venture Interest
Name _____
Location _____
Type of business _____
Gross value $_____
Your share held _____
Your net value .... $ _____

Bonds and mutual bond funds

Company _____
CUSIP or Certificate # _____
and Type of shares _____
Value.. $ _____

Company _____
CUSIP or Certificate # _____
and Type of shares _____
Value.. $ _____

Accounts receivable

Accounts owed to you .... $ _____
Due from _____
Address _____

Accounts owed to you .... $ _____
Due from _____
Address _____

Alimony, support, or property settlements owed to you

Alimony .... $ _____
Due from _____
Address _____

Property settlement .... $ _____
Due from _____
Address _____

Other debts owed to you

Other debts owed to you .... $ _____
Due from _____
Address _____

Other debts owed to you .... $ _____
Due from _____
Address _____

Tax refunds due you

Federal Income Tax .... $ _____
Address of IRS office _____

State Income Tax .... $ _____
Name of state _____
Address of tax authority _____

Other Tax .... $ _____
Name tax authority _____
Address of tax authority _____

Miscellaneous property interests

Future interest, life estates .... $ _____
Description _____
Location _____

Interests in estates of decedents, etc. .... $ _____
Description _____
Location _____

Interests in another's life insurance policy .... $ _____
Description _____
Location _____

Other contingent or unliquidated claims .... $ _____
Description _____
Location _____

Royalties, patents, copyrights, etc... $ _____
Description _____
Location _____

Licenses, franchises, etc. .... $ _____
Description _____
Location _____

Auto, truck, or other vehicles .... $ _____
Description _____
Location _____

Boat, marine motor, etc. .... $ _____
Description _____
Location _____

Airplane and accessories .... $ _____
Description _____
Location _____

Office equipment, supplies, and furnishings .... $ _____
Description _____
Location _____

Machinery, business equipment, etc. .... $ _____
Description _____
Location _____

Business inventory .... $ _____
Description _____
Location _____

Animals .... $ _____
Description _____
Location _____

Crops (growing or harvested) .... $ _____
Description _____
Location _____

Farm equipment .... $ _____
Description _____
Location _____

Farm supplies and seed .... $ _____
Description _____
Location _____

Tools .... $ _____
Description _____
Location _____

Season tickets .... $ _____
Description _____
Location _____

Any other personal property not listed .... $ _____
Description _____
Location _____

Any other personal property not listed .... $ _____
Description _____
Location _____

Any other personal property not listed .... $ _____
Description _____
Location _____

Total personal property

(Insert totals from previous pages)

Cash and bank accounts Total .... $ _____
Security deposits Total .... $ _____
Miscellaneous household and personal property Total .... $ _____
Insurance and annuity Total .... $ _____
IRA, Keogh, pension Total.. $ _____
Stocks Total .... $ _____
Business interests Total.. $ _____
Bonds Total.. $ _____
Accounts receivable Total .... $ _____
Alimony Total.. $ _____
Other debts owed to you Total.. $ _____
Tax refunds Total .... $ _____
Miscellaneous property interests Total.. $ _____

TOTAL Personal Property .... $ _____

What Are Your Debts?

Mortgages you owe (home or business)

Payable to _____ Mortgage # _____

Address _____

Property location _____

Reason for debt _____

Place debt originated _____ Date incurred _____

Do you dispute debt? _____ Did you sign contract? _____

Any legal action on this debt? _____ Name of co-signer (if any)? _____

Term _____ Interest rate _____

Total amount now due.. $ _____

Payable to _____ Loan # _____

Address _____

Property location _____

Reason for debt _____

Has there been any legal action regarding this debt? _____

Place debt originated _____ Date incurred _____

Do you dispute debt? _____ Did you sign contract? _____

Any legal action on this debt? _____ Name of co-signer (if any)? _____

Term _____ Interest rate _____

Total amount now due.. $ _____

Loans you owe (finance company, bank, auto, or personal loans)

Payable to _____ Loan # _____

Address _____

Collateral _____ Reason for debt _____

Place debt originated _____ Date incurred _____

Do you dispute debt? _____ Did you sign loan contract? _____

Any legal action on this debt? _____ Name of co-signer (if any)? _____

Length of Term _____ Interest rate _____

Total amount now due.. $ _____

Payable to _____ Loan # _____

Address _____

Collateral _____ Reason for debt _____

Place debt originated _____ Date incurred _____

Do you dispute debt? _____ Did you sign loan contract? _____

Any legal action on this debt? _____ Name of co-signer (if any)? _____

Length of Term _____ Interest rate _____

Total amount now due.. $ _____

Accounts payable you owe (medical, dental, stores, etc.)

Payable to _____ Account # _____
Address _____
Reason for debt _____
Place debt originated _____ Date incurred _____
Do you dispute debt? _____ Did you sign contract? _____
Is account past due? _____ Interest rate _____
Total amount now due.. $ _____

Payable to _____ Account # _____
Address _____
Reason for debt _____
Place debt originated _____ Date incurred _____
Do you dispute debt? _____ Did you sign contract? _____
Is account past due? _____ Interest rate _____
Total amount now due.. $ _____

Rent you owe

Payable to _____
Address _____
Address of rental property _____ Date incurred _____
Do you dispute debt? _____ Did you sign lease? _____
Is rent past due? _____ Late charge _____
Total amount now due.. $ _____

Taxes due

Federal Income (name of Tax authority _____) .... $ _____
State Income (name of Tax authority _____) .... $ _____
Personal Property (name of Tax authority _____) .... $ _____
Real Estate (name of Tax authority _____) .... $ _____
Other (name of Tax authority _____) .... $ _____

Credit card accounts

Credit Card Company _____ Credit Card Account # _____
Address _____
Reason for debt _____
Place debt originated _____ Date incurred _____
Do you dispute debt? _____ Did you sign contract? _____
Amount Due.. $ _____

Credit Card Company _____ Credit Card Account # _____
Address _____
Reason for debt _____
Place debt originated _____ Date incurred _____
Do you dispute debt? _____ Did you sign contract? _____
Amount Due... $ _____

Miscellaneous debts

To Whom Due _____
Address _____
Collateral _____ Reason for debt _____
Place debt originated _____ Date incurred _____
Do you dispute debt? _____ Did you sign contract? _____
Any legal action on this debt? ____ Name of co-signer (if any)? _____
Term _____ Interest rate _____
Amount Due... $ _____

To Whom Due _____
Address _____
Collateral _____ Reason for debt _____
Place debt originated _____ Date incurred _____
Do you dispute debt? _____ Did you sign contract? _____
Any legal action on this debt? ____ Name of co-signer (if any)? _____
Term _____ Interest rate _____
Amount Due... $ _____

Total debts

(Insert totals from previous pages)

Total Mortgages you owe .... $ _____
Total Loans you owe .... $ _____
Total Accounts you owe .... $ _____
Total Rent you owe .... $ _____
Total Taxes you owe .... $ _____
Total Credit Card Accounts you owe .... $ _____
Total Miscellaneous Debts you owe .... $ _____

TOTAL Debts .... $ _____

What Is Your Monthly Income?

Occupation _____ How long employed? _____

Name of Employer _____

Address of Employer _____

Monthly Wage Income   You   Spouse

Gross wages, salary, and commissions: $ _____ $ _____

(pro rate if not paid monthly)

Estimated monthly overtime: $ _____ $ _____

Total Monthly Wages: $ _____ $ _____

Less Payroll Deductions: You   Spouse

    Taxes $ _____ $ _____

    Social Security: $ _____ $ _____

    Insurance: $ _____ $ _____

    Union dues: $ _____ $ _____

    Other (Specify: $ _____ $ _____

Subtotal Of Payroll Deductions $ _____ $ _____

Total Net Monthly Wage Income (take home pay):

(Total monthly wages minus payroll deductions):$ _____ $ _____

Non-Wage Income:

Income from business, profession, or farm: $ _____ $ _____

Income from real property: $ _____ $ _____

Interest and dividends: $ _____ $ _____

Alimony or child support payments: $ _____ $ _____

Social Security or other government assistance: $ _____ $ _____

Pension or retirement income: $ _____ $ _____

Other monthly income: $ _____ $ _____

Total Monthly Non-Wage Income: $ _____ $ _____

TOTAL MONTHLY INCOME:

Combined Wage and Non-Wage Income: $ _____ $ _____

Do you anticipate any change of more than 10% in any of the above categories within the next year? Explain. _____

What Are Your Monthly Expenses?

Rent or home mortgage payment (include lot rent for mobile home): $ _____

Are real estate taxes included? _____   Property insurance? _____

Utilities: Electricity and heating fuel .... $ _____

       Water and sewer .... $ _____

       Telephone .... $ _____

       Other .... $ _____

Home maintenance (repairs and upkeep) .... $ _____

Food .... $ _____

Clothing .... $ _____

Laundry and dry cleaning .... $ _____

Medical and dental expenses .... $ _____

Transportation (not including car payments) .... $ _____

Recreation, clubs and entertainment, newspapers, magazines, etc...... $ _____

Charitable contributions .... $ _____

Insurance (not deducted from wages or included in mortgage payments)

       Homeowner's or renter's .... $ _____

       Life .... $ _____

       Health .... $ _____

       Auto .... $ _____

       Other .... $ _____

Taxes (not deducted from wages or included in mortgage payments)

       Taxes .... $ _____

Installment payments:

       Auto .... $ _____

       Other .... $ _____

       Other .... $ _____

Alimony, maintenance, and support paid to others .... $ _____

Support of dependents not living at your home .... $ _____

Regular expenses from operation of business, profession, or farm ...... $ _____

Other .... $ _____

TOTAL MONTHLY EXPENSES .... $ _____

Chapter 4

Filling Out the Official Bankruptcy Forms

On the following pages you will find instructions for filling in each of the required forms for a Chapter 7 bankruptcy. The instructions for each form will explain who will need to use the form and, specifically, how to fill in the form. After each set of instructions, you will also find a sample filled-in form, showing information from a fictional bankruptcy proceeding. Before you begin, you should carefully read through this entire chapter to gain an understanding of the entire procedure of bankruptcy form completion and to determine which forms you will personally need to use. You should then make photocopies of the necessary forms from the blank originals included in Appendix A of this book. The photocopies must be on single-side white 8.5" X 11" paper. You should make two blank copies of each needed form: the first copy will be for your first draft, which you may fill in with pencil. The other copy of the blank forms will be used for your final copy, which should be completed by typing or with very neat handwriting in black ink. Please note that on page 63 are instructions for a *Supplemental Sheet to Schedules*. This particular form is to be used, if necessary, to add additional information to bankruptcy schedules. Bankruptcy Schedules B, D, E, and F already have pre-printed continuation sheets which you should use for additional information for those forms. As you prepare each of the necessary forms, you should have before you a copy of your completed Bankruptcy Questionnaire from Chapter 3. Virtually all of the information needed for filling in the official forms will be readily available to you by referring to your completed Questionnaire. Referring to a client questionnaire is, in fact, the same method that a bankruptcy attorney would use to fill in these forms. The difference, of course, is that they would be charging you over $100 per hour to fill in these forms.

Instructions for Voluntary Petition (Official Form 1)

This form is your official request for bankruptcy. By filing this form, you are voluntarily agreeing to give control over everything you own to the court. In turn, you will be allowed to keep all of your property which is exempt from bankruptcy and all of your debts which are dischargeable in bankruptcy will be wiped out. A sample form follows.

Court Name: Fill in the full name of the judicial district in which you will be filing your papers (such as "<u>Southern</u> District of <u>Illinois</u>).

In RE: Fill in your full name (last name first) that you regularly use to sign checks, etc.

Name of Joint Debtor: Fill in your spouse's name, if you are married and filing a joint petition with your spouse. Use the name he or she regularly uses (last name first).

All Other Names: Fill in any other names which you or your spouse have used (nick names, shortened, maiden, or initials-only names, etc.). If you have recently operated a business, fill in any business or fictitious name which you used.

Soc. Sec./Tax I.D. No.: Fill in you and your spouse's Social Security # and/or Federal Employer Tax ID #, if applicable.

Street Address of Debtor: Here fill-in the actual street address of your home. This may not be a post office box or other address where you merely receive mail.

Mailing Address of Debtor: Here is where you list your actual mailing address. This may be a post office box.

Location of Principal Assets of Business Debtor: This is only for those debtors who have operated a business. Normally, this address will be that of your business, but if not, specify where the majority of your business possessions are located. If you have not operated a business, enter **N/A**.

Venue: This indicates your residency. Put an **X** in the top box.

Type of Debtor: Place an **X** in front of either "Individual" or "Joint."

Nature of Debt: Most will place an **X** in front of "Non-Business/Consumer". However, if you have operated a business in the last few years and many of your debts are business-related, place an **X** in front of "Business."

Type of Business: Check the appropriate box which most clearly describes your type of business. If not listed, check "Other Business."

Briefly Describe Nature of Business: In plain language, describe what your business is.

Chapter or Section of Bankruptcy Code Under Which the Petition is Filed: Place an **X** before "Chapter 7." Skip the **Small Business** section; it is only for Chapter 11.

Filing Fee: Check the first box if you will attach the entire filing fee of $160. Check the second box if you will be requesting to pay the fee in installments. In a few states, low-income debtors may request a waiver of the entire filing fee. Check with the bankruptcy court clerk if you wish to pursue this option and don't check any box.

Name and Address of Law Firm or Attorney: Enter N/A.

Name of Attorney Designated to Represent Debtor: Enter N/A.

Debtor is not represented by an attorney: Check this box and list your phone number.

Statistical/Administrative Information: When you have a clear idea of the necessary amounts, check the appropriate boxes. Ignore the last two questions.

Form 1. Voluntary Petition

United States Bankruptcy Court Northern **District of** Illinois	VOLUNTARY PETITION
In RE (Name of debtor-if individual, enter Last, First, Middle) Smith, Mary Ellen	NAME OF JOINT DEBTOR (Spouse)(Last, First, Middle) Smith, John Alan
ALL OTHER NAMES used by the debtor in the last 6 years (Include married, maiden, and trade names) Ellen Smith Ellen Harris (maiden)	ALL OTHER NAMES used by the joint debtor in the last 6 years (Include married, maiden, and trade names) J.A. Smith
SOC. SEC/TAX I.D. NO. (If more than one, state all) 555-55-5555	SOC. SEC/TAX I.D. NO. (of joint debtor)(If more than one, state all) 444-44-4444

STREET ADDRESS OF DEBTOR (No. and street, city, state, and zip code) 16 Main Street Centerville IL 61111	COUNTY OF RESIDENCE OR PRINCIPAL PLACE OF BUSINESS Superior County	STREET ADDRESS OF JOINT DEBTOR (No. and street, city, state, and zip code) 16 Main Street Centerville IL 61111	COUNTY OF RESIDENCE OR PRINCIPAL PLACE OF BUSINESS Superior County

MAILING ADDRESS OF DEBTOR (If different from street address) P.O. Box 120 Centerville IL 61111	MAILING ADDRESS OF JOINT DEBTOR (If different from street address) P.O. Box 120 Centerville IL 61111
LOCATION OF PRINCIPAL ASSETS OF BUSINESS DEBTOR (If different from addresses listed above N/A	VENUE (Check one box) ☒ Debtor has been domiciled or has had a residence, principal place of business or principal assets in this District for 180 days immediately preceding the date of this petition or for a longer part of such 180 days than in any other District. ☐ There is a bankruptcy case concerning debtor's affiliate, general partner, or partnership pending in this District.

INFORMATION REGARDING DEBTOR (Check applicable boxes)

TYPE OF DEBTOR ☐ Individual ☒ Joint (Husband and Wife)) ☐ Partnership ☐ Other _____ ☐ Corporation publicly held ☐ Corporation not publicly held ☐ Municipality NATURE OF DEBT ☒ Non-business/Consumer ☐ Business–Complete A & B below A. TYPE OF BUSINESS (Check one box) ☐ Farming ☐ Transportation ☐ Commodity broker ☐ Professional ☐ Manufacturing ☐ Construction ☐ Retail/Wholesale ☐ Mining ☐ Real Estate ☐ Railroad ☐ Stockbroker ☐ Other business B. BRIEFLY DESCRIBE NATURE OF BUSINESS N/A	CHAPTER OR SECTION OF BANKRUPTCY CODE UNDER WHICH THE PETITION IS FILED (Check one box) ☒ Chapter 7 ☐ Chapter 11 ☐ Chapter 13 ☐ Chapter 9 ☐ Chapter 12 ☐ Sec. 304-Case ancillary to foreign proceeding SMALL BUSINESS (Chapter 11 only) ☐ Debtor is a small business as defined in 11 U.S.C. 101. ☐ Debtor is and elects to be considered a small business under 11 U.S.C. 101. FILING FEE (Check one box) ☒ Filing fee attached ☐ Filing fee to be paid in installments (Applicable to individuals only). Must attach signed application for the court's consideration certifying that the debtor is unable to pay the fee except in installments. Rule 1006(b)-Form 3. NAME AND ADDRESS OF LAW FIRM OR ATTORNEY N/A NAME(S) OF ATTORNEY DESIGNATED TO REPRESENT DEBTOR (Print or type names) N/A ☐ Debtor is not represented by an attorney. Telephone Number of debtor not represented by an attorney: (708) 555-5555

STATISTICAL/ADMINISTRATIVE INFORMATION (28 U.S.C. Section 604) (Estimates only–Check applicable boxes). ☐ Debtor estimate that funds will be available for distribution to unsecured creditors. ☒ Debtor estimates that after any exempt property is excluded and administrative expenses paid, there will be no funds available for distribution to unsecured creditors.	THIS SPACE FOR COURT USE ONLY

ESTIMATED NUMBER OF CREDITORS

1-15	16-49	50-99	100-199	200-999	1000 +
☒	☐	☐	☐	☐	☐

ESTIMATED ASSETS (In thousands of dollars)

-50	50-99	100-499	500-999	1000-9,999	10,000-99,999	100,000+
☐	☒	☐	☐	☐	☐	☐

ESTIMATED LIABILITIES (In thousands of dollars)

-50	50-99	100-499	500-999	1000-9,999	10,000-99,999	100,000+
☐	☒	☐	☐	☐	☐	☐

ESTIMATED NUMBER OF EMPLOYEES (Chapter 11 & 12 Only)

0	1-19	20-99	100-999	1000 +
☐	☐	☐	☐	☐

ESTIMATED NUMBER OF SECURITY HOLDERS (Chapter 11 & 12 Only)

0	1-19	20-99	100-999	1000 +
☐	☐	☐	☐	☐

Instructions for Voluntary Petition (Page 2)

Name of Debtor: Enter your full name. If you are filing jointly, also enter your spouse's full name.

Case No.: Leave this line blank. The court clerk will assign you a case number.

Filing of Plan: Enter N/A. This does not apply to Chapter 7 bankruptcy.

Prior Bankruptcy Case Filed Within Last Six Years: Enter N/A if you (or your spouse if you are both filing jointly) have not filed for bankruptcy in the last six years. If you have filed for bankruptcy within the last 6 years, you may not be allowed to refile. In that case, you should consult a reputable bankruptcy attorney.

Pending Bankruptcy Case Filed: Enter N/A if there are no other bankruptcy cases currently pending which involve your spouse, a partnership, or other business of which you are an owner. If there is a bankruptcy pending, consult an attorney.

Request for Relief: This is your official request to the court for your debts to be discharged.

Signatures: Enter N/A in the box for the attorney signature. Sign the top line in the "Individual/Joint Debtor(s)" box and enter the appropriate date. If you are filing jointly, your spouse should sign the "Signature of Joint Debtor" line and enter the date. Enter N/A on the lines in the "Corporate or Partnership Debtor" box.

To Be Completed by Individual Chapter 7 Debtor: Again, you must sign the top line and enter the appropriate date. If you are filing jointly, your spouse should sign the "Signature of Joint Debtor" line and enter the date.

Exhibit B: Enter N/A.

Certification and Signature of Non-Attorney Bankruptcy Petition Preparer: Enter N/A unless you are using the services of a paid bankruptcy form preparer.

On the following pages are the forms and instructions for filling in the bankruptcy schedules and official forms. The schedules are the forms on which you will enter the information regarding what you own (your *assets*), what you owe (your *debts*) and to whom you owe it, what you make (your *income*), and what you spend (your *expenditures*). As you complete these forms, keep these guidelines in mind:

Be absolutely honest in filling out these forms. Do not, in any way, attempt to hide property from the court. You must list every single piece of property that you own and every source of income that you have. If the court discovers any evidence of deceit, your case will most likely be dismissed and you will not be allowed to attempt to refile for bankruptcy for at least 6 months. You may also be subject to fines or imprisonment.

Be extremely thorough. As you list your debts, assets, income, and expenditures, be certain that you have listed every possible item. It is very easy to overlook many common items or debts. Read the instructions and forms very carefully for clues on what you should include. The only debts that the bankruptcy court will eliminate are those which you list. If the debt is not listed by you on the appropriate schedule, you may go through bankruptcy and still owe the debt. Equally important is the careful listing of the exact address of each person you owe. Creditors must be given notice that you are filing for bankruptcy or your debt to them will not be discharged. Recall that you need to include all transactions for a full year prior to your filing for bankruptcy.

Name of Debtor <u>Mary Ellen and John Alan Smith</u>

Case No. <u>(Will be supplied by court clerk)</u>
(Court Use Only)

FILING OF PLAN

For Chapter 9, 11, 12, and 13 use only. Check appropriate box.

☐ A copy of debtor's proposed plan dated _____ is attached   ☐ Debtor intends to file a plan within the time allowed by statute, rule, or court order.

PRIOR BANKRUPTCY CASE FILED WITHIN LAST 6 YEARS (If more than one, attach additional sheet)

Location where filed	Case Number	Date filed
N/A		

PENDING BANKRUPTCY CASE FILED BY ANY SPOUSE, PARTNER, OR AFFILIATE OF THIS DEBTOR (If more than one, attach additional sheet)

Location where filed	Case Number	Date
N/A		
Relationship N/A	District	Judge

REQUEST FOR RELIEF

Debtor requests relief in accordance with the chapter of Title 11, United States Code, specified in this petition.

SIGNATURES

Attorney

X N/A

Signature   Date

INDIVIDUAL/JOINT DEBTOR(S) I declare under penalty of perjury that the information provided in this petition is true and correct.	**CORPORATE OR PARTNERSHIP DEBTOR** I declare under penalty of perjury that the information provided in this petition is true and correct and that the filing of this petition on behalf of the debtor has been authorized.
X *Mary Ellen Smith*	X N/A
Signature of Debtor November 1, 1995	Signature of Authorized Individual
Date	Print or type name of Authorized Individual
X *John Alan Smith*	
Signature of Joint Debtor November 1, 1995	Title of Individual Authorized by Debtor to file this Petition
Date	Date If debtor is a corporation filing under Chapter 11, Exhibit "A" is attached and made part of this petition

---

TO BE COMPLETED BY INDIVIDUAL CHAPTER 7 DEBTOR WITH PRIMARILY CONSUMER DEBTS (SEE P.L. 96-353, SECTION 322) I am aware that I may proceed under Chapter 7, 11, 12, or 13 of title 11, United States Code, understand the relief available under each chapter, and choose to proceed under Chapter 7 of such title. If I am represented by an attorney, Exhibit "B" has been completed.	**CERTIFICATION AND SIGNATURE OF NON-ATTORNEY BANKRUPTCY PETITION PREPARER** I certify that I am a bankruptcy petition preparer as defined in 11 U.S.C. Section 110, that I prepared this document for compensation, and that I have provided the debtor with a copy of this document.
X *Mary Ellen Smith* November 1, 1995	N/A
Signature of Debtor Date	Printed or Typed Name of Bankruptcy Petition Preparer
	Social Security Number
X *John Alan Smith* November 1, 1995	
Signature of Joint Debtor Date	Address Telephone
EXHIBIT "B" (To be completed by attorney for individual Chapter 7 debtor(s) with primarily consumer debts.) I, the attorney for the debtor(s) named in the foregoing petition, declare that I have informed the debtor(s) that (he, she, or they) may proceed under Chapter 7, 11, 12, or 13 of Title 11, United States Code, and chapter.	Names and Social Security numbers of all other individuals who prepared or assisted in preparing this document. If more than one person prepared this document, attach additional signed sheets conforming to the appropriate Official Form for each person. have explained the relief available under each such
	Signature of Bankruptcy Petition Preparer
X N/A	A bankruptcy petition preparer's failure to comply with the provisions of title 11 and the Federal Rules of Bankruptcy Procedure may result in fines and imprisonment or both. 11 U.S.C. Sec. 110; 18 U.S.C. Sec. 156.
Signature of Attorney Date	

Instructions for Schedule A: Real Property

All of the real estate which you own or have an interest in will be listed on Schedule A. However, don't include leases: these will go on Schedule G. Note that if you own a home, you may lose it in a Chapter 7 Bankruptcy. You may be better off using a Chapter 13 Bankruptcy and should consult an attorney for advice in this situation.

In re: Enter your full name. If you're filing jointly, include your spouse's name.

Case No.: Leave this blank. The court clerk will assign you a case number.

Description and Location of Property: Here enter a brief description of the property and its street address. You should enter all homes, land, condos, business property, and buildings in which you have any ownership interest. Your description can simply be "home" or "lot" or some other simple description and the address or location. If you do not own any real estate, enter **None**.

Nature of Debtor's Interest in Property: Check the ownership language on your deed or mortgage, but in most cases property is held as "fee simple". Enter the term "**fee simple**", unless you are certain that your property is held in some other form.

Husband, Wife, Joint or Community : If single, enter **N/A**. If married, enter **H, W, J** or **C**, depending if the property is owned individually by the husband or wife, is owned jointly by both (as joint tenants or tenants-by-the-entireties), or is owned as community property in a community property state. Check the ownership language on the deed or other document of ownership. In community property states (Arizona, California, Idaho, Louisiana, Nevada, New Mexico, Texas, Washington, and Wisconsin) property which was acquired during a marriage is generally considered community property. In all other states, the ownership of property depends on the names on the title document or deed.

Current Market Value of Debtor's Interest in Property Without Deducting any Secured Claim or Exemption: Here you should enter the full value at which the property could be sold today. Do not deduct any money which you may owe on the property, like a mortgage. You may need to obtain market value estimate from a real estate broker. However, you may determine the value yourself by checking the value of other similar property for sale in your locale. If you own the property jointly with someone who is not filing for bankruptcy with you, you should indicate your percentage of ownership and only note the market value of your share of the property (for example: your 33.33% ownership of home owned jointly with your parents with a full market value of $60,000.00 would constitute a market value of $20,000.00 for your interest in the property).

Amount of Secured Claim: A *secured claim* is any mortgage, deed of trust, loan, lien, or other claim against the property which is in writing and for which the property acts as collateral. Enter the amount which is left to be paid on the mortgage or other obligation. You can get the current amount from the financial institution to which the money is owed. If there are no secured claims, enter **None**.

Total: Total the amounts in the "Current Market Value" column and enter here and also on the *Summary of Schedules* form (which follows later in this Chapter).

In re <u>Mary Ellen and John Alan Smith</u>   Case No. <u>(Will be supplied by clerk)</u>

       Debtor   (If known)

SCHEDULE A-REAL PROPERTY

Except as directed below, list all real property in which the debtor has any legal, equitable, or future interest, including all **property** owned as a co-tenant, community property, or in which the debtor has a life estate. Include any property in which the debtor holds rights and **powers** exercisable for the debtor's own benefit. If the debtor is married, state whether husband, wife, or both own the property by placing an "H," "W," or "C" in the column labeled "Husband, Wife, Joint, or Community." If the debtor holds no interest in real property, write "None" under "Description and Location of Property."

Do not include interests in executory contracts and unexpired leases on this schedule. List them in Schedule G-Executory Contracts and Unexpired Leases.

If an entity claims to have a lien or hold a secured interest in any property, state the amount of the secured claim. See Schedule D. If no entity claims to hold a secured interest in the property, write "None" in the column labeled "Amount of Secured Claim."

If the debtor is an individual or if a joint petition is filed, state the amount of any exception claimed in the property only in Schedule C-Property Claimed as Exempt.

DESCRIPTION AND LOCATION OF PROPERTY	NATURE OF DEBTOR'S INTEREST IN PROPERTY	HUSBAND, WIFE, JOINT OR COMMUNITY	CURRENT MARKET VALUE OF DEBTOR'S INTEREST IN PROPERTY WITHOUT DEDUCTING ANY SECURED CLAIM OR EXEMPTION	AMOUNT OF SECURED CLAIM
Personal home located at 16 Main Street Centerville IL 61111	Fee Simple	J	48,000	37,000
		Total	$ 48,000	

(Report also on Summary of Schedules.)

Instructions for Schedule B: Personal Property

On this form, you will list every other property which you own or have any claim of ownership in. Personal property includes all other property except real estate. This form includes extensive lists for many specific types of property. If your specific property is not listed, line #33 should be used for "other" property.

In re: Enter your full name. If you're filing jointly, include your spouse's name.

Case No.: Leave this blank. The court clerk will assign you a case number.

None: If you do not own any of the type of property for that number, enter an **X**.

Description and Location of Property: Here enter a brief description of the property and the street address of its location. You should separately enter each piece of individual property worth more than $25.00 in which you have any ownership interest at all. List wages which are owed to you under #17 (unliquidated debts). Your property should be listed under the appropriate number for that specific type of property (for example: enter an auto under line #23.) Include a clear description of the property. For cash and bank accounts, list the source of the money (for example: from wages). At the top of this box, you may note that all of your property is located at a single address unless noted otherwise.

Husband, Wife, Joint or Community : If you are single, enter **N/A**. If you are married, enter **H**, **W**, **J** or **C**, depending if the property is owned individually by the husband or wife, is owned jointly by both (as joint tenants or tenants-by-the-entireties), or is owned as community property in a community property state. Check the ownership language on the title or other document of ownership. In community property states (Arizona, California, Idaho, Louisiana, Nevada, New Mexico, Texas, Washington, and Wisconsin) property which was acquired during a marriage is considered community property. In all other states, the ownership of property depends on the names on the title document and if no title, then is generally jointly owned if it was acquired while you were married. In most states, property which was individually owned prior to a marriage is still considered individually-owned during the marriage.

Current Market Value of Debtor's Interest in Property Without Deducting any Secured Claim or Exemption: Here you should enter the full value at which the property could be sold today. Do not deduct any money which you may owe on the property, like a loan. For life insurance, enter the cash surrender value only, not the amount of the policy. For other property, you may need to obtain market value estimates from a used car Blue Book at the library or by checking the value of other similar property for sale in your area. For very valuable property, you may need to consult an appraiser. If you own the property jointly with someone who is not filing for bankruptcy with you, you should indicate your percentage of ownership and only note the market value of your share of the property.

Total: On the last page, total the amounts in the "Current Market Value" column on each page and enter here. Also enter this amount on the *Summary of Schedules* form (which follows later in this Chapter).

In re Mary Ellen and John Alan Smith   Case No. (will be supplied by clerk)
_____   _____
          Debtor   (If known)

SCHEDULE B-PERSONAL PROPERTY

Except as directed below, list all personal property of the debtor of whatever kind. If the debtor has no property in one or more of the categories, place an "X" in the appropriate position in the column labeled "None." If additional space is needed in any category, attach a separate sheet properly identified with the case name, case number, and the number of the category. If the debtor is married, state whether husband, wife, or both own the property by placing an "H," "W" "J," or "C" in the column labeled "Husband, Wife, Joint, or Community." If the debtor is an individual or a joint petition is filed, state the amount of any exemptions claimed only in Schedule C-Property Claimed as Exempt.

Do not include interests in executory contracts and unexpired leases on this schedule. List them in Schedule G-Executory Contracts and Unexpired Leases.

If the property is being held for the debtor by someone else, state that person's name and address under "Description and Location of Property."

TYPE OF PROPERTY	NONE	DESCRIPTION AND LOCATION OF PROPERTY	HUSBAND, WIFE, JOINT OR COMMUNITY	CURRENT MARKET VALUE OF DEBTOR'S INTEREST IN PROPERTY, WITHOUT DEDUCTING ANY SECURED CLAIM OR EXEMPTION
1. Cash on hand.		cash with debtors	J	$ 90
2. Checking, savings or other financial accounts, certificates of deposit, or shares in banks, savings and loan, thrift, building and loan, and homestead associations, or credit unions, brokerage houses, or cooperatives.		checking account at First Bank of Centerville,120 Broadway, Centerville IL 61111	J	$ 137
3. Security deposits with public utilities, telephone companies, landlords, and others.		Centerville Electric Company, 14 Center Street Centerville IL 61111	J	$ 100
4. Household goods and furnishings, including audio, video, and computer equipment.		washer,dryer, refrigerator, tv, stereo, and various household furnishings: all at family home	J	$ 2,500

In re <u>Mary Ellen and John Alan Smith</u>   Case No.<u>(will be supplied by clerk)</u>
            Debtor   (If known)

SCHEDULE B-PERSONAL PROPERTY
(Continuation Sheet)

TYPE OF PROPERTY	NONE	DESCRIPTION AND LOCATION OF PROPERTY	HUSBAND, WIFE, JOINT OR COMMUNITY	CURRENT MARKET VALUE OF DEBTOR'S INTEREST IN PROPERTY, WITHOUT DEDUCTING ANY SECURED CLAIM OR EXEMPTION
5. Books, pictures and other art objects, antiques, stamp, coin, record, tape, compact disc, and other collections or collectibles.		personal books, family photos, and 3 paintings	J	$ 150
6. Wearing apparel.		personal clothing of debtors	J	$ 400
7. Furs and jewelry.		wedding rings	J	$ 1000
8. Firearms and sports, photographic, and other hobby equipment.		Nikon camera	J	$ 100
9. Interests in insurance policies. Name insurance company of each policy and itemize surrender or refund value of each.		Prudential Insurance Co., Policy #1234567, Cash surrender value	W	$ 1200
10. Annuities. Itemize and name each issuer.	X			
11. Interests in IRA, ERISA, Keogh, or other pension or profit sharing plans. Itemize.		IRA accounts held at First Bank of Centerville, 120 Broadway, Centerville IL 61111	H/W	$ 2,600
12. Stock and interests in incorporated and unincorporated businesses. Itemize.	X			
13. Interests in partnerships or joint ventures. Itemize.	X			

In re <u>Mary Ellen and John Alan Smith</u>   Case No. <u>(will be supplied by clerk)</u>
_____Debtor_____   (If known)

SCHEDULE B-PERSONAL PROPERTY
(Continuation Sheet)

TYPE OF PROPERTY	NONE	DESCRIPTION AND LOCATION OF PROPERTY	HUSBAND, WIFE, JOINT OR COMMUNITY	CURRENT MARKET VALUE OF DEBTOR'S INTEREST IN PROPERTY, WITHOUT DEDUCTING ANY SECURED CLAIM OR EXEMPTION
14. Government and corporate bonds and other negotiable non-negotiable instruments.	X			
15. Accounts receivable.	X			
16. Alimony, maintenance, support, and property settlements to which the debtor is or may be entitled. Give particulars.	X			
17. Other liquidated debts owing debtor including tax refunds. Give particulars.	X			
18. Equitable or future interest, life estates, and rights or powers exercisable for the benefit of the debtor other than those listed in Schedule A - Real Property.	X			
19. Contingent and non-contingent interests in estate of a decedent, death benefit plan, life insurance policy, or trust.	X			

In re Mary Ellen and John Alan Smith   Case No. (will be supplied by clerk)
       Debtor   (If known)

SCHEDULE B-PERSONAL PROPERTY
(Continuation Sheet)

TYPE OF PROPERTY	NONE	DESCRIPTION AND LOCATION OF PROPERTY	HUSBAND, WIFE, JOINT OR COMMUNITY	CURRENT MARKET VALUE OF DEBTOR'S INTEREST IN PROPERTY, WITHOUT DEDUCTING ANY SECURED CLAIM OR EXEMPTION
20. Other contingent and unliquidated claims of every nature, including tax refunds, counterclaims of the debtor, and rights to setoff claims. Give estimated value of each.	X			
21. Patents, copyrights, and other intellectual property. Give particulars	X			
22. Licenses, franchises, and other general intangibles. Give particulars.	X			
23. Automobiles, trucks, trailers, and other vehicles and accessories.		1985 Honda Accord 1978 Chevy pick-up	W H	$ 1,000 $ 700
24. Boats, motors, and accessories.	X			
25. Aircraft and accessories.	X			
26. Office equipment, furnishings, and supplies.	X			
27. Machinery, fixtures, equipment, and supplies used in business.	X			

In re <u>Mary Ellen and John Alan Smith</u>   Case No. <u>(will be supplied by clerk)</u>
　　　　　　Debtor　　　　　　　　　　　　　　　　　　　　(If known)

SCHEDULE B-PERSONAL PROPERTY
(Continuation Sheet)

TYPE OF PROPERTY	NONE	DESCRIPTION AND LOCATION OF PROPERTY	HUSBAND, WIFE, JOINT OR COMMUNITY	CURRENT MARKET VALUE OF DEBTOR'S INTEREST IN PROPERTY, WITHOUT DEDUCTING ANY SECURED CLAIM OR EXEMPTION
28. Inventory.	X			
29. Animals.		1 dog (pet)	J	$ 50
30. Crops growing or harvested. Give particulars.	X			
31. Farming equipment and implements.	X			
32. Farm supplies, chemicals, and feed.	X			
33. Other personal property of any kind not already listed, such as season tickets, etc. Itemize.		Tools used in trade as mechanic piano	H W	$ 1,000 $ 800

_____4_____ continuation sheets attached   Total $ $11,827

(Include amounts from any continuation sheets attached. Report total also on Summary of Schedules.)

Instructions for Schedule C: Exempt Property

You will use this form to claim the property that is exempt from being taken in your bankruptcy. Please consult Appendix B for details on the specific exemptions available in your state. In some states (Arkansas, Connecticut, District of Columbia, Hawaii, Massachusetts, Michigan, Minnesota, New Jersey, New Mexico, Pennsylvania, Rhode Island, South Carolina, Texas, Vermont, Washington, and Wisconsin) you have a choice between federal or state exemptions. In those states, fill in a separate copy of Schedule C for each set of exemptions and then decide which is the better choice. (Note: California residents may choose between two different sets of state exemptions).

In re: Enter your full name. If you're filing jointly, include your spouse's name.

Case No.: Leave this blank. The court clerk will assign you a case number.

Debtor elects the exemptions to which debtor is entitled under: Select the top box if your choose to use the federal bankruptcy exemptions and the second box if you choose state and federal non-bankruptcy exemptions.

Description of Property: Carefully go through the exemption list which you have chosen and your Schedules A and B and decide which property can be claimed as exempt. For each item of property that you decide is exempt, use the same description of that property that you used on Schedules A or B. List each grouping of property under sub-headings such as "Real Estate", "Household Goods", "Tools", etc. For pensions, all ERISA pensions are exempt under either federal or state bankruptcy exemptions. Check with your employer to see if yours is an "ERISA" pension. If not, your state may specifically exempt your particular pension. If in doubt, you may need to consult a lawyer to be certain that you do not lose your pension.

Specify Law Providing Each Exemption: Using your state's listing in Appendix B, list the exact name and chapter of your state's law which provides the exemption. You may state at the top of the form that "All references are to ... " and then list the name of your state's statute (for example: *Idaho Code*). Then just list the chapter numbers for each exemption.

Value of Claimed Exemption: Based on the statute exemption limits, list the amount which you claim as exempt for each piece of property. If you are married and filing jointly, you may double the amount of most exemptions, unless noted in Appendix B that your state does not allow such doubling. Some states have separate exemptions which may apply to a single piece of property. If so, list both exemption amounts up to the market value of the property. If the exemption amount is more than the value of the property, you may use the rest of the exemption on another piece of similar property until the exemption limit is reached. If the exemption amount is less than the market value of the property, the property may be sold by the court and the exemption amount given to you as cash and the rest of the proceeds used to pay off your creditors.

Current Market Value of Property Without Deducting Exemptions: Enter the full market value of each piece of property exactly as you have previously listed it on Schedules A or B. Don't make any deduction for your exemption amount.

In re: <u>Mary Ellen and John Alan Smith</u>   Case No. <u>(Will be supplied by Court Clerk)</u>
      Debtor

SCHEDULE C-PROPERTY CLAIMED AS EXEMPT

Debtor elects the exemptions to which debtor is entitled under:

(Check one box)

☐ 11 U.S.C.§ 522(b)(1): Exemptions provided in 11 U.S.C.§522(d). Note: These exemptions are available only in certain states.

☐ 11 U.S.C.§ 522(b)(2): Exemptions available under applicable nonbankruptcy federal laws, state or local law where the debtor's domicile has been located for the 180 days immediately preceding the filing of the petition, or for a longer portion of the 180-day period than in any other place, and the debtor's interest as a tenant by the entirety or joint tenant to the extent the interest is exempt from process under applicable nonbankruptcy law.

DESCRIPTION OF PROPERTY	SPECIFY LAW PROVIDING EACH EXEMPTION	VALUE OF CLAIMED EXEMPTION	CURRENT MARKET VALUE OF PROPERTY WITHOUT DEDUCTING EXEMPTIONS
	All references are to Illinois Annotated Statutes. Each debtor claims a full set of exemptions.		
Personal residence	735-5/12-901	$15,000	$48,000
Cash with debtors	735-5/12-1001(b)	$ 90	$ 90
Checking account at First Bank of Centerville	735-5/12-1001(b)	$ 137	$ 137
Security deposit with Centerville Electric Company	735-5/12-1001(b)	$ 100	$ 100
Household goods and furnishings including washer, dryer, tv, refrigerator and stereo	735-5/12-1001(b)	$ 2,500	$ 2,500
Pet dog	735-5/12-1001(b)	$ 50	$ 50
Nikon camera	735-5/12-1001(b)	$ 100	$ 100
Wedding rings	735-5/12-1001(b)	$ 1,000	$ 1,000
Paintings	735-5/12-1001(b)	$ 23	$ 50
Prudential insurance policy-cash surrender value	735-5/12-1001(f)	$ 1,200	$ 1,200
IRA accounts at First Bank of Centerville	735-5/12-1006	$ 2,600	$ 2,600
Personal clothing of debtors	735-5/12-1001(a)	$ 400	$ 400
Family pictures	735-5/12-1001(a)	$ 50	$ 50
Books	735-5/12-1001(a)	$ 50	$ 50
Tools used in trade	735-5/12-1001(d)	$ 750	$ 1,000
Piano (used in trade-piano lessons)	735-5/12-1001(d)	$ 750	$ 800
Honda Accord	735-5/12-1001(c)	$ 1,000	$ 1,000
Chevy pick-up	735-5/12-1001(c)	$ 700	$ 700

Instructions for Schedule D: Creditors Holding Secured Claims

A secured debt is a debt for which you pledged some type of collateral (like a mortgage, consumer loan, car loan, etc.) or a debt based on a lien against your property (as where a judgement, tax or mechanic's lien has been filed against property which you own). You may cancel these debts, but you are required to either give up the collateral or buy it back from the court for its market value. Use the official continuation sheet if necessary.

In re: Enter your full name. If you're filing jointly, include your spouse's name.

Case No.: Leave this blank. The court clerk will assign you a case number.

Check this box if debtor has no creditors holding secured claims: If so, check box.

Creditor's Name and Mailing Address: Fill in the complete name and address of each creditor (in alphabetical order). Include an account number if there is one.

Codebtor: If someone else co-signed the debt documents, is a non-filing spouse or joint owner, or otherwise can be held liable for the debt, place an **X** in this box. In community property states, non-filing spouses are generally liable for debts undertaken during a marriage. In common law states, non-filing spouses are generally liable for debts for necessities (food, clothing, shelter, etc.).

Husband, Wife, Joint or Community : If you are single, enter **N/A**. If you are married, enter **H**, **W**, **J** or **C**, depending if the particular debt is owed individually by the husband or wife, is owed jointly by both (as joint tenants or tenants-by-the-entireties), or is owed as a community debt in a community property state. Check the language on the debt document. In common-law states, the liability for the debt generally depends on the names on the debt document. In most states, debts which were individually undertaken prior to a marriage are considered individual debts during the marriage.

Date Claim Was Incurred, Nature of Lien, and Description and Market Value of Property Subject to Lien: Here list all pertinent information about each secured debts. List the date you signed the debt documents or that the lien was recorded. The *nature of lien* is either a tax, judgement, child support, or mechanic's lien for a lien; or for debts: a *purchase money debt* (the property purchased is the collateral), a *non-purchase money debt* (the property purchased was not the collateral), or a *possessory non-purchase money debt* (you obtained a loan on property which the creditor has possession of, such as a pawn-shop loan). To describe the property and market value of the collateral for any debt or lien, use the Schedule A or B description and value.

Contingent, Unliquidated, or Disputed: *Contingent* means the debt is based on an event that has not yet occurred. *Unliquidated* means an outstanding loan whose amount has not yet been fixed by court action. *Disputed* means that you dispute either the amount or even the existence of the debt. You may check more than one box.

Amount of Claim Without Deducting Value of Collateral: Here list the amount required to pay off the entire debt or lien.

Unsecured portion, if any: If the value of the collateral is less than the amount of the debt, enter the difference here. If the collateral is worth more than the debt, enter zero.

Subtotal and Total: Total the amounts in the "Current Market Value" column and enter here and also on the *Summary of Schedules* form (which follows later in this Chapter).

In re _Mary Ellen and John Alan Smith_   Case No. _(Will be supplied by clerk)_
              Debtor   (If known)

SCHEDULE D-CREDITORS HOLDING SECURED CLAIMS

State the name, mailing address, including zip code, and account number, if any, of all entities holding claims secured by property of the debtor as of the date of filing of the petition. List creditors holding all types of secured interest such as judgment liens, garnishments, statutory liens, mortgages, deeds of trust, and other security interests. List creditors in alphabetical order to the extent practicable. If all secured creditors will not fit on this page, use the continuation sheet provided.

If any entity other than a spouse in a joint case may be jointly liable on a claim, place an "X" in the column labeled "Codebtor," include the entity on the appropriate schedule of creditors, and complete Schedule H-Codebtors. If a joint petition is filed, state whether husband, wife, both of them, or the marital community may be liable on each claim by placing an "H", "W", "J", or "C" in the column labeled "Husband, Wife, Joint, or Community."

If the claim is contingent, place an "X" in the column labeled "Contingent." If the claim is unliquidated, place an "X" in the column labeled "Unliquidated." If the claim is disputed, place an "X" in the column labeled "Disputed." (You may need to place an "X" in more than one of these three columns.)

Report the total of all claims listed on this schedule in the box labeled "Total" on the last sheet of the completed schedule. Report this total also on the Summary of Schedules.

☐ Check this box if debtor has no creditors holding secured claims to report on this Schedule D.

CREDITOR'S NAME AND MAILING ADDRESS INCLUDING ZIP CODE	CODEBTOR	HUSBAND, WIFE, JOINT, OR COMMUNITY	DATE CLAIM WAS INCURRED, NATURE OF LIEN, AND DESCRIPTION AND MARKET VALUE OF PROPERTY SUBJECT TO LIEN	CONTINGENT	UNLIQUIDATED	DISPUTED	AMOUNT OF CLAIM WITHOUT DEDUCTING VALUE OF COLLATERAL	UNSECURED PORTION, IF ANY
Account No. 987654321 Centerville Savings and Loan, 169 Front St. Centerville IL 61111			Mortgage on personal home at 16 Main St. Centerville dated 1/1/93 Value $ 48,000		X		$37,000	none
Account No.			Value $					
Account No.			Value $					
Account No.			Value $					

_0_ Continuation sheets attached

Subtotal (Total of this page) $ 37,000

TOTAL (Use only on last page) $ 37,000

(Report total also on Summary of Schedules)

Instructions for Schedule E: Creditors Unsecured Priority Claims

Unsecured priority claims are certain debts which are given priority in being paid off in a bankruptcy, but which have no collateral pledged. They include taxes which you might owe, wages you may owe to employees, alimony, child support, and certain other claims. Use the official Schedule E continuation sheet if necessary.

In re: Enter your full name. If you're filing jointly, include your spouse's name.

Case No.: Leave this blank. The court clerk will assign you a case number.

Check this box if debtor has no creditors holding unsecured priority claims to report on this Schedule E: If so, check the box and go on to Schedule F.

Type of Priority Claims: Read through each definition of the various priority claims carefully and check them against your list of debts on your questionnaire. The most likely unsecured priority claim will be for back taxes owed. Place an **X** before any of your debts which are considered priority claims.

Continuation Sheet Instructions:

Creditor's Name and Mailing Address: Fill in the complete name and address of each creditor (in alphabetical order). Include an account number if there is one.

Codebtor: If someone else has co-signed the debt documents, is a non-filing spouse or joint owner, or otherwise can be held liable for the debt, place an **X** in this box. In community property states, debts undertaken during a marriage are generally considered community debts, and non-filing spouses are liable. In common law states, non-filing spouses are generally only liable for debts for necessities (food, clothing, shelter, etc.).

Husband, Wife, Joint or Community : If you are single, enter **N/A**. If you are married, enter **H**, **W**, **J** or **C**, depending if the particular debt is owed individually by the husband or wife, is owed jointly by both (as joint tenants or tenants-by-the-entireties), or is owed as a community debt in a community property state. Check the language on the debt document. In common-law states, the liability for the debt generally depends on the names on the debt document. In most states, debts which were individually undertaken prior to a marriage are considered individual debts during the marriage.

Date Claim Was Incurred and Consideration For Claim: List the date that the debt was incurred and a description of the debt or claim.

Contingent, Unliquidated, or Disputed: *Contingent* means the debt is based on an event that has not yet occurred. *Unliquidated* means an outstanding loan whose amount has not yet been fixed by court action. *Disputed* means that you dispute either the amount or even the existence of the debt. You may check more than one box.

Total Amount of Claim: List the total amount of the claimed debt, including any amount over the actual priority amount limit listed under *Types of Priority Claims* on the first page of *Schedule E*.

Amount Entitled to Priority: Here list the lesser of the total amount of claim or the maximum priority amount from the list under *Types of Priority Claims*.

Subtotal and Total: Total the amounts in the "Current Market Value" column and enter here and also on the *Summary of Schedules* form (which follows later in this Chapter).

In re: <u>Mary Ellen and John Alan Smith</u>   Case No. <u>(Will be supplied by Court Clerk)</u>
       Debtor

SCHEDULE E-CREDITORS HOLDING UNSECURED PRIORITY CLAIMS

A complete list of claims entitled to priority, listed separately by type of priority, is to be set forth on the sheets provided. Only holders of unsecured claims entitled to priority should be listed in this schedule. In the boxes provided on the attached sheets, state the name and mailing address, including zip code, and account number, if any, of all entities holding priority claims against the debtor or the property of the debtor, as of the date of the filing of the petition.

If any entity other than a spouse in a joint case may be jointly liable on a claim, place an "X" in the column labeled "Codebtor," include the entity on the appropriate schedule of creditors, and complete Schedule H-Codebtors. If a joint petition is filed, state whether husband, wife, both of them, or the marital community may be liable on each claim by placing an "H", "W", "J", or "C" in the column labeled "Husband, Wife, Joint, or Community."

If the claim is contingent, place an "X" in the column labeled "Contingent." If the claim is unliquidated, place an "X" in the column labeled "Unliquidated." If the claim is disputed, place an "X" in the column labeled "Disputed." (You may need to place an "X" in more than one of these three columns.)

Report the total of all claims listed on each sheet in the box labeled "Subtotal" on each sheet. Report the total of all claims listed on this Schedule E in the box labeled "Total" on the last sheet of the completed schedule. Repeat this total also on the Summary of Schedules.

❑   Check this box if **debtor** has no **creditors** holding **unsecured priority claims to report** on **this** Schedule E.

TYPES OF PRIORITY CLAIMS (Check the appropriate box(es) below if claims in that category are listed on the attached sheets)

❑   **Extensions of credit in an involuntary case**
     Claims arising in the ordinary course of the debtor's business or financial affairs after the commencement of the case but before the earlier Of the appointment of a trustee or the order for relief. 11 U.S.C. § 507(a)(2).

❑   **Wages, salaries, and commissions**
     Wages, salaries, and commissions, including vacation, severance, and sick leave pay owing to employees and commissions owing to qualifying independent sales representatives up to $4000* per person, earned within 90 days immediately preceding the filing of the original petition, or the cessation of business, whichever occurred first, to the extent provided in 11 U.S.C. § 507(a)(3).

❑   **Contributions to employee benefit plans**
     Money owed to employee benefit plans for services rendered within 180 days immediately preceding the filing of the original petition, or the cessation of business, whichever occurred first, to the extent provided in 11 U.S.C. § 507(a)(4).

❑   **Certain farmers and fishermen**
     Claims of certain farmers and fishermen, up to a maximum of $4000* per farmer or fisherman, against the debtor, as provided in I 1 U.S.C. § 507(a)(5).

❑   **Deposits by individuals**
     Claims of individuals up to a maximum of $1800* for deposits for the purchase, lease, or rental of property or services for personal, family, or household use, that were not delivered or provided. 11 U.S.C. § 507(a)(6).

❑   **Alimony, Maintenance, or Support**
     Claims of a spouse, former spouse, or child of the debtor for alimony, maintenance, or support, to the extent provided in I I U.S.C. § 507(a)(7).

☒   **Taxes and Certain Other Debts Owed to Governmental Units**
     Taxes, customs, duties, and penalties owing to federal, state, and local governmental units as set forth in 1 1 U.S.C. § 507(a)(8).

❑   **Commitments to Maintain the Capital of an Insured Depository Institution**
     Claims based on commitments to the FDIC, RTC, Director of the Office of Thrift Supervision, Comptroller of the Currency, or Board of Governors of the Federal Reserve system, or their predecessors or successors, to maintain the capital of an insured depository institution. 1 1 U.S.C. § 507 (a)(9).

* Amounts are subject to adjustment on April 1, 1998, and every three years thereafter with respect to cases commenced on or after the date of adjustment.

        <u>   1   </u>   continuation sheets attached

In re <u>Mary Ellen and John Alan Smith</u>   Case No. <u>(will be supplied by clerk)</u>
      Debtor   (If known)

SCHEDULE E-CREDITORS HOLDING UNSECURED PRIORITY CLAIMS
(Continuation Sheet)

CREDITOR'S NAME AND MAILING ADDRESS INCLUDING ZIP CODE	CODEBTOR	HUSBAND, WIFE, JOINT, OR COMMUNITY	DATE CLAIM WAS INCURRED AND CONSIDERATION FOR CLAIM	CONTINGENT	UNLIQUIDATED	DISPUTED	TOTAL AMOUNT OF CLAIM	AMOUNT ENTITLED TO PRIORITY
Account No. 555-12-5555 Internal Revenue Serv Kansas City MO 64999		J	Federal Income taxes due on joint return filed April 15,1995 for 1994 taxes	X			$ 850	$ 850
Account No.								
Account No.								
Account No.								
Account No.								
Account No.								

Sheet no. 1 of 1 Continuation sheets attached
to Schedule E - Creditors Holding Unsecured Priority Claims

Subtotal (Total of this page)	$ 850
TOTAL (Use only on last page)	$ 850

(Report total also on Summary of Schedules)

Instructions for Schedule F: Creditors Unsecured NonPriority Claims

Unsecured non-priority claims are any other debts which you owe, other than leases or contractual obligations: that is, any debts which are not secured debts or unsecured priority debts. This includes, generally, all of your bills, including credit cards, medical bills, utility bills, personal loans with no collateral, and bills owed to stores. These debts will usually be cancelled by your bankruptcy. Every debt must be listed, even those that you dispute are valid debts; those you wish to pay off; and those which are non-dischargeable (such as a student loan or court-ordered fine).

In re: Enter your full name. If you're filing jointly, include your spouse's name.

Case No.: Leave this blank. The court clerk will assign you a case number.

Check this box if debtor has no creditors holding unsecured non-priority claims to report on this Schedule F: If so, check the box and go on to Schedule G.

Creditor's Name and Mailing Address: Fill in the complete name and address of each creditor (in alphabetical order). Include an account number if there is one. Include all collection agencies and attorneys who have contacted you regarding a debt; all co-signers on a debt you owe; all debtors which you have co-signed for a debt; and anyone who has sued you for a monetary amount.

Codebtor: If someone else has co-signed the debt documents, is a non-filing spouse or joint owner, or otherwise can be held liable for the debt, place an **X** in this box. In community property states, debts undertaken during a marriage are generally considered community debts, and non-filing spouses are liable. In common law states, non-filing spouses are generally liable for debts for necessities.

Husband, Wife, Joint or Community: If you are single, enter **N/A**. If you are married, enter **H**, **W**, **J** or **C**, depending if the particular debt is owed individually by the husband or wife, is owed jointly by both (as joint tenants or tenants-by-the-entireties), or is owed as a community debt in a community property state. Check the language on the debt document. In common-law states, the liability for the debt generally depends on the names on the debt document. In most states, debts which were individually undertaken prior to a marriage are considered individual debts during the marriage.

Date Claim Was Incurred and Consideration For Claim If Claim Subject to Set-Off, so State: List the date that the debt was incurred and a brief but clear description of the debt or claim. A *set-off* means that the creditor owes you money and will apply it to a debt. If there is a set-off, state the amount and reason for the set-off.

Contingent, Unliquidated, or Disputed: *Contingent* means the debt is based on an event that has not yet occurred. *Unliquidated* means an outstanding loan whose amount has not yet been fixed by court action. *Disputed* means that you dispute either the amount or even the existence of the debt. You may check more than one box.

Amount of Claim: List the total amount of the claimed debt. If there are multiple creditors for the same amount (as when a collection agency has taken over a debt) only list the total amount for one creditor (preferably the original creditor).

Subtotal and Total: Total the amounts in the "Current Market Value" column and enter here and also on the *Summary of Schedules* form (which follows later in this Chapter).

In re __Mary Ellen and John Alan Smith__ Case No(_Will be supplied by clerk_)
　　　　Debtor　　　　　　　　　　　　　　　　　　　　　(If known)

SCHEDULE F-CREDITORS HOLDING UNSECURED NONPRIORITY CLAIMS

State the name, mailing address, including zip code, and account number, if any, of all entities holding unsecured claims without priority against the debtor or the property of the debtor as of the date of filing of the petition. Do not include claims listed in Schedules D and E. If all creditors will not fit on this page, use the continuation sheet provided.

If any entity other than a spouse in a joint case may be jointly liable on a claim, place an "X" in the column labeled "Codebtor," include the entity on the appropriate schedule of creditors, and complete Schedule H-Codebtors. If a joint petition is filed, state whether husband, wife, both of them, or the marital community may be liable on each claim by placing an "H", "W", "J", or "C" in the column labeled "Husband, Wife, Joint, or Community."

If the claim is contingent, place an "X" in the column labeled "Contingent." If the claim is unliquidated, place an "X" in the column labeled "Unliquidated." If the claim is disputed, place an "X" in the column labeled "Disputed." (You may need to place an "X" in more than one of these three columns.)

Report the total of all claims listed on this schedule in the box labeled "Total" on the last sheet of the completed schedule. Report this total also on the Summary of Schedules.

❑　　　Check this box if debtor has no creditors holding unsecured nonpriority claims to report on this Schedule F.

CREDITOR'S NAME AND MAILING ADDRESS INCLUDING ZIP CODE	CODEBTOR	HUSBAND, WIFE, JOINT, OR COMMUNITY	DATE CLAIM WAS INCURRED AND CONSIDERATION FOR CLAIM. IF CLAIM IS SUBJECT TO SETOFF, SO STATE.	CONTINGENT	UNLIQUIDATED	DISPUTED	AMOUNT OF CLAIM
Account No. 1234567 American Bank 1234 First Ave Chicago IL 60606		J	Visa credit card charges, 1994-1995		X		3,500
Account No. 87654321 Barker Bank 654321 66th St. Springfield IL 62700		J	MasterCard credit card charges 1994-1995		X		5,800
Account No. N/A Carter Car Repair' 345 Oak St. Centerville IL 61111		J	Car repair September 1994			X	600
Account No. 123-456 Centerville Bank 9876 Main St. Centerville IL 61111		W	Student loan October 1987		X		5,000

__1__　　Continuation sheets attached

Subtotal (Total of this page)　$ 14,900

TOTAL (Use only on last page)　$ N/A

(Report total also on Summary of Schedules)

In re Mary Ellen and John Alan Smith   Case No. (Will be supplied by clerk)
        Debtor   (If known)

SCHEDULE F-CREDITORS HOLDING UNSECURED NONPRIORITY CLAIMS
(Continuation Sheet)

CREDITOR'S NAME AND MAILING ADDRESS INCLUDING ZIP CODE	CODEBTOR	HUSBAND, WIFE, JOINT, OR COMMUNITY	DATE CLAIM WAS INCURRED AND CONSIDERATION FOR CLAIM. IF CLAIM IS SUBJECT TO SETOFF, SO STATE.	CONTINGENT	UNLIQUIDATED	DISPUTED	AMOUNT OF CLAIM
Account No. 567890 Centerville Hospital 3 Hospital Lane Centerville IL 61111		H	Hospital bills June 1995		X		$12,000
Account No. 34567 Dwight Furniture 7878 Second St. Centerville IL 61111		J	Furniture October 1994		X		$ 1,000
Account No. N/A Dr. William Fredericks 35 Doctors Court Centerville IL 61111		H	Doctor's bills 1994-1995		X		$ 4,300
Account No. 24681357 Mobil Oil Company Box 12345 Houston TX 77777		J	Gas company credit card 1993-1994		X		$ 1,235
Account No. A-234 Personal Finance Co. 6666 LaSalle St Chicago IL 60606		J	Personal Loan November 1994		X		$ 5,000
Account No. 1111-2222 Northern Illinois Elec. 7778 Coal St Centerville IL 61111		J	Electric service 1994-1995		X		$ 3,590

Sheet no. 1 of 1 Continuation sheets attached
to Schedule F - Creditors Holding Unsecured Nonpriority Claims

Subtotal (Total of this page) $ 27,125

TOTAL (Use only on last page) $ 42,025

(Report total also on Summary of Schedules)

Instructions for Schedule G: Executory Contracts and Unexpired Leases

Executory contracts are contracts which are still in force and contain obligations which you or another party must still fulfill. *Unexpired leases* are leases which are still in force, either for residential or business property. These include any type of contract or lease which you have signed and is still in force, including real estate contracts, insurance contracts, and business contracts. If you are past due on payments on a lease or contract, that should be listed as a debt on Schedules D, E, or F. Schedule G is a master list of all leases and contracts which are outstanding, whether or not you are delinquent in payments. This includes leases where someone leases property from you.

In re: Enter your full name. If you're filing jointly, include your spouse's name.

Case No.: Leave this blank. The court clerk will assign you a case number.

Check this box if debtor has no executory contracts or unexpired leases: If so, check the box and continue to Schedule H.

Name and Mailing Address of Other Parties to Lease or Contract: Here list the name and address of every person who is a party to any current lease or contract. This will include anyone who signed the lease or contract and every company who is involved with the lease or contract. Don't list yourself, however.

Description of Contract or Lease and Nature of Debtor's Interest. State Whether Lease is for Non-Residential Real Property. State Contract Number of any Government Contract: State the date the lease or contract was signed and give a brief general description of the type of lease or contract which is included. In addition, briefly describe what the lease or contract requires of each party. If the contract is with any government agency or authority, list the contract number.

Instructions for Schedule H: Codebtors

This schedule is a master list of all of the codebtors which you have listed on Schedules D, E, and F. Review those forms and enter all of the codebtors on this form.

In re: Enter your full name. If you're filing jointly, include your spouse's name.

Case No.: Leave this blank. The court clerk will assign you a case number.

Check this box if debtor has no codebtors: If so, check the box and continue to Schedule I.

Name and Address of Codebtor: Here enter the name and address of each codebtor which is listed on Schedules D, E, or F.

Name and Address of Creditor: Here enter the name and address of each creditor for each of the codebtors listed in the first column. This should be identical to the information for creditors which you listed on Schedules D, E, or F for which there were codebtors indicated.

In re: <u>Mary Ellen and John Alan Smith</u>   Case No. <u>(Will be supplied by Court Clerk)</u>
                 Debtor

SCHEDULE G-EXECUTORY CONTRACTS AND UNEXPIRED LEASES

Describe all executory contracts of any nature and all unexpired leases of real personal property. Include any timeshare interests.

State nature of debtor's interest in contract, i.e., "Purchaser," "Agent," etc. State whether debtor is the lessor or lessee of a lease.

Provide the names and complete mailing addresses of all other parties to each lease or contract described.

NOTE: A party listed on this schedule will not receive notice of the filing of this case unless the party is also scheduled in the appropriate schedule of creditors.

❑   Check this box if debtor has no executory contracts or unexpired leases.

NAME AND MAILING ADDRESS, INCLUDING ZIP CODE, OF OTHER PARTIES TO LEASE OR CONTRACT.	DESCRIPTION OF CONTRACT OR LEASE AND NATURE OF DEBTOR'S INTEREST. STATE WHETHER LEASE IF FOR NONRESIDENTIAL REAL PROPERTY. STATE CONTRACT NUMBER OF ANY GOVERNMENT CONTRACT.
Centerville Business Products 234 Business Lane Centerville IL 61111	Co-signer with brother, William David Smith on contract dated September 15, 1994 to buy computer

In re: <u>Mary Ellen and John Alan Smith</u>   Case No. <u>(Will be supplied by Court Clerk)</u>
          Debtor

SCHEDULE H-CODEBTORS

Provide the information requested concerning any person or entity, other than a spouse in a joint case, that is also liable on any debts listed by debtor in the schedules of creditors. Include all guarantors and co-signers. In community property states, a married debtor not filing a joint case should report the name and address of the nondebtor spouse on this schedule. Include all names used by the nondebtor spouse during the six years

☐   Check this box if debtor has no codebtors.

NAME AND ADDRESS OF CODEBTOR	NAME AND ADDRESS OF CREDITOR
William David Smith 567 Elm Street Centerville IL 61111	Centerville Business Products 234 Business Lane Centerville IL 61111

Instructions for Schedule I: Current Income of Individual Debtor

Schedule I will contain information on all of your current income, whether from wages, salary, self-employment, farm, real estate, investments, alimony, social security, pensions or any other source. You will calculate your income on a monthly basis. Include a copy of your latest tax return with Schedule I when you file it with the court.

In re: Enter your full name. If you're filing jointly, include your spouse's name.

Case No.: Leave this blank. The court clerk will assign you a case number.

Debtor's Marital Status: Indicate single, married, divorced, or widowed.

Dependents of Debtor and Spouse: Enter the names, age, and relationship of dependant children and others for whom you provide over half of the support.

Employment: Enter the name, address, length and type of employment for you and your spouse's employer. Enter retired, disabled, or unemployed if applicable.

Income: For you and your spouse (if filing jointly) enter your total gross monthly income from a regular job. Enter your average monthly overtime, if applicable. If your income varies monthly or seasonally, divide the last full year's income by 12.

Less Payroll Deductions: List the average monthly amount of all taxes, insurance, pensions, dues, or other deductions which are taken out of your paycheck.

Total Net Monthly Take Home Pay: Deduct the *Subtotal of Payroll Deductions* from the *Subtotal of Monthly Wages* and enter here.

Regular Income from Operation of a Business or Profession or Farm: Enter the average monthly amount of income from a farm, business, or self-employment. Divide the last year's total income (taken from your latest tax return) by 12.

Income from Real Property: Here list the average monthly income which you make from rental of real estate, either commercial or residential.

Interest and Dividends: Enter the average monthly income from stocks, bank accounts, or other income-producing investments.

Alimony, maintenance, or support payments payable: Enter the monthly average amount which you receive for yourself or the support of any dependent child.

Social Security or other government assistance: Here list the monthly amount of any social security, unemployment, worker's compensation, disability, aid to families with dependent children, foodstamps, veteran's benefits, or other government assistance. Specify the type of assistance.

Pension or retirement income: Here enter the average monthly amount of any retirement benefits, including IRA's, KEOGH's, or annuities. Specify the type.

Other monthly income: Include the average monthly amount of any other type of income which you receive on a regular basis. Specify the source of the income.

Total non-wage monthly income: Total all columns below *Total Net Monthly Take Home Pay* and enter here.

Total Combined Monthly Income: Add your *Total Net Take Home Pay* amount and your *Total Non-Wage Monthly Income* amount and enter here.

Describe any increase or decrease of more than 10%: If you know or anticipate any reason why your income will change in the next 12 months, explain here.

In re: <u>Mary Ellen and John Alan Smith</u>   Case No. <u>(Will be supplied by Court Clerk)</u>
     Debtor

SCHEDULE I-CURRENT INCOME OF INDIVIDUAL DEBTOR(S)

The column labeled "Spouse" must be completed in all cases filed by joint debtors and by a married debtor in a Chapter 12 or 13 case whether or not a joint petition is filed, unless the spouses are separated and a joint petition is not filed.

Debtor's Marital Status	DEPENDENTS OF DEBTOR AND SPOUSE		
	NAMES	AGE	RELATIONSHIP
Married	None		
Employment:	DEBTOR	SPOUSE	
Occupation	Teacher	Mechanic	
Name of Employer	Centerville Elementary School	Centerville Auto Repair	
How long employed?	3 years	2 years	
Address of Employer	987 W. Main, Centerville IL 61111	765 Elm, Centerville IL 61111	

Income: (Estimate of average monthly income)   DEBTOR   SPOUSE

Current monthly gross wages, salary, and commissions
        (pro rate if not paid monthly) $ 1,000 $ 2,000

Estimated monthly overtime $ 0 $ 0

SUBTOTAL OF MONTHLY WAGES $ 1,000 $ 2,000

LESS PAYROLL DEDUCTIONS

        a. Payroll taxes and Social Security $ 127 $ 234

        b. Insurance $ $

        c. Union dues $ 23 $ 0

        d. Other (Specify: _____) $ $

SUBTOTAL OF PAYROLL DEDUCTIONS $ 150 $ 234

TOTAL NET MONTHLY TAKE HOME PAY $ 850 $ 1,766

Regular income from operation of business or profession or farm
        (attach detailed statement) $ $

Income from real property $ $

Interest and dividends $ $

Alimony, maintenance or support payments payable to the debtor
        for the debtor's use or that of dependents listed above $ $

Social Security or other government assistance
(Specify: _____) $ $

Pension or retirement income $ $

Other monthly income
(Specify: _____) $ $

TOTAL MONTHLY NON-WAGE INCOME $ 0 $ 0

TOTAL COMBINED MONTHLY INCOME $ 2,616   (Report also on Summary of Schedules)

Describe any increase or decrease of more than 10% in any of the above categories anticipated to occur within the year following the filing of this document:

Instructions for Schedule J: Current Expenses of Individual Debtor

On this schedule, you will estimate your average monthly expenses. The amounts you list will be for your entire family's expenses, whether you are filing jointly or are married and filing alone. If you are filing jointly, but you and your spouse do not live together, see below under *Check this box*. For all amounts, determine the average monthly expense amount. For expenditures which are made on a weekly, quarterly, or annual basis, calculate the monthly amount and enter.

In re: Enter your full name. If you're filing jointly, include your spouse's name.

Case No.: Leave this blank. The court clerk will assign you a case number.

Check this box if a joint petition is filed: Do so if you and your spouse are separated but are filing a joint petition. You will then need to complete separate *Schedule J's* for you and your spouse. Clearly label your spouse's Schedule J as "**Spouses**."

Expenses: For each of the listed expense items, list your average monthly amount. If the amount is paid other than monthly (ie. weekly, annually, etc.), calculate the monthly average amount. Include any types of expenses not listed under *Other*.

Total Monthly Expenses: Here total all expenses and list this amount also on your *Summary of Schedules* (later in this chapter).

For Chapter 12 and Chapter 13 Debtors Only: Enter **N/A**.

Instructions for Supplemental Sheet to Schedules:

You will use this form if you need to include any additional information on any of your schedules. If you use this form, it will be considered a continuation sheet and should be counted as a sheet when you need to list the total number of sheets for each schedule and on your *Summary of Schedules* (later in this chapter).

In re: Enter your full name. If you're filing jointly, include your spouse's name.

Case No.: Leave this blank. The court clerk will assign you a case number.

Supplemental Sheet to Schedule: Here list the letter of the Schedule which the sheet will supplement (for example: Schedule A).

On the rest of the sheet include any information which you may need to add in order to complete or explain anything on the official schedule.

In re: Mary Ellen and John Alan Smith   Case No. (Will be supplied by Court Clerk)
        Debtor

SCHEDULE J-CURRENT EXPENDITURES OF INDIVIDUAL DEBTOR(S)

Complete this schedule by estimating the average monthly expenses of the debtor and the debtor's family. Pro rate any payments made biweekly, quarterly, semi-annually, or annually to show monthly rate.

❑   Check this box if a joint petition is filed and debtor's spouse maintains a separate household. Complete a separate schedule of expenditures labeled "Spouse."

Rent or home mortgage payment (include lot rented for mobile home)	$ 650
Are real estate taxes included? Yes X No	
Is property insurance included? Yes x No	
Utilities: Electricity and heating fuel	$ 175
Water and sewer	$ 78
Telephone	$ 109
Other (Cable Tv)	$ 24
Home maintenance (repairs and upkeep)	$ 121
Food	$ 375
Clothing	$ 100
Laundry and dry cleaning	$ 50
Medical and dental expenses	$ 700
Transportation (not including car payments)	$ 20
Recreation, clubs and entertainment, newspapers, magazines, etc.	$ 100
Charitable contributions	$1200
Insurance (not deducted from wages or included in home mortgage payments)	
Homeowner's or renter's	$
Life	$ 140
Health	$ 100
Auto	$ 125
Other ( )	$
Taxes (not deducted from wages or included in home mortgage payments)	
(Specify:)	$
Installment payments: (In Chapter 12 and 13 cases, do not list payments to be included in the plan)	
Auto	$
Other (personal loan)	$ 250
Other (credit cards)	$ 450
Alimony, maintenance, and support paid to others	$
Payments for support of additional dependents not living at your home	$
Regular expenses from operation of business, profession, or farm (attach detailed statement)	$
Other (See attached Supplemental Sheet)	$1,500
TOTAL MONTHLY EXPENSES (Report also on Summary of Schedules)	
	$ 6,267

[FOR CHAPTER 12 AND CHAPTER 13 DEBTORS ONLY]
Provide the information requested below, including whether plan payments are to be made biweekly, monthly, annually, or at some other regular interval.

A. Total projected monthly income $

B. Total projected monthly expenses $

C. Excess income (A minus B) $

D. Total amount to be paid into plan each _____ $
                        (interval)

In re: Mary Ellen and John Alan Smith   Case No. (Will be supplied by Court Clerk)
           Debtor

SUPPLEMENTAL SHEET TO SCHEDULE __J

Explanation of Other monthly expenses:

```
    Prescription drugs for Mary Ellen Smith      $   500
    Physical therapy for Mary Ellen Smith        $1,000
```

Instructions for Summary of Schedules:

Here you will enter information from all Schedules to act as a summary for the court.

Court Name: Fill in the full name of the judicial district in which you will be filing (as listed on your Voluntary Petition).

In re: Fill in your full name (last name first) that you regularly use to sign checks, etc.

Case No.: Leave this line blank. The court clerk will assign you a case number.

Attached (Yes/No): Indicate that all schedules are attached.

Number of sheets: For each schedule, count the number of pages. Include any continuation pages that you have used.

Amounts Scheduled: Enter Asset totals from *Schedules A* and *B*; Liability totals from *Schedules D, E,* and *F*; and Income and Expenditure totals from *Schedules I* and *J*.

Totals: Total the columns for the *Number of Sheets, Total Assets* and *Total Liabilities*.

Instructions for Declarations Concerning Debtor's Schedules:

This form is where you state that everything which you entered on all of the Schedules is true and correct to the best of your knowledge. Everything which you enter on your bankruptcy forms must be absolutely true and you must be able to prove it with documents, receipts, bills, or other paper records. Keep in mind that the penalty for making a false statement on a bankruptcy form is a fine of up to $500,000.00 and imprisonment for up to 5 years, or both, and, of course, denial of your request to discharge your debts in bankruptcy.

In re: Enter your full name. If you're filing jointly, include your spouse's name.

Case No.: Leave this blank. The court clerk will assign you a case number.

Declaration Under Penalty of Perjury by Individual Debtor: List the total number of sheets from your *Summary of Schedules* plus 1 (for the *Summary of Schedules*). Sign and date (if joint, both spouses must sign).

Certification and Signature of Non-Attorney Bankruptcy Petition Preparer: Enter N/A, unless you are using a bankruptcy petition preparer.

Declaration Under Penalty of perjury on Behalf of Corporation or Partnership: Enter N/A.

In re: <u>Mary Ellen and John Alan Smith</u>   Case No. <u>(Will be supplied by Court Clerk)</u>
          Debtor

SUMMARY OF SCHEDULES

Indicate as to each schedule whether that schedule is attached and state the number of pages in each. Report the totals from Schedules A, B, D, E, F, I, and J in the boxes provided. Add the amounts from Schedules A and B to determine the total amount of the debtor's assets. Add the amounts from Schedules D, E, and F to determine the total amount of the debtor's liabilities.

NAME OF SCHEDULE	ATTACHED (YES/NO?)	# SHEETS	AMOUNTS SCHEDULED		
			ASSETS	DEBTS	OTHER
A: Real Property	yes	1	$ 48,000		
B: Personal Property	yes	5	$ 11827		
C: Property Claimed as Exempt	yes	1			
D: Creditors Holding Secured Claims	yes	1		$ 37,000	
E: Creditors with Unsecured Priority Claims	yes	1		$ 850	
F: Creditors with Unsecured Nonpriority Claims	yes	2		$ 42,025	
G: Executory Contracts and Unexpired Leases	yes	1			
H: Codebtors	yes	1			
I: Current Income of Individual Debtor(s)	yes	1			$ 2,616
J: Current Expenditures of Individual Debtor(s)	yes	2			$ 6,267
TOTAL # SHEETS ALL SCHEDULES ⇒		12			
TOTAL ASSETS ⇒			$ 59,827		
TOTAL DEBTS ⇒				$ 79,875	

In re: <u>Mary Ellen and John Alan Smith</u>   Case No. <u>(Will be supplied by Court Clerk)</u>
      Debtor

DECLARATION CONCERNING DEBTOR'S SCHEDULES

DECLARATION UNDER PENALTY OF PERJURY BY INDIVIDUAL DEBTOR

I declare under penalty of perjury that I have read the foregoing summary and schedules consisting of _____ 13 _____
sheets, and that they are true and correct to the best of my knowledge, information, and belief. *(Total shown on summary page plus 1)*

Date   November 1, 1995 _____   Signature *Mary Ellen Smith* _____
                                                       Debtor

Date   November 1, 1995 _____   Signature *John Alan Smith* _____
                                                   (Joint Debtor, if any)

(If joint case, both spouses must sign.)

CERTIFICATION AND SIGNATURE OF NON-ATTORNEY BANKRUPTCY PETITION PREPARER (See 11 U.S.C. §110)

I certify that I am a bankruptcy petition preparer - as defined in 11 U.S.C. § 110, that I prepared this document for compensation, and that I have provided the debtor with a copy of this document.

     N/A

_____   _____
Printed or Typed Name of Bankruptcy Petition Preparer   Social Security No.

_____
_____
Address

Names and Social Security numbers of all other individuals who prepared or assisted in preparing this document:

If more than one person prepared this document, attach additional signed sheets conforming to the appropriate Official Form for each person.

X _____   _____
Signature of Bankruptcy Petition Preparer   Date

A bankruptcy petition preparer's failure to comply with the provisions of title 11 and the Federal Rules of Bankruptcy Procedure may result in fines or imprisonment or both. 11 U.S.C. § 110, 18 U.S.C. § 156.

DECLARATION UNDER PENALTY OF PERJURY ON BEHALF OF CORPORATION OR PARTNERSHIP

     N/A

I, the _____ (the president or other officer or an authorized agent of the corporation or an authorized agent of the partnership] of the _____ (corporation or partnership) named as debtor in this case, declare under penalty of perjury that I have read the foregoing summary and schedules, consisting of _____sheets, and that they are true and correct to the best of my knowledge, information, and belief.
(Total shown on summary page plus 1)

     N/A
Date _____.   Signature _____

                                           _____
                                           (Print or type name of individual signing on behalf of debtor]

[An individual signing on behalf of a partnership or corporation must indicate position or relationship to debtor.)

Penalty for making a false statement or concealing property: Fine of up to $500,000, imprisonment for up to 5 years, or both. 18 U.S.C. §§ 152 and 3571.

Instructions for Form 7: Statement of Financial Affairs:

This form is used to describe your financial transactions over the last 2 years. You must truthfully answer all questions on this form. The answers on this form will be checked very carefully by the court. In certain cases, the bankruptcy court may void certain transactions and take control of money or property that you transferred to others before you filed for bankruptcy. If you are filing jointly, list the information for each of you separately.

In re: Enter your full name. If you're filing jointly, include your spouse's name.

Case No.: Leave this blank. The court clerk will assign you a case number.

Income from employment or operation of business: Here list all income from your job or business for this calendar year. Also list the total amount of income during the 2 years prior to this calendar year. Use your tax return.

Income other than from employment or operation of business: Here list all other income you have received from any source in the 2 years prior to filing for bankruptcy (bank account interest, for example).

Payments to creditors: Under (a.) list any payments totaling over $600 which you have made on any debts within the 90 days prior to filing for bankruptcy. Under (b.) list any payments for any amount made within 1 year prior to filing which were made to *insiders* (relatives, business partners, or other closely-related parties).

Suits, executions, garnishments and attachments: Under (a.) list any lawsuits which you or your spouse were parties to within 1 year prior to filing for bankruptcy. Under (b.) list any property which has been garnished, attached or seized within 1 year prior to filing.

Repossessions, foreclosures and returns: Here enter any property which was repossessed, foreclosed, or returned to a seller within 1 year prior to filing.

Assignments and receiverships: Under (a.) list any assignment of property made within 120 days prior to filing. Under (b.) list any property held by a receiver or other court official within 1 year prior to filing.

Gifts: List every gift that you or your spouse made within 1 year prior to filing if they total over $200 worth of gifts to a family member or over $100 worth of gifts to any single charity.

Losses: List all fire, theft, gambling, or other losses within 1 year prior to filing or since filing.

Payments related to debt counseling or bankruptcy: List any payments or property transferred to any party for any bankruptcy or debt counseling or assistance within 1 year prior to filing.

Other transfers: List any other property which was transferred within 1 year prior to filing, except ordinary business or financial transactions.

Closed financial accounts: Here list information regarding any financial or bank accounts which were closed or transferred within 1 year prior to filing for bankruptcy.

Safe deposit boxes: List all safety deposit boxes in which you or your spouse held any valuables within 1 year prior to filing.

Setoff: List any set-offs made against a debt by a creditor or bank within 90 days prior to filing. Set-offs are money which a creditor owes you which the creditor has applied against a debt which you owe the creditor.

Property held for another person: List any property which you or your spouse are holding for someone else.

Prior address of debtor: List any addresses where you or your spouse have lived within the last 2 years.

Questions #16-21 should only be answered if you or your spouse have been in business within the past 2 years, either as a corporation, partnership, sole proprietorship, or otherwise self-employed. These questions must be answered even if you are no longer in business at the time you file for bankruptcy.

Nature, location and name of business: Under (a.) list the type, name, and address of every business which you or your spouse owned 5 percent or more within the 2 years prior to filing for bankruptcy. Under (b.) enter **N/A** and under (c.) enter **N/A**.

Books, records and financial statements: Under (a.) list the names and addresses of any bookkeepers and accountants who handled any of your business records within the 6 years prior to filing for bankruptcy. Under (b.) list any person or firm which has audited or prepared financial records for your business within the 2 years prior to filing. Under (c.) list any person or firm who had possession of any books or records of your business on the date of filing for bankruptcy. Under (d.) list any financial institution or creditor to which the business gave a financial statement within the 2 years prior to filing for bankruptcy.

Inventories: Under (a.) list the dates and amounts for each of the last 2 business inventories. Also list the name of the person who supervised each inventory. Under (b.) enter the name and address of the person who has possession of the records of those inventories.

Current partners, officers, directors and shareholders: Under both (a.) and (b.), enter **N/A**.

Former partners, officers, directors and shareholders: Under both (a.) and (b.), you should enter **N/A**.

Withdrawals from a partnership or distributions by a corporation: Enter **N/A**.

If completed by an individual or individual and spouse: Sign and date. If a joint petition, your spouse must also sign and date.

Certification and signature of non-attorney bankruptcy petition preparer: Enter **N/A**, unless you were assisted by a bankruptcy petition preparer.

If completed on behalf of a partnership or corporation: Enter **N/A**.

FORM 7. STATEMENT OF FINANCIAL AFFAIRS

UNITED STATES BANKRUPTCY COURT
<u>Northern</u> District of <u>Illinois</u>

In re: <u>Mary Ellen and John Alan Smith</u>   Case No. <u>(Will be supplied by Court Clerk)</u>
            Debtor

STATEMENT OF FINANCIAL AFFAIRS

This statement is to be completed by every debtor. Spouses filing a joint petition may file a single statement on which the information for both spouses is combined. If the case is filed under Chapter 12 or Chapter 13, a married debtor must furnish information for both spouses whether or not a joint petition is filed, unless the spouses are separated and a joint petition is not filed. An individual debtor engaged in business as a sole proprietor, partner, family farmer, or self-employed professional, should provide the information requested on this statement concerning all such activities as well as the individual's personal affairs.

Questions 1-15 are to be completed by all debtors. Debtors that are or have been in business, as defined below, also must complete Questions 16-21. **Each question must be answered. If the answer to any question is "None," or the question is not applicable, mark the box labeled "None."** If additional space is needed for the answer to any question, use and attach a separate sheet properly identified with the case name, case number (if known), and the number of the question.

DEFINITIONS

"In business." A debtor is "in business" for the purpose of this form if the debtor is a corporation or partnership. An individual debtor is "in business" for the purpose of this form if the debtor is or has been, within the two years immediately preceding the filing of this bankruptcy case, any of the following: an officer, director, managing executive, or person in control of a corporation; a partner, other than a limited partner, of a partnership; a sole proprietor or self-employed.

"Insider." The term "insider" includes but is not limited to: relatives of the debtor; general partners of the debtor and their relatives; corporations of which the debtor is an officer, director, or person in control; officers, directors, and any person in control of a corporate debtor and their relatives; affiliates of the debtor and insiders of such affiliates; any managing agent of the debtor. 11 U.S.C. § 101(30).

1. Income from employment or operation of business

None
☐

State the gross amount of income the debtor has received from employment, trade, or profession, or from operation of the debtor's business from the beginning of this calendar year to the date this case was commenced. State also the gross amounts received during the **two years** immediately preceding this calendar year. (A debtor that maintains, or has maintained, financial records on the basis of a fiscal rather than a calendar year may report fiscal year income. Identify the beginning and ending dates of the debtor's fiscal year.) If a joint petition is filed, state income for each spouse separately. (Married debtors filing under Chapter 12 or Chapter 13 must state income of both spouses whether or not a joint petition is filed, unless the spouses are separated and a joint petition is not filed.)

AMOUNT	SOURCE (If more than one)	
$ 8,000	Debtor	Wages from Centerville Elementary School
$ 9,500	Joint Debtor	Wages from Centerville Car Repair

71

2. Income other than from employment or operation of business

None
☒

State the amount of income received by the debtor other than from employment, trade, profession, or operation of the debtor's business during the **two years** immediately preceding the commencement of this case. Give particulars. If a joint petition is filed, state income for each spouse separately. (Married debtors filing under Chapter 12 or Chapter 13 must state income for each spouse whether or not a joint petition is filed, unless the spouses are separated and a joint petition is not filed.)

AMOUNT	SOURCE

3. Payments to creditors

None
☐

a. List all payments on loans, installment purchases of goods or services, and other debts, aggregating more than $600 to any creditor, made within **90 days** immediately preceding the commencement of this case. (Married debtors filing under Chapter 12 or Chapter 13 must include payments by either or both spouses whether not a joint petition is filed, unless the spouses are separated and a joint petition is not filed.)

NAME AND ADDRESS OF CREDITOR	DATES OF PAYMENTS	AMOUNT PAID	AMOUNT STILL OWING
American Bank 1234 First Ave Chicago IL 60606	7/5/95 8/10/95	$550 $400	$3,500

None
☒

b. List all payments made within **one year** immediately preceding the commencement of this case, to or for the benefit of, creditors who are or **were** insiders. (Married debtors filing under Chapter 12 or Chapter 13 must include payments by either or both spouses whether or not a joint petition is filed, unless the spouses are separated and a joint petition is not filed.)

NAME AND ADDRESS OF CREDITOR RELATIONSHIP TO DEBTOR	DATES OF PAYMENTS	AMOUNT PAID	AMOUNT STILL OWING

4. Suits, executions, garnishments and attachments

None
☒

a. List all suits to which the debtor is or was a party within **one year** immediately preceding the filing of this bankruptcy case. (Married debtors filing under Chapter 12 or Chapter 13 must include information concerning either or both spouses whether or not a joint petition is filed, unless the spouses are separated and a joint petition is not filed.)

CAPTION OF SUIT AND CASE NUMBER	NATURE OF PROCEEDING	COURT AND LOCATION	STATUS OR DISPOSITION

None
☒

b. Describe all property that has been attached, garnished or seized under any legal or equitable process within **one year** immediately preceding the commencement of this case. (Married debtors filing under Chapter 12 or Chapter 13 must include information concerning property of either or both spouses whether or not a joint petition is filed, unless the spouses are separated and a joint petition is not filed.)

NAME AND ADDRESS OF PERSON FOR WHOSE BENEFIT PROPERTY WAS SEIZED	DATE OF SEIZURE	DESCRIPTION AND VALUE OF PROPERTY

5. Repossessions, foreclosures and returns

None
☐

List all property that has been repossessed by a creditor, sold at a foreclosure sale, transferred through a deed in lieu of foreclosure or returned to the seller, within **one year** immediately preceding the commencement of this case. (Married debtors filing under Chapter 12 or Chapter 13 must include information concerning property of either or both spouses whether or not a joint petition is filed, unless the spouses are separated and a joint petition is not filed.)

NAME AND ADDRESS OF CREDITOR OR SELLER	DATE OF REPOSSESSION, FORECLOSURE SALE, TRANSFER OR RETURN	DESCRIPTION AND VALUE OF PROPERTY
Hunt Ford Motor Company 444 Main St Centerville IL 61111	6/19/95	1994 Ford Truck $15,995

6. Assignments and receiverships

None
☒

a. Describe any assignment of property for the benefit of creditors made within **120 days** immediately preceding the commencement of this case. (Married debtors filing under Chapter 12 or Chapter 13 must include any assignment by either or both spouses whether or not a joint petition is filed, unless the spouses are separated and a joint petition is not filed.)

NAME AND ADDRESS OF ASSIGNEE	DATE OF ASSIGNMENT	TERMS OF ASSIGNMENT OR SETTLEMENT

None
☒

b. List all property which has been in the hands of a custodian, receiver, or court-appointed official within **one year** immediately preceding the commencement of this case. (Married debtors filing under Chapter 12 or Chapter 13 must include information concerning property of either or both spouses whether or not a joint petition is filed, unless the spouses are separated and a joint petition is not filed.)

NAME AND ADDRESS OF CUSTODIAN	NAME AND LOCATION OF COURT; CASE TITLE & NUMBER	DATE OF ORDER	DESCRIPTION AND VALUE OF PROPERTY

7. Gifts

None
☐

List all gifts or charitable contributions made within **one year** immediately preceding the commencement of this case except ordinary and usual gifts to family members aggregating less than $200 in value per individual family member and charitable contributions aggregating less than $100 per recipient. (Married debtors filing under Chapter 12 or Chapter 13 must include gifts or contributions by either or both spouses whether or not a joint petition is filed, unless the spouses are separated and a joint petition is not filed.)

NAME AND ADDRESS OF PERSON OR ORGANIZATION	RELATIONSHIP TO DEBTOR, IF ANY	DATE OF GIFT	DESCRIPTION AND VALUE OF GIFT
First Church of God Church 34 Main St Centerville IL 61111		Monthly	$1,200

8. Losses

None
☒

List all losses from fire, theft, other casualy or gambling within **one year** immediately preceding the commencement of this case **or since the commencement of this case.** (Married debtors filing under Chapter 12 or Chapter 13 must include losses by either or both spouses whether or not a joint petition is filed, unless the spouses are separated and a joint petition is not filed.)

DESCRIPTION AND VALUE OF PROPERTY	DESCRIPTION OF CIRCUMSTANCES AND, IF LOSS WAS COVERED IN WHOLE OR IN PART BY INSURANCE, GIVE PARTICULARS	DATE OF LOSS

9. Payments related to debt counseling or bankruptcy

None
☒

List all payments made or property transferred by or on behalf of the debtor to any person, including attorneys, for consultation concerning debt consolidation, relief under the bankruptcy law or preparation of a petition in bankruptcy within **one year** immediately preceding the commencement of this case.

NAME AND ADDRESS OF PAYEE	DATE OF PAYMENT NAME OF PAYOR IF OTHER THAN DEBTOR	AMOUNT OF MONEY OR DESCRIPTION AND VALUE OF PROPERTY

10. Other transfers

None
☐

a. List all other property, other than property transferred in the ordinary course of the business or financial affairs of the debtor, transferred either absolutely or as security within **one year** immediately preceding the commencement of this case. (Married debtors filing under Chapter 12 or Chapter 13 must include transfers by either or both spouses whether or not a joint petition is filed, unless the spouses are separated and a joint petition is not filed.)

NAME AND ADDRESS OF TRANSFEREE; RELATIONSHIP TO DEBTOR	DATE	DESCRIBE PROPERTY TRANSFERRED AND VALUE RECEIVED
William David Smith 567 Elm St Centerville IL 61111	1/15/95	Boat and trailer $1,500

11. Closed financial accounts

None

☐

List all financial accounts and instruments held in the name of the debtor or for the benefit of the debtor which were closed, sold, or otherwise transferred within **one year** immediately preceding the commencement of this case. Include checking, savings, or other financial accounts, certificates of deposit, or other instruments; shares and share accounts held in banks, credit unions, pension funds, cooperatives, associations, brokerage houses and other financial institutions. (Married debtors filing under Chapter 12 or Chapter 13 must include information concerning accounts or instruments held by or for either or both spouses whether or not a joint petition is filed, unless the spouses are separated and a joint petition is not filed.)

NAME AND ADDRESS OF INSTITUTION	TYPE AND NUMBER OF ACCOUNT AND AMOUNT OF FINAL BALANCE	AMOUNT AND DATE OF SALE OR CLOSING
Centerville Credit Union 567 Broadway Centerville IL 61111	Checking Account Account #122222 $12	4/5/95

12. Safe deposit boxes

None

☒

List each safe deposit or other box or depository in which the debtor has or had securities, cash, or other valuables within **one year** immediately preceding the commencement of this case. (Married debtors filing under Chapter 12 or Chapter 13 must include boxes or depositories of either or both spouses whether or not a joint petition is filed, unless the spouses are separated and a joint petition is not filed.)

NAME AND ADDRESS OF BANK OR OTHER DEPOSITORY	NAMES AND ADDRESSES OF THOSE WITH ACCESS TO BOX OR DEPOSITORY	DESCRIPTION OF CONTENTS	DATE OF TRANSFER OR SURRENDER, IF ANY

13. Setoff

None

☒

List all setoffs made by any creditor, including a bank, against a debt or deposit of the debtor within **90 days** preceding the commencement of this case. (Married debtors filing under Chapter 12 or Chapter 13 must include information concerning either or both spouses whether or not a joint petition is filed, unless the spouses are separated and a joint petition is not filed.)

NAME AND ADDRESS OF CREDITOR	DATE OF SETOFF	AMOUNT OF SETOFF

14. Property held for another person

None

❑

List all property owned by another person that the debtor holds or controls.

NAME AND ADDRESS OF OWNER	DESCRIPTION AND VALUE OF PROPERTY	LOCATION OF PROPERTY
Jennifer Jones 167 Main Street Centerville IL 61111	Mountain Bike $350	16 Main Street Centerville IL 61111

15. Prior address of debtor

None

☒

If the debtor has moved within the **two years** immediately preceding the commencement of this case, list all premises which the debtor occupied during that period and vacated prior to the commencement of this case. If a joint petition is filed, report also any separate address of either spouse.

ADDRESS	NAME USED	DATES OF OCCUPANCY

The following questions are to be completed by every debtor that is a corporation or partnership and by any individual debtor who is or has been, within the two years immediately preceding the commencement of this case, any of the following: an officer, director, managing executive, or owner of more than 5 percent of the voting securities of a corporation; a partner, other than a limited partner, of a partnership; a sole proprietor or otherwise self-employed.

*(An individual or joint DEBTOR should complete this portion of the statement **only** if the debtor is or has been in business, as defined above, within the two years immediately preceding the commencement of this case.)*

16. Nature, location and name of business

None
☒

a. If the debtor is an individual, list the names and addresses of all businesses in which the debtor was an officer, director, partner, or managing executive of a corporation, partnership, sole proprietorship, or was a self-employed professional within the **two years** immediately preceding the commencement of this case, or in which the debtor owned 5 percent or more of the voting or equity securities, within the **two years** immediately preceding the commencement of this case.

b. If the debtor is a partnership, list the names and addresses of all businesses in which the debtor was a partner or owned 5 percent or more of the voting securities, within the **two years** immediately preceding the commencement of this case.

c. If the debtor is a corporation, list the names and addresses of all businesses in which the debtor was a partner or owned 5 percent or more of the voting securities, within the **two years** immediately preceding the commencement of this case.

NAME	ADDRESS	NATURE OF BUSINESS	BEGINNING AND ENDING DATES OF OPERATION

17. Books, records and financial statements

None
☒

a. List all bookkeepers and accountants who within the **six years** immediately preceding the filing of this bankruptcy case kept or supervised the keeping of books of account and records of the debtor.

NAME AND ADDRESS	DATES SERVICES RENDERED

None
☒

b. List all firms or individuals who within the **two years** immediately preceding the filing of this bankruptcy case have audited the books of account and records, or prepared a financial statement of the debtor.

NAME AND ADDRESS	DATES SERVICES RENDERED

None

c. List all firms or individuals who at the time of the commencement of this case were in possession of the books of account and records of the debtor. If any of the books of account and records are not available, explain.

NAME   ADDRESS

None

d. List all financial institutions, creditors and other parties, including mercantile and trade agencies, to whom a financial statement was issued within the **two years** immediately preceding the commencement of this case by the debtor.

NAME AND ADDRESS   DATE ISSUED

18. Inventories

None

a. List the dates of the last two inventories taken of your property, the name of the person who supervised the taking of each inventory, and the dollar amount and basis of each inventory.

| | | DOLLAR AMOUNT OF INVENTORY |
| DATE OF INVENTORY | INVENTORY SUPERVISOR | (Specify cost, market or other basis) |

None

b. List the name and address of the person having possession of the records of each of the two inventories reported in a., above.

| | NAME AND ADDRESSES OF |
| DATE OF INVENTORY | CUSTODIAN OF INVENTORY RECORDS |

19. Current partners, officers, directors and shareholders

None
☒

a. If the debtor is a partnership, list the nature and percentage of partnership interest of each member of the partnership.

NAME AND ADDRESS	NATURE OF INTEREST	PERCENTAGE OF INTEREST

None
☒

b. If the debtor is a corporation, list all officers and directors of the corporation, and each stockholder who directly or indirectly owns, controls, or holds 5 percent or more of the voting securities of the corporation.

NAME AND ADDRESS	TITLE	NATURE AND PERCENTAGE OF STOCK OWNERSHIP

20. Former partners, officers, directors and shareholders

None
☒

a. If the debtor is a partnership, list each member who withdrew from the partnership within **one year** immediately preceding the commencement of this case.

NAME	ADDRESS	DATE OF WITHDRAWAL

None
☒

b. If the debtor is a corporation, list all officers or directors whose relationship with the corporation terminated within **one year** immediately preceding the commencement of this case.

NAME AND ADDRESS	TITLE	DATE OF TERMINATION

21. Withdrawals from a partnership or distributions by a corporation

None
☒

If the debtor is a partnership or corporation, list all withdrawals or distributions credited or given to an insider, including compensation in any form, bonuses, loans, stock redemptions, options exercised and any other perquisite during **one year** immediately preceding the commencement of this case.

NAME AND ADDRESS OF RECIPIENT; RELATIONSHIP TO DEBTOR	DATE AND PURPOSE OF WITHDRAWAL	AMOUNT OF MONEY OR DESCRIPTION AND VALUE OF PROPERTY

[If completed by an individual or individual and spouse]

I declare under penalty of perjury that I have read the answers contained in the foregoing statement of financial affairs and any attachments thereto and that they are true and correct.

Date ___November 1, 1995___ Signature of Debtor _*Mary Ellen Smith*_____

Date ___November 1, 1995___ Signature of Joint Debtor (if any) ___*John Alan Smith*___

CERTIFICATION AND SIGNATURE OF NON-ATTORNEY BANKRUPTCY PETITION PREPARER (See 11 U.S.C. § 110)

I certify that I am a bankruptcy petition preparer as defined in 11 U.S.C. § 110, that I prepared this document for compensation, and that I have provided the debtor with a copy of this document.

N/A
_____   _____
Printed or Typed Name of Bankruptcy Petition Preparer   Social Security No.

_____

_____
Address

Names and Social Security numbers of all other individuals who prepared or assisted in preparing this document:

If more than one person prepared this document, attach additional signed sheets conforming to the appropriate Official Form for each person.

X_____   _____
Signature of Bankruptcy Petition Preparer   Date

A bankruptcy petition preparer's failure to comply with the provisions of title 11 and the Federal Rules of Bankruptcy may result in fine or imprisonment or both. 11 U.S.C. §110, 18 U.S.C. §156.

[If completed on behalf of a partnership or corporation]

I declare under penalty of perjury that I have read the answers contained in the foregoing statement of financial affairs and any attachments thereto and that they are true and correct to the best of my knowledge, information and belief.

Date ___N/A_____   Signature _____

_____
Print Name and Title

[An individual signing on behalf of a partnership or corporation must indicate position or relationship to debtor.]

Penalty for presenting fraudulent claim.- Fine of up to $500,00 or imprisonment for up to 5 years, or both. 18 U.S.C. §§ 152 and 3571

Instructions for Form 8: Individual Debtor's Statement of Intention:

This form is required if you have a secured debt (a debt for which you have pledged some type of collateral or which has a lien against it). It is crucial if you wish to keep the collateral and/or eliminate the creditor's claims on the collateral. If you have secured debts, refer to your completed *Schedule D*. You must separate all debts listed on that schedule into 2 categories: debts for which you will surrender the collateral and debts for which you wish to keep the collateral. For those debts for which you wish to keep the collateral, there are 3 additional choices. You may reaffirm the debt; you may claim the property as exempt and redeem the property; or you may claim the property as exempt *and* seek to eliminate the creditor's lien on the property. Note that you must perform your stated intentions within 45 days of filing Form 8 with the Bankruptcy Court. **If you do not wish to surrender your collateral, you should seek legal advice.**

Court Name: Fill in the full name of the judicial district in which you will be filing (as listed on your Voluntary Petition).

In re: Fill in your full name (last name first) that you regularly use to sign checks, etc.

Case No.: Leave this line blank. The court clerk will assign you a case number.

Property to be surrendered: Here describe each item of property listed on your *Schedule D* as collateral which you choose to voluntarily surrender to the bankruptcy court. Use the property descriptions and creditor's names as shown on your *Schedule D*. Under this option, you are free from the debt entirely, however, you also lose the property. If there is an exemption for the property which is less than the claim against the property, the secured property will generally be surrendered to the bankruptcy trustee and sold. You will receive the amount of the exemption in cash and the remaining proceeds will be used to pay off the secured creditor. If you have no debts listed on *Schedule D*, enter **N/A** here and skip to the signature line.

Property to be retained: **If you wish to retain your secured property either by reaffirmation; redemption; or exemption/lien avoidance, you are advised to seek the assistance of a competent attorney.** There are additional forms which must be prepared which are beyond the scope of this book. In this section, you list all property on Schedule D which you do not wish to surrender to the court. Describe the property and list the creditor's names as shown on your Schedule D. For each property listed in this section, you must choose to either reaffirm the debt, claim it as exempt and redeem it, or claim it as exempt *and* seek to avoid any lien against the property. Be very careful not to reaffirm any of your debts without legal advice. In a few judicial districts, there is another option available. You may seek to retain the property by keeping up on your payments, but not reaffirming the debt. The districts which currently allow this are: Colorado, Kansas, Maryland, New Mexico, North Carolina, Oklahoma, Pennsylvania (Western District only), South Carolina, Utah, Virginia, West Virginia, and Wyoming. Consult an attorney if you wish to pursue this option.

Date and Signature of Debtor: Date and sign the form. If filing jointly, spouse should also sign.

Certification and signature of non-attorney bankruptcy petition preparer: Enter **N/A**, unless you were assisted by a bankruptcy petition preparer.

FORM 8. CHAPTER 7 INDIVIDUAL DEBTOR'S STATEMENT OF INTENTION

UNITED STATES BANKRUPTCY COURT
<u>Northern</u> District of <u>Illinois</u>

In re: <u>Mary Ellen and John Alan Smith</u>   Case No. <u>(Will be supplied by Court Clerk)</u>
         Debtor

1. I, the debtor, have filed a schedule of assets and liabilities which includes consumer debts secured by property of the estate.

2. My intention with respect to the property of the estate which secures those consumer debts is as follows:

a. *Property to be surrendered.*

	Description of Property	Creditor's Name
1.	Personal home, 16 Main St, Centerville IL	Centerville Savings & Loan
2.		
3.		

b. *Property to be retained.* [Check applicable statement of debtor's intention concerning reaffirmation, redemption or lien avoidance.]

	Description of property	Creditor's name	Debt will be reaffirmed pursuant to § 524(c)	Property is claimed as exempt and will be redeemed pursuant to § 722	Lien will be avoided pursuant to § 522(f) and property will be be claimed as exempt
1.					
2.					
3.					
4.					
5.					

3. I understand that § 521(2)(B) of the Bankruptcy Code requires that I perform the above stated intentions within 45 days of the filing of this statement with the court or within such additional time as the court, for cause, within such 45-day period fixes.

Date: <u>November 1, 1995</u>   *Mary Ellen Smith*
                                  Signature of Debtor

CERTIFICATION AND SIGNATURE OF NON-ATTORNEY BANKRUPTCY PETITION PREPARER (See 11 U.S.C. § 110)

I certify that I am a bankruptcy petition preparer as defined in 11 U.S.C. § 110, that I prepared this document for compensation, and that I have provided the debtor with a copy of this document.

N/A

_____   _____
Printed or Typed Name of Bankruptcy Petition Preparer   Social Security No.

_____

Address

Names and Social Security numbers of all other individuals who prepared or assisted in preparing this document:

If more than one person prepared this document, attach additional signed sheets conforming to the appropriate Official Form for each person.

X_____   _____
Signature of Bankruptcy Petition Preparer   Date

A bankruptcy petition preparer's failure to comply with the provisions of title 11 and the Federal Rules of Bankruptcy may result in fine or imprisonment or both. 11 U.S.C. §110, 18 U.S.C. §156.

Instructions for Form 3: Application to Pay Filing Fee in Installments:

This form is used to request permission to pay your filing fees in installments. You have the right to request this under bankruptcy law. Using this form, you make an initial payment with the filing of your bankruptcy papers and then indicate that you will make up to 4 further installment payments over a period of up to 120 days in order to pay the filing fee in full. There are a few restrictions, however:

- You must certify that you are unable to pay the entire fee at one time. Be certain that this request coincides with your description of your current financial situation. If your petition and schedules indicate that you have sufficient cash to pay the filing fee, your request will be denied.

- If you have already paid an attorney or bankruptcy petition preparer for assistance with your case, you can not request permission to pay your fee in installments.

- If your request is granted, you may not pay anyone for any services or assistance related to your bankruptcy until you have first paid your filing fee in full. Additionally, you may not transfer any property to anyone as payment for services in connection with your bankruptcy until your entire filing fee is paid.

Court Name: Fill in the full name of the judicial district in which you will be filing (as listed on your Voluntary Petition).

In re: Fill in your full name (last name first) that you regularly use to sign checks, etc.

Case No.: Leave this line blank. The court clerk will assign you a case number.

Application to Pay Filing Fee in Installments: On the first line indicate the amount of your initial payment on the filing fee. Subtract your initial payment from $160.00 and list the balance due on the second line. Also indicate on the second line how many installments you will use to pay the entire fee. You may use up to 4 installments (plus your down payment). On the next 4 lines indicate the amount of each of your installment payments and the date before which you will make each payment. The final payment must be made within 120 days of the granting of your request for permission to make the installment payments.

Date and Signature of Debtor: Date and sign the form. If filing jointly, spouse should also sign.

Certification and signature of non-attorney bankruptcy petition preparer: Enter N/A, unless you were assisted by a bankruptcy petition preparer.

Order: Leave this area blank. This is where the bankruptcy court judge will sign if your request is granted.

FORM 3. APPLICATION TO PAY FILING FEE IN INSTALLMENTS

UNITED STATES BANKRUPTCY COURT
<u>Northern</u> District of <u>Illinois</u>

In re: <u>Mary Ellen and John Alan Smith</u>   Case No. <u>(Will be supplied by Court Clerk)</u>
　　　　　Debtor

APPLICATION TO PAY FILING FEE IN INSTALLMENTS

In accordance with Federal Rules of Bankruptcy Procedure 1006, application is made for permission to pay the filing fee on the following terms:

$ ____30_____ with the filing of the petition, and the balance of
$ __120_____ in __4____ installments, as follows:

$ __30_____ on or before <u>November 15, 1995</u>
$ __30_____ on or before <u>December 1, 1995'</u>
$ __30_____ on or before <u>December 15, 1995</u>
$ __30_____ on or before <u>December 31, 1995</u>

I certify that I am unable to pay the filing fee except in installments. I further certify that I have not paid any money or transferred any property to an attorney or any other person for services in connection with this case or in connection with any other pending bankruptcy case and I will not make any payment or transfer of property for services in connection with the case until the filing fee is paid in full.

Date: _____November 1, 1995_____   *Mary Ellen Smith*
　　　　　　　　　　　　　　　　　　　　　　　　　_____
　　　　　　　　　　　　　　　　　　　　　　　　　Applicant
　　　　　　　　　　　　　　　　　　　　　　　　　John Alan Smith
　　　　　　　　　　　　　　　　　　　　　　　　　_____
　　　　　　　　　　　　　　　　　　　　　　　　　Joint Applicant

CERTIFICATION AND SIGNATURE OF NON-ATTORNEY BANKRUPTCY PETITION PREPARER (See 11 U.S.C. § 110)

I certify that I am a bankruptcy petition preparer as defined in 1 1 U.S.C. § 1 10, that I prepared this document for compensation, and that I have provided the debtor with a copy of this document.

N/A
_____   _____
Printed or Typed Name of Bankruptcy Petition Preparer   Social Security No.

_____

_____
Address

Names and Social Security numbers of all other individuals who prepared or assisted in preparing this document:

If more than one person prepared this document, attach additional signed sheets conforming to the appropriate Official Form for each person.

X_____   _____
Signature of Bankruptcy Petition Preparer   Date

A bankruptcy petition preparer's failure to comply with the provisions of title 11 and the Federal Rules of Bankruptcy may result in fine or imprisonment or both. 11 U.S.C. §110, 18 U.S.C. §156.

ORDER

IT IS ORDERED that the debtor pay the filing fee in installments on the terms set forth in the foregoing application.

IT IS FURTHER ORDERED that until the filing fee is paid in full the debtor shall not pay, and no person shall accept, any money for services in connection with this case, and the debtor shall not relinquish, and no person shall accept, any property as payment for services in connection with this case.

BY THE COURT

Date: _____   _____
　　　　　　　　　　　　　　　　　　　　　　United States Bankruptcy Judge

Instructions for Mailing Label Matrix:

You will use a Mailing Label Matrix in most bankruptcy courts. However, certain courts have their own specific instructions and forms for preparing mailing lists. Be sure to check with your particular court for any additional instructions for preparing mailing lists. Some courts will require you also to prepare a separate single column creditor-only mailing list to be used in a computer-scanned mailing system. In general, however, the instructions below are applicable.

1. Place plain bond paper on top of the matrix. The dark black lines of the matrix will show through. In the first box in the upper left hand corner, you should type your own name and address on the plain sheet of paper, within the black lines which show through. Inside the next box in the first column, you should type your spouse's name and address, if you are filing jointly. Next, going down in the first column, type the name and address of each creditor and security holder which you have listed on your Schedules D, E, and F. The creditors should be listed alphabetically. Each creditor should only be listed one time, regardless of the number of debts which you owe to a single debtor. Going down the first column, type each creditor's name and address. Move to the second column when the first column is full. Move to the third column when the second column is full. If necessary, type similar additional sheets.

2. You must type this form; handwriting is unacceptable. You may need to pay a typist to do it for you if you do not have a typewriter. You should only use Courier 10, Prestige, or Elite type or printstyle. Type the names and addresses in upper and lower case. Do not use all capitals. Type the Zip Code for each address on the last line of the address at the end of the line. Make sure that you have a good ribbon in your typewriter or printer. Do not make any marks on the matrix and do not include any other information other than the creditor's names and addresses. Make certain that each creditor's name and address is aligned properly and is within the black-lined boxes. Do not staple this form to any other forms.

Instructions for Verification of Mailing Label Matrix:

Using this form you will swear to the court that the information on your Mailing List Matrix is true and correct to the best of your knowledge.

Court Name: Fill in the full name of the judicial district in which you will be filing (as listed on your Voluntary Petition).

In re: Fill in your full name (last name first) that you regularly use to sign checks, etc.

Case No.: Leave this line blank. The court clerk will assign you a case number.

Consisting of: Here simply list the number of pages of the mailing list which contains your list of creditors.

Date and Signature of Debtor: Date and sign the form. If filing jointly, your spouse should also sign.

Mary Ellen Smith
16 Main Street
Centerville IL 61111

Centerville Hospital
3 Hospital Lane
Centerville IL 61111

John Alan Smith
16 Main Street
Centerville IL 61111

Dwight Furniture
7878 Second St
Centerville IL 61111

American Bank
1234 First Ave
Chicago IL 60606

Dr. William
Fredericks
35 Doctors Court
Centerville IL 61111

Barker Bank
654321 66th St
Springfield IL 62700

Internal Revenue
Sevice
Service Center
Kansas City MO 64999

Carter Car Repair
345 Oak Street
Centerville IL 61111

Mobil Oil Company
P.O. Box 12345
Houston TX 77777

Centerville Bank
9876 Main St
Centerville IL 61111

Northern Illinois
Electric
7778 Coal Street
Centerville IL 61111

Centerville Business
Products
234 Business Lane
Centerville IL 61111

Personal Finance
Company
6666 LaSalle Street
Chicago IL 60606

Centerville Electric
Company
14 Center Street
Centerville IL 61111

William David Smith
567 Elm Street
Centerville IL 61111

Centerville Savings
and Loan
169 Front Street
Centerville IL 61111

United States Bankruptcy Court

<u>Northern</u> District of <u>Illinois</u>

In re: <u>Mary Ellen and John Alan Smith</u>   Case No. <u>(Will be supplied by Court Clerk)</u>
                    Debtor

VERIFICATION OF CREDITOR MATRIX

The above named debtor(s) in this case, declare under penalty of perjury that the information set forth in the attached list of creditors, consisting of 1   pages, is true and correct to the best of my (our) information and belief.

November 1, 1995
Dated: _____

_____   _____
Mary Ellen Smith   *John Alan Smith*
Signature of Debtor   Signature of Joint Debtor (if any)

Instructions for Cover Sheet and Information Summary:

You will fill this form out upon completion of all of your other forms. This is the cover sheet which will give the bankruptcy court a quick overview of your complete filing of bankruptcy papers. Check with your local court clerk, however. Some courts require a slightly different version of this cover sheet, which you will need to use.

Court Name: Fill in the full name of the judicial district in which you will be filing (as listed on your Voluntary Petition).

In re: Fill in your full name (last name first) that you regularly use to sign checks, etc.

Case No.: Leave this line blank. The court clerk will assign you a case number.

Presented to the court are the original and one copy of the following documents: Here check each document which you will file. You should generally check all boxes, except the *Individual Debtor's Statement of Intention*. This form will be filed with the court later, after you have mailed copies of it to your creditors. In addition, the *Application to Pay Filing Fee in Installments* should only be checked if you are requesting permission to make installment payments of this fee.

Name of Debtor(s): Here list your full name and your spouses, if filing jointly. Enter last name first.

Social Security #: Here list your social security # (and your spouse's, if filing jointly).

EIN #: Here list your Employer Identification Number if you have operated a business in the last 2 years (and your spouse's EIN#, if filing jointly and it is a separate EIN).

A/K/A: Here list any names which you have used other than that listed above (and your spouse's, if filing jointly).

D/B/A: Here list any fictitious business names which you have used in the past 2 years (and your spouse's, if filing jointly).

Address of Debtor(s): Enter the street address where you actually reside.

Check All Applicable Boxes: Here you should check *Voluntary Chapter 7*; *Pro-Se Petition* (which means you are not using an attorney); *Business* or *Non-Business* (depending on your case); *Filing fee paid in installments* or *Filing fee paid in full* (depending on your situation); and if you are filing a *Joint* or *Individual Petition*.

Obligations, Assets, and Number of Creditors of Debtor(s) as scheduled: Here you should enter the amount totals as listed on your Summary of Schedules. Under Priority, you should list the amount which is listed on your Summary for Schedule E. Under Unsecured Non-Priority, list the total from your Summary for Schedule F. Under Secured list the amount from your Summary for Schedule D. For Total Assets, list the total amounts from your Summary for Schedules A and B together. Take the number of creditors total from your Mailing List Matrix.

Date and Signature of Debtor: Date and sign the form. If filing jointly, your spouse should also sign.

United States Bankruptcy Court

__Northern__ District of __Illinois__

In re:__Mary Ellen and John Alan Smith__   Case No. __(Will be supplied by Court Clerk)__
      Debtor

COVER SHEET and INFORMATION SUMMARY

Presented to the court are the original and one copy of the following documents:

- ☒ Voluntary Petition
- ☒ Schedule A-Real Property
- ☒ Schedule B-Personal Property
- ☒ Schedule C-Property Claimed as Exempt
- ☒ Schedule D-Creditors Holding Secured Claims
- ☒ Schedule E-Creditors Holding Unsecured Priority Claims
- ☒ Schedule F-Creditors Holding Unsecured Nonpriority Claims
- ☒ Schedule G-Executory Contracts and Unexpired Leases
- ☒ Schedule H-Codebtors
- ☒ Schedule I-Current Income of Individual Debtor(s)
- ☒ Schedule J-Current Expenditures of Individual Debtor(s)
- ☒ Declaration Concerning Debtor's Schedules
- ☒ Summary of Schedules
- ☒ Statement of Financial Affairs
- ☒ Individual Debtor's Statement of Intention
- ☒ Application to Pay Filing Fee in Installments
- ☒ Creditor Mailing List Matrix
- ☒ Verification of Creditor Mailing List

NAME OF DEBTOR(S)	Smith	, Mary	Ellen	
	Last	First	Middle	
Spouse (if Joint Petition)	Smith	, John	Alan	
	Last	First	Middle	
Social Security #	(Debtor) 555-55-5555		(Spouse) 444-44-4444	
EIN # (if applicable)	(Debtor) N/A		(Spouse) N/A	
A/K/A (if applicable)	(Debtor) Ellen Smith/Ellen Harris		(Spouse) J.A. Smith	
D/B/A (if applicable)	(Debtor) N/A		(Spouse) N/A	
Address of Debtor(s)	16 Main Street			
	Number Street		Apt. #	
	Centerville, Superior County, IL		61111	
	City	County	State	Zip

Check all applicable boxes:

- ☒ Voluntary Chapter 7
- ☒ Pro-Se Petition
- ☐ Business
- ☒ Non-Business
- ☒ Filing fees paid in installments
- ☐ Filing fees paid in full
- ☒ Joint Petition
- ☐ Individual Petition

Obligations, assets, and number of creditors of Debtor(s) as scheduled:

Priority:	$ 850 .00	Unsecured:	$ 42,025 .00	
Secured:	$ 37,000 .00	TOTAL ASSETS:	$ 59,827 .00	
Number of Creditors:	14			

The above named debtor(s) in this case, declare under penalty of perjury that the information set forth in this summary and the attached documents, consisting of __37__ pages, is true and correct to the best of my (our) information and belief.

Dated: __November 1, 1995__

Mary Ellen Smith   _John Alan Smith_
Signature of Debtor   Signature of Joint Debtor (if any)

Instructions for Proof of Service by Mail:

You will fill out this form only if you have secured debts listed on Schedule D and if you have prepared a copy of Official Form #8: *Individual Debtor's Statement of Intention* regarding those secured debts. Each of the creditors which you have listed on Schedule D and your *Individual Debtor's Statement of Intention* must be provided with a copy of your *Individual Debtor's Statement of Intention* within 30 of the date on which you file your bankruptcy papers. In addition, the court-appointed bankruptcy trustee who will oversee your case must also get a copy of your *Individual Debtor's Statement of Intention*. Following the instructions in Chapter 5, a friend or relative over the age of 18 will send each of these parties a copy of your *Individual Debtor's Statement of Intention* by first class mail. Then you will complete this particular form, have the person who mailed the letters sign it, and send the original of this form and your *Individual Debtor's Statement of Intention* to the bankruptcy court within 30 days of your filing. You then will have 45 days from when you initially filed your bankruptcy papers to complete the actions which you have indicated that you will perform on your *Individual Debtor's Statement of Intention*.

Court Name: Fill in the full name of the judicial district in which you will be filing (as listed on your *Voluntary Petition*).

In re: Fill in your full name (last name first) that you regularly use to sign checks, etc.

Case No.: Leave this line blank until the court clerk assigns you a case number. Then fill in the Case number.

I: After the first "I," enter the full first and last name of the person who will mail your *Individual Debtor's Statements of Intention* to your secured creditors and trustee. On the next lines, enter the county and state of their residence. Next fill in their correct actual street address (not a post office box).

On the: After these words in the second paragraph, enter the day, month, and year that the person actually mailed the copies of your *Individual Debtor's Statements of Intentions*.

U.S. Post Office located at: Here enter the street address of the post office at which the letters were mailed.

After **addressed exactly as follows**: Enter the exact names and addresses of all of your creditors who are listed on your *Individual Debtor's Statement of Intentions*. Also list the name and address of your bankruptcy trustee. If you need additional room, complete another sheet of names and addresses and add a line at the bottom of this sheet which states: "Additional names and addresses contained on continuation sheet".

Signed and Dated: This form should be dated and then signed on the date listed by the person who actually did the mailing. You or your spouse should **not** sign this form.

Congratulations, you have completed all of the forms necessary for filing your Chapter 7 Bankruptcy.

United States Bankruptcy Court

<u>Northern</u> District of <u>Illinois</u>

In re: <u>Mary Ellen and John Alan Smith</u>   Case No. <u>(Will be supplied by Court Clerk)</u>
Debtor

PROOF OF SERVICE BY MAIL

I, <u>Jennifer Jones</u>, declare that I am over the age of 18 years and not a party to this

bankruptcy. I reside in the County of <u>Superior</u>, and the State of <u>Illinois</u>.

My address is <u>167 Main Street, Centerville IL 61111</u>.

On the <u>1st</u> day of <u>November</u>, 19<u>95</u>, I served the following listed parties a copy of **Official Bankruptcy Form #8,**

Chapter 7 Individual Debtor's Statement of Intention of the debtor in this case, by placing a true and correct copy of it in a sealed

envelope with correct first-class postage fully prepaid, and depositing it in the United States mail at the U.S. Post Office located at

<u>200 West Main Street, Centerville IL 61111</u> addressed exactly as follows:

Centerville Savings and Loan
169 Front Street
Centerville IL 61111

I declare under penalty of perjury that the foregoing is true and correct.

Signed and dated on the <u>1st</u> day of <u>November</u>, 19 <u>95</u>

Jennifer Jones
Signature

Chapter 5

Completing Your Bankruptcy

Once you have completed filling in your official bankruptcy forms, you are ready to complete your bankruptcy. There are three basic steps left. First, you must file the original and copies of your complete set of papers with the bankruptcy court in your area and pay the required fees. Next, you will be required to attend a creditors meeting and surrender any non-exempt property. Finally, you will receive a discharge in bankruptcy which will officially eliminate your dischargeable debts and leave you with full possession of your exempt property. These three steps are not difficult to complete. From start to finish, the entire process will take around 4 months to complete. You may wish to review the two *Checklists* located at the end of Chapter 2 for an overview of the needed actions and the necessary items to file.

Filing Your Bankruptcy Papers

There are several steps you should take prior to actually filing your papers with the bankruptcy court.

Determine Which Bankruptcy Court: First, you should determine which bankruptcy court is the correct court for you to use. Appendix C contains a listing of the names, addresses, and phone numbers of all of the federal bankruptcy courts. You should file your bankruptcy papers in the federal district where you have lived or conducted your business for the last six months. If you are in doubt as to which court, call and ask the clerk of the bankruptcy court. Although court employees are prohibited from giving you legal advice, they should be able to answer basic informational questions.

Contact the Bankruptcy Court Clerk: You will also need to contact the clerk of your local bankruptcy court to determine if there are any additional local forms which may be required. The official forms in this book are acceptable in all bankruptcy courts in the United States. However, each federal district can also require its own local forms for organizational purposes. These generally consist of cover sheets or other forms to assist the court employees in filing the forms. When you check with the court clerk, you will also need to ask how many copies of your bankruptcy papers will be required. You will generally be required to file the original and at least 2 sets of photocopies of all of your papers. In addition, you will need to have a copy for yourself. Also, ask the court clerk for a list of the order in which they prefer the papers to be filed. If no particular order is required, file your papers with the *Cover Sheet* first and then in the order listed on your *Cover Sheet*.

Emergency Filing: If you have decided to pursue an emergency filing, you will only need to file your *Voluntary Petition*, any additional required local court forms (check with the court clerk), and a complete *Mailing List Matrix* of your creditors with verification. You will also need to either pay the filing fees in full or file an application to pay your filing fee in installments, if you desire. You will have 15 days to file all of the additional required forms. If you miss the 15-day deadline, your case will likely be dismissed and you won't be able to file again for 6 months. You may also be unable to discharge the debts you owed at the time of your emergency filing. Follow the rest of the instructions for filing your forms.

Check Your Papers Carefully: Go over each of the official documents which you have filled in. Carefully check every item for accuracy, particularly the names and addresses of your creditors. These names and addresses will be used for notifying the creditors of your bankruptcy. If the creditors are not notified properly, your debt to them may not be erased by your bankruptcy. Your creditors must have an opportunity to attend the creditors meeting or challenge your bankruptcy (although this seldom happens). Be also very certain that you have included every item of property that you own and every debt you owe, regardless how small. Check also that each continuation sheet that you may have used is properly completed. Any required local forms should also be filled in and checked.

Once you have determined that all of your forms are neatly and properly filled in, you should sign and date the originals of each form where indicated. If you are filing jointly, your spouse must also sign the forms. After signing, you should make certain that you have all of the sheets in proper order. Where indicated on each form, note if any continuation sheets are included. *Schedules B, D, E, F* and your *Statement of Financial Affairs* have lines on the lower left-hand side of their first page for this information. On your *Summary of Schedules*, note the number of total pages you are filing.

Make Copies of Your Bankruptcy Papers: You will now need to make several copies of your complete set of bankruptcy papers. Check with the court clerk to determine how many copies are required to be filed. Using your original, you will need to make the required number *plus* an additional copy for yourself. Your additional copy should be taken with you to the court when you file all of your papers. Have the court clerk stamp this copy with a dated "Filed" stamp to indicate that you have filed your bankruptcy papers. All copies and the original of your bankruptcy papers should be 2-hole punched at the top. You can have a quick-print shop do the copying and hole punching if you desire. Be certain that you have your forms in the correct order. If you have debts secured by property listed on Schedule D and you are filing a *Individual Debtor's Statement of Intention* for those debts, you will need to also make an additional copy of your *Individual Debtor's Statement of Intention* for each creditor listed on this form and one for the bankruptcy trustee. You will also then need to make two copies of your *Proof of Service by Mail*. Please see below under **Mailing Your Individual Debtor's Statement of Intention** for further instructions.

File Your Papers and Pay Your Fees: You should now either mail or go in person to the correct bankruptcy court armed with the following items:

- The complete set of the originals of all of your official bankruptcy forms (except your *Individual Debtor's Statement of Intention*);

- The required number of copies of your full set of bankruptcy forms (except your *Individual Debtor's Statement of Intention*);

- Your own copy of the full set of bankruptcy forms (except your *Individual Debtor's Statement of Intentions*).

- A completed original and the required copies of your *Application and Order to Pay Filing Fees in Installments* (if you are asking for this);

- A money order or certified bank check for $160.00 made out to the "U.S. Bankruptcy Court." If you are asking for permission to pay your filing fee in installments, make the check out for the down payment amount which you have listed on your *Application and Order to Pay Filing Fees in Installments*.

Mail or take these items to the court. Either in person or by mail, ask that the original and copies of your bankruptcy papers be filed. Pay your fee. Ask the court clerk to "File" stamp your own copy of your bankruptcy papers. Request the name and address of the bankruptcy trustee for your case.

Automatic Stay: Once you have filed your bankruptcy papers, the automatic stay goes into effect. The bankruptcy court will notify each of the creditors which you have listed of your filing and of the automatic stay. However, if you are in an emergency situation, you yourself can notify any creditors, collection agencies, landlords, police, or others. To do this, simply make a copy of the **file-stamped** version of *Official Form 1*, your *Voluntary Petition* (pages 1 and 2) for each person whom you wish to notify. Using your creditor mailing list matrix, mail a copy of the **file-stamped** *Vol-

untary Petition to each person whom you wish to immediately notify. This will prevent any further action on their part to evict you, shut off your utilities, harass you, or take any actions to collect on any of your debts. These creditors, however, have the right to ask the bankruptcy court to lift the automatic stay for their particular situation. If they do petition the court to lift the stay, you will be notified by the court.

Sending Your Individual Debtor's Statement of Intention: If you have any secured debts listed on Schedule D and **if** you have completed a *Individual Debtor's Statement of Intention* with regard to those debts, you have one more step to complete in filing your papers. If you did not list any debts on *Schedule D*, skip this step.

You must personally notify each of your secured creditors of your intentions with regard to their debt. To do this, follow these simple steps:

♦ Within 30 days of filing your papers with the court, have a friend or relative over the age of 18 mail (by first class mail) a copy of your *Individual Debtor's Statement of Intention* to each creditor listed on *Schedule D* and also to your bankruptcy trustee.

♦ Have this friend or relative sign your completed *Proof of Service by Mail* which lists the names and addresses of all of the creditors from your *Schedule D* and of your bankruptcy trustee. Make a copy of the signed *Proof of Service by Mail*.

♦ Mail or take the signed original *Individual Debtor's Statement of Intention* and the signed original *Proof of Service by Mail* to the bankruptcy court within 30 days of filing your other papers. File these two documents with the clerk and ask the clerk to "file-stamp" your copies of these two forms.

The Creditors Meeting

For you, the next step in your bankruptcy is the creditors meeting. After you have filed your bankruptcy papers, the court assigns a bankruptcy trustee to handle your case. The trustee sends notice of your bankruptcy, notice of the automatic stay, and notice of a creditors meeting to all of the creditors which you have listed on your mailing list matrix. You will also be notified of the time and place of this meeting. It will usually be held about a month after the filing of your papers. You **must** attend this meeting. If you do not, you may be fined, your bankruptcy may be dismissed, and you may be prevented from filing again for 6 months. Both you and your spouse must attend if you filed jointly. If you have a major schedule conflict, you may be able to contact the court and reschedule the meeting.

Unless you have significant non-exempt assets which can be sold or a creditor suspects you of fraudulent activities with regard to your bankruptcy, creditors rarely attend the meeting. The meeting should take about a half-hour. Generally, at the meeting, the bankruptcy trustee goes over your papers and may question you regarding specific debts or property. The trustee will also likely ask you questions regarding your understanding of bankruptcy. They are supposed to be certain that you understand the effect of bankruptcy on your credit; the consequences of a bankruptcy discharge; the availability of other types of bankruptcies; and the effect of reaffirming a debt. If you have read this entire book, you should have no difficulty in answering these questions. Prior to the meeting, review this book and look over your bankruptcy papers so that you will be able to honestly and easily answer any questions regarding your financial circumstances. You should also bring with you any of your financial records which you used to fill in your bankruptcy questionnaire and official forms. The meeting should be relatively brief and business-like. If you feel that you are being intimidated by the trustee or a creditor, you have the right stop the meeting and ask for a court hearing.

Within 30 days of your creditors meeting, the bankruptcy trustee or your creditors can object to your listing certain property as exempt. They must do so in writing and a court hearing will be scheduled. Generally, you need not attend the court hearing unless you wish to contest their claim that the property should not be exempt. Additionally, creditors can specifically object to the discharge of a particular debt. This may be done if they claim it is a non-dischargeable debt or if they feel that you incurred the debt by fraud or dishonesty of some kind. If a creditor challenges the discharge of a particular debt, you will be served court papers informing you of this challenge. If you wish to defend the dischargeability of the debt, you will need to seek the advice of a competent attorney. Finally, a creditor, on rare occasions, can seek to prevent you from obtaining a bankruptcy at all on the basis that you have incurred the bulk of your debts by fraud. If this happens, you will be notified and you should immediately seek the assistance of an attorney skilled in bankruptcy law.

Surrendering Your Property: After your creditors meeting, your bankruptcy trustee will notify you which of your non-exempt property will have to be surrendered to the court. Excess cash and any valuable property which could be sold to pay your creditors will likely be the only non-exempt property you will need to surrender. You may also be able to negotiate with your trustee to buy back any non-exempt property for cash or trade some of your exempt property for particular non-exempt property which you wish to keep. Most trustees are flexible, as long as they are able to collect property with an equivalent value. You must deal with any secured property (collateral) in the manner in which you have indicated on your *Individual Debtor's Statement of Intention*. You have 45 days from the date you filed your bankruptcy papers with the court to complete your stated intentions. If you indicated on your *Individual Debtor's Statement of Intention* that you would surrender secured property, it is up to your creditor to repossess the property.

Your Final Discharge

The final step in your bankruptcy will come about 3 months after your creditors meeting. Generally, you will be notified by the court of the scheduling of a very brief court hearing. At this quick hearing, the bankruptcy judge will determine that all of the proper steps have been taken and that your bankruptcy should be approved. The judge will then also generally inform you of the effects of bankruptcy. Finally, the judge will issue an order of discharge and your bankruptcy will be over. All of your dischargeable debts will be forever wiped clean. You will receive a final notice of your discharge in the mail a few weeks later. Congratulations.

After your Bankruptcy

Once your bankruptcy is over, all of the debts listed on your bankruptcy papers which were not successfully challenged by a creditor are wiped out. You are not liable to pay them in any way. Debts which are non-dischargeable are still valid. If a creditor claims you still owe them, write them and state that your bankruptcy has discharged your debt. There are, of course, several other consequences to your bankruptcy.

Your Credit Record: By law, the fact that you have obtained a personal bankruptcy can remain on your credit record for up to 10 years.

Filing Another Bankruptcy: Once you have obtained a personal bankruptcy, you will not be allowed to file another bankruptcy for a period of 6 years.

Discrimination: All governmental agencies are prohibited from taking action against you based on your bankruptcy. This includes firing you, evicting you, refusing to issue you a license, or other discriminatory actions. In addition, private employers are prohibited from firing you or otherwise discriminating against you because of your bankruptcy.

If You Made a Mistake on Your Bankruptcy Papers: If, after your final discharge, you discover that you have made a mistake on the bankruptcy papers which you filed, you must notify the bankruptcy trustee. This is particularly important if you neglected to include non-exempt property which might have been sold to pay your creditors. The bankruptcy trustee has the power to reopen your case and seek recovery of any non-exempt property which you owned at the time of your discharge and which was not included on your bankruptcy papers. Generally, this will not be done for small amounts of property. If you neglected to list a creditor, unfortunately the debt you owe to that creditor will not be discharged, unless you can show that the creditor actually knew of your bankruptcy in time to file a claim. If the debt is substantial, you may need to seek legal assistance.

If You Receive an Inheritance, Divorce Settlement, or Insurance Proceeds: If within 6 months of the date which you filed for bankruptcy (not the date of your discharge) you receive or are informed of an inheritance, or divorce or insurance settlement, you must notify your bankruptcy trustee. In the situation of such windfalls which you receive shortly after your bankruptcy, the bankruptcy trustee also has the power to reopen your case and seek to claim such property.

Rebuilding Your Credit: Once you have eliminated your debts through a bankruptcy, you must then begin the process of rebuilding your credit rating. If you have a steady job and are able to build a record of making on-time rental or utility payments, it should take only a few years to be eligible for credit of some kind. The first credit which will generally be available to you will be collateralized consumer loans or credit for consumer goods. Next, within as little as 3 to 4 years, credit cards and auto loans may become available. Finally, if you maintain a clear financial record, home mortgages will again be available to you. Be very careful, however, about once again getting into the credit traps which caused your first bankruptcy. Good credit is a valuable asset which can assist you in reaching your goals and achieving a better life. Bankruptcy will have given you a new start on the road to that life.

Appendix A

Federal Bankruptcy Forms

On the following pages, you will find copies of all of the necessary official bankruptcy forms which you will need to complete your personal bankruptcy. These forms should not be removed from this book (particularly if this is a library book!) Instead, you should make photo-copies of the forms in this book for your use. You will need to make at least 2 photo-copies of each of the forms. The first copy will be used to make a rough draft of your answers on each form. The final copy will be used to create a clean, legible final version of each completed form. This final draft version will be considered your *original*. On this completed original, you will sign and date each form if necessary before filing it with the bankruptcy court.

In general, you will use every form provided. However, 3 of the forms (*Individual Debtor's Statement of Intention*; *Application and Order to Pay Filing Fees in Installments*; and *Proof of Service by Mail*) are only used if your particular situation warrants their use. Please refer to the instructions for each individual form in Chapter 4. When filling in your copy of these forms, please be careful that your information is listed in the proper columns or on the correct form. Some of these forms are complicated and several forms are very similar. Do not make any stray marks on the forms. Type your information if possible. You may use legible black-ink handwriting to complete them (except the *Mailing Label Matrix* which must be typed).

Form 1. Voluntary Petition

<table>
<tr><td colspan="2">United States Bankruptcy Court
_____ District of _____</td><td colspan="2">VOLUNTARY
PETITION</td></tr>
<tr><td colspan="2">In RE (Name of debtor-if individual, enter Last, First, Middle)</td><td colspan="2">NAME OF JOINT DEBTOR (Spouse)(Last, First, Middle)</td></tr>
<tr><td colspan="2">ALL OTHER NAMES used by the debtor in the last 6 years
(Include married, maiden, and trade names)</td><td colspan="2">ALL OTHER NAMES used by the joint debtor in the last 6 years
(Include married, maiden, and trade names)</td></tr>
<tr><td colspan="2">SOC. SEC/TAX I.D. NO. (If more than one, state all)</td><td colspan="2">SOC. SEC/TAX I.D. NO. (of joint debtor)(If more than one, state all)</td></tr>
<tr><td>STREET ADDRESS OF DEBTOR (No. and street, city, state, and zip code)</td><td>COUNTY OF RESIDENCE OR PRINCIPAL PLACE OF BUSINESS</td><td>STREET ADDRESS OF JOINT DEBTOR (No. and street, city, state, and zip code)</td><td>COUNTY OF RESIDENCE OR PRINCIPAL PLACE OF BUSINESS</td></tr>
<tr><td colspan="2">MAILING ADDRESS OF DEBTOR (If different from street address)</td><td colspan="2">MAILING ADDRESS OF JOINT DEBTOR (If different from street address)</td></tr>
</table>

LOCATION OF PRINCIPAL ASSETS OF BUSINESS DEBTOR
(If different from addresses listed above

VENUE (Check one box)
- ☐ Debtor has been domiciled or has had a residence, principal place of business or principal assets in this District for 180 days immediately preceding the date of this petition or for a longer part of such 180 days than in any other District.
- ☐ There is a bankruptcy case concerning debtor's affiliate, general partner, or partnership pending in this District.

INFORMATION REGARDING DEBTOR (Check applicable boxes)

TYPE OF DEBTOR

- ☐ Individual
- ☐ Joint (Husband and Wife))
- ☐ Partnership
- ☐ Other _____
- ☐ Corporation publicly held
- ☐ Corporation not publicly held
- ☐ Municipality

NATURE OF DEBT
- ☐ Non-business/Consumer
- ☐ Business—Complete A & B below

A. TYPE OF BUSINESS (Check one box)
- ☐ Farming
- ☐ Professional
- ☐ Retail/Wholesale
- ☐ Railroad
- ☐ Transportation
- ☐ Manufacturing
- ☐ Mining
- ☐ Stockbroker
- ☐ Commodity broker
- ☐ Construction
- ☐ Real Estate
- ☐ Other business

B. BRIEFLY DESCRIBE NATURE OF BUSINESS

CHAPTER OR SECTION OF BANKRUPTCY CODE UNDER WHICH THE PETITION IS FILED (Check one box)
- ☐ Chapter 7
- ☐ Chapter 9
- ☐ Chapter 11
- ☐ Chapter 12
- ☐ Chapter 13
- ☐ Sec. 304-Case ancillary to foreign proceeding

SMALL BUSINESS (Chapter 11 only)
- ☐ Debtor is a small business as defined in 11 U.S.C. 101.
- ☐ Debtor is and elects to be considered a small business under 11 U.S.C. 101.

FILING FEE (Check one box)
- ☐ Filing fee attached
- ☐ Filing fee to be paid in installments (Applicable to individuals only). Must attach signed application for the court's consideration certifying that the debtor is unable to pay the fee except in installments. Rule 1006(b)-Form 3.

NAME AND ADDRESS OF LAW FIRM OR ATTORNEY

NAME(S) OF ATTORNEY DESIGNATED TO REPRESENT DEBTOR
(Print or type names)

- ☐ Debtor is not represented by an attorney. Telephone Number of debtor not represented by an attorney: (   )

STATISTICAL/ADMINISTRATIVE INFORMATION (28 U.S.C. Section 604,
(Estimates only–Check applicable boxes).

THIS SPACE FOR COURT USE ONLY

- ☐ Debtor estimate that funds will be available for distribution to unsecured creditors.
- ☐ Debtor estimates that after any exempt property is excluded and administrative expenses paid, there will be no funds available for distribution to unsecured creditors.

ESTIMATED NUMBER OF CREDITORS

1-15	16-49	50-99	100-199	200-999	1000 +
☐	☐	☐	☐	☐	☐

ESTIMATED ASSETS (In thousands of dollars)

- 50	50-99	100-499	500-999	1000-9,999	10,000-99,999	100,000+
☐	☐	☐	☐	☐	☐	☐

ESTIMATED LIABILITIES (In thousands of dollars)

- 50	50-99	100-499	500-999	1000-9,999	10,000-99,999	100,000+
☐	☐	☐	☐	☐	☐	☐

ESTIMATED NUMBER OF EMPLOYEES (Chapter 11 & 12 Only)

0	1-19	20-99	100-999	1000 +
☐	☐	☐	☐	☐

ESTIMATED NUMBER OF SECURITY HOLDERS (Chapter 11 & 12 Only)

0	1-19	20-99	100-999	1000 +
☐	☐	☐	☐	☐

Name of Debtor _____

Case No. _____

(Court Use Only)

FILING OF PLAN

For Chapter 9, 11, 12, and 13 use only. Check appropriate box.

☐ A copy of debtor's proposed plan dated _____ is attached   ☐ Debtor intends to file a plan within the time allowed by statute, rule, or court order.

PRIOR BANKRUPTCY CASE FILED WITHIN LAST 6 YEARS (If more than one, attach additional sheet)

Location where filed	Case Number	Date filed

PENDING BANKRUPTCY CASE FILED BY ANY SPOUSE, PARTNER, OR AFFILIATE OF THIS DEBTOR (If more than one, attach additional sheet)

Location where filed	Case Numbere	Date
Relationship	District	Judge

REQUEST FOR RELIEF

Debtor requests relief in accordance with the chapter of Title 11, United States Code, specified in this petition.

SIGNATURES

Attorney

X _____

Signature   Date

INDIVIDUAL/JOINT DEBTOR(S)
I declare under penalty of perjury that the information provided in this petition is true and correct.

X _____

Signature of Debtor

Date

X _____

Signature of Joint Debtor

Date

CORPORATE OR PARTNERSHIP DEBTOR
I declare under penalty of perjury that the information provided in this petition is true and correct and that the filing of this petition on behalf of the debtor has been authorized.

X _____

Signature of Authorized Individual

Print or type name of Authorized Individual

Title of Individual Authorized by Debtor to file this Petition

Date
If debtor is a corporation filing under Chapter 11, Exhibit "A" is attached and made part of this petition

TO BE COMPLETED BY INDIVIDUAL CHAPTER 7 DEBTOR WITH PRIMARILY CONSUMER DEBTS (SEE P.L. 96-353, SECTION 322)
I am aware that I may proceed under Chapter 7, 11, 12, or 13 of title 11, United States Code, understand the relief available under each chapter, and choose to proceed under Chapter 7 of such title.
If I am represented by an attorney, Exhibit "B" has been completed.

X _____

Signature of Debtor   Date

X _____

Signature of Joint Debtor   Date

CERTIFICATION AND SIGNATURE OF NON-ATTORNEY BANKRUPTCY PETITION PREPARER
I certify that I am a bankruptcy petition preparer as defined in 11 U.S.C. Section 110, that I prepared this document for compensation, and that I have provided the debtor with a copy of this document.

Printed or Typed Name of Bankruptcy Petition Preparer

Social Security Number

Address   Telephone
Names and Social Security numbers of all other individuals who prepared or assisted in preparing this document.
If more than one person prepared this document, attach additional signed sheets conforming to the appropriate Official Form for each person.
have explained the relief available under each such

Signature of Bankruptcy Petition Preparer

A bankruptcy petition preparer's failure to comply with the provisions of title 11 and the Federal Rules of Bankruptcy Procedure may result in fines and imprisonment or both. 11 U.S.C. Sec. 110; 18 U.S.C. Sec. 156.

EXHIBIT "B"
(To be completed by attorney for individual Chapter 7 debtor(s) with primarily consumer debts.)

I, the attorney for the debtor(s) named in the foregoing petition, declare that I have informed the debtor(s) that (he, she, or they) may proceed under Chapter 7, 11, 12, or 13 of Title 11, United States Code, and chapter.

X _____

Signature of Attorney   Date

In re _____   Case No. _____
                    Debtor   (If known)

SCHEDULE A-REAL PROPERTY

Except as directed below, list all real property in which the debtor has any legal, equitable, or future interest, including all **property** owned as a co-tenant, community property, or in which the debtor has a life estate. Include any property in which the debtor holds rights and **powers** exercisable for the debtor's own benefit. If the debtor is married, state whether husband, wife, or both own the property by placing an "H," "W," or "C" in the column labeled "Husband, Wife, Joint, or Community." If the debtor holds no interest in real property, write "None" under "Description and Location of Property."

Do not include interests in executory contracts and unexpired leases on this schedule. List them in Schedule G-Executory Contracts and Unexpired Leases.

If an entity claims to have a lien or hold a secured interest in any property, state the amount of the secured claim. See Schedule D. If no entity claims to hold a secured interest in the property, write "None" in the column labeled "Amount of Secured Claim."

If the debtor is an individual or if a joint petition is filed, state the amount of any exception claimed in the property only in Schedule C-Property Claimed as Exempt.

DESCRIPTION AND LOCATION OF PROPERTY	NATURE OF DEBTOR'S INTEREST IN PROPERTY	HUSBAND, WIFE, JOINT OR COMMUNITY	CURRENT MARKET VALUE OF DEBTOR'S INTEREST IN PROPERTY WITHOUT DEDUCTING ANY SECURED CLAIM OR EXEMPTION	AMOUNT OF SECURED CLAIM
			Total $	

(Report also on Summary of Schedules.)

In re _____   Case No. _____
           Debtor   (If known)

SCHEDULE B-PERSONAL PROPERTY

Except as directed below, list all personal property of the debtor of whatever kind. If the debtor has no property in one or more of the categories, place an "X" in the appropriate position in the column labeled "None." If additional space is needed in any category, attach a separate sheet properly identified with the case name, case number, and the number of the category. If the debtor is married, state whether husband, wife, or both own the property by placing an "H," "W "J," or "C" in the column labeled "Husband, Wife, Joint, or Community." If the debtor is an individual or a joint petition is filed, state the amount of any exemptions claimed only in Schedule C-Property Claimed as Exempt.

Do not include interests in executory contracts and unexpired leases on this schedule. List them in Schedule G-Executory Contracts and Unexpired Leases.

If the property is being held for the debtor by someone else, state that person's name and address under "Description and Location of Property."

TYPE OF PROPERTY	NONE	DESCRIPTION AND LOCATION OF PROPERTY	HUSBAND, WIFE, JOINT OR COMMUNITY	CURRENT MARKET VALUE OF DEBTOR'S INTEREST IN PROPERTY, WITHOUT DEDUCTING ANY SECURED CLAIM OR EXEMPTION
1. Cash on hand.				
2. Checking, savings or other financial accounts, certificates of deposit, or shares in banks, savings and loan, thrift, building and loan, and homestead associations, or credit unions, brokerage houses, or cooperatives.				
3. Security deposits with public utilities, telephone companies, landlords, and others.				
4. Household goods and furnishings, including audio, video, and computer equipment.				

In re _____   Case No. _____
                  Debtor   (If known)

SCHEDULE B-PERSONAL PROPERTY
(Continuation Sheet)

TYPE OF PROPERTY	NONE	DESCRIPTION AND LOCATION OF PROPERTY	HUSBAND, WIFE, JOINT OR COMMUNITY	CURRENT MARKET VALUE OF DEBTOR'S INTEREST IN PROPERTY, WITHOUT DEDUCTING ANY SECURED CLAIM OR EXEMPTION
5. Books, pictures and other art objects, antiques, stamp, coin, record, tape, compact disc, and other collections or collectibles.				
6. Wearing apparel.				
7. Furs and jewelry.				
8. Firearms and sports, photographic, and other hobby equipment.				
9. Interests in insurance policies. Name insurance company of each policy and itemize surrender or refund value of each.				
10. Annuities. Itemize and name each issuer.				
11. Interests in IRA, ERISA, Keogh, or other pension or profit sharing plans. Itemize.				
12. Stock and interests in incorporated and unincorporated businesses. Itemize.				
13. Interests in partnerships or joint ventures. Itemize.				

In re _____   Case No. _____
                    Debtor   (If known)

SCHEDULE B-PERSONAL PROPERTY
(Continuation Sheet)

TYPE OF PROPERTY	NONE	DESCRIPTION AND LOCATION OF PROPERTY	HUSBAND, WIFE, JOINT OR COMMUNITY	CURRENT MARKET VALUE OF DEBTOR'S INTEREST IN PROPERTY, WITHOUT DEDUCTING ANY SECURED CLAIM OR EXEMPTION
14. Government and corporate bonds and other negotiable non-negotiable instruments.				
15. Accounts receivable.				
16. Alimony, maintenance, support, and property settlements to which the debtor is or may be entitled. Give particulars.				
17. Other liquidated debts owing debtor including tax refunds. Give particulars.				
18. Equitable or future interest, life estates, and rights or powers exercisable for the benefit of the debtor other than those listed in Schedule A - Real Property.				
19. Contingent and non-contingent interests in estate of a decedent, death benefit plan, life insurance policy, or trust.				

In re _____   Case No. _____
　　　　　　Debtor　　　　　　　　　　　　　　　　　　　　　　(If known)

SCHEDULE B-PERSONAL PROPERTY
(Continuation Sheet)

TYPE OF PROPERTY	NONE	DESCRIPTION AND LOCATION OF PROPERTY	HUSBAND, WIFE, JOINT OR COMMUNITY	CURRENT MARKET VALUE OF DEBTOR'S INTEREST IN PROPERTY, WITHOUT DEDUCTING ANY SECURED CLAIM OR EXEMPTION
20. Other contingent and unliquidated claims of every nature, including tax refunds, counterclaims of the debtor, and rights to setoff claims. Give estimated value of each.				
21. Patents, copyrights, and other intellectual property. Give particulars.				
22. Licenses, franchises, and other general intangibles. Give particulars.				
23. Automobiles, trucks, trailers, and other vehicles and accessories.				
24. Boats, motors, and accessories.				
25. Aircraft and accessories.				
26. Office equipment, furnishings, and supplies.				
27. Machinery, fixtures, equipment, and supplies used in business.				

In re _____   Case No. _____
             Debtor   (If known)

SCHEDULE B-PERSONAL PROPERTY
(Continuation Sheet)

TYPE OF PROPERTY	NONE	DESCRIPTION AND LOCATION OF PROPERTY	HUSBAND, WIFE, JOINT OR COMMUNITY	CURRENT MARKET VALUE OF DEBTOR'S INTEREST IN PROPERTY, WITHOUT DEDUCTING ANY SECURED CLAIM OR EXEMPTION
28. Inventory.				
29. Animals.				
30. Crops-growing or harvested. Give particulars.				
31. Farming equipment and implements.				
32. Farm supplies, chemicals, and feed.				
33. Other personal property of any kind not already listed, such as season tickets, etc. Itemize.				

_____ continuation sheets attached   **Total** | $

(Include amounts from any continuation sheets attached. Report total also on Summary of Schedules.)

In re _____   Case No. _____
            Debtor   (If known)

SCHEDULE C-PROPERTY CLAIMED AS EXEMPT

Debtor elects the exemptions to which debtor is entitled under:

(Check one box)

❑   11 U.S.C.§ 522(b)(1): Exemptions provided in 11 U.S.C.§522(d). Note: These exemptions are available only in certain states.

❑   11 U.S.C.§ 522(b)(2): Exemptions available under applicable nonbankruptcy federal laws, state or local law where the debtor's domicile has been located for the 180 days immediately preceding the filing of the petition, or for a longer portion of the 180-day period than in any other place, and the debtor's interest as a tenant by the entirety or joint tenant to the extent the interest is exempt from process under applicable nonbankruptcy law.

DESCRIPTION OF PROPERTY	SPECIFY LAW PROVIDING EACH EXEMPTION	VALUE OF CLAIMED EXEMPTION	CURRENT MARKET VALUE OF PROPERTY WITHOUT DEDUCTING EXEMPTIONS

In re _____   Case No. _____
             Debtor   (If known)

SCHEDULE D-CREDITORS HOLDING SECURED CLAIMS

State the name, mailing address, including zip code, and account number, if any, of all entities holding claims secured by property of the debtor as of the date of filing of the petition. List creditors holding all types of secured interest such as judgment liens, garnishments, statutory liens, mortgages, deeds of trust, and other security interests. List creditors in alphabetical order to the extent practicable. If all secured creditors will not fit on this page, use the continuation sheet provided.

If any entity other than a spouse in a joint case may be jointly liable on a claim, place an "X" in the column labeled "Codebtor," include the entity on the appropriate schedule of creditors, and complete Schedule H-Codebtors. If a joint petition is filed, state whether husband, wife, both of them, or the marital community may be liable on each claim by placing an "H", "W", "J", or "C" in the column labeled "Husband, Wife, Joint, or Community."

If the claim is contingent, place an "X" in the column labeled "Contingent." If the claim is unliquidated, place an "X" in the column labeled "Unliquidated." If the claim is disputed, place an "X" in the column labeled "Disputed." (You may need to place an "X" in more than one of these three columns.)

Report the total of all claims listed on this schedule in the box labeled "Total" on the last sheet of the completed schedule. Report this total also on the Summary of Schedules.

☐ Check this box if debtor has no creditors holding secured claims to report on this Schedule D.

CREDITOR'S NAME AND MAILING ADDRESS INCLUDING ZIP CODE	CODEBTOR	HUSBAND, WIFE, JOINT, OR COMMUNITY	DATE CLAIM WAS INCURRED, NATURE OF LIEN, AND DESCRIPTION AND MARKET VALUE OF PROPERTY SUBJECT TO LIEN	CONTINGENT	UNLIQUIDATED	DISPUTED	AMOUNT OF CLAIM WITHOUT DEDUCTING VALUE OF COLLATERAL	UNSECURED PORTION, IF ANY
Account No.								
			Value $					
Account No.								
			Value $					
Account No.								
			Value $					
Account No.								
			Value $					

_____ Continuation sheets attached

Subtotal (Total of this page)	$	
TOTAL (Use only on last page)	$	

(Report total also on Summary of Schedules)

In re _____ Case No. _____
            Debtor   (If known)

SCHEDULE D-CREDITORS HOLDING SECURED CLAIMS
(Continuation Sheet)

CREDITOR'S NAME AND MAILING ADDRESS INCLUDING ZIP CODE	CODEBTOR	HUSBAND, WIFE, JOINT, OR COMMUNITY	DATE CLAIM WAS INCURRED, NATURE OF LIEN, AND DESCRIPTION AND MARKET VALUE OF PROPERTY SUBJECT TO LIEN	CONTINGENT	UNLIQUIDATED	DISPUTED	AMOUNT OF CLAIM WITHOUT DEDUCTING VALUE OF COLLATERAL	UNSECURED PORTION, IF ANY
Account No.			Value $					
Account No.			Value $					
Account No.			Value $					
Account No.			Value $					
Account No.			Value $					
Account No.			Value $					

Sheet no. ____ of ____ Continuation sheets attached
to Schedule D - Creditors Holding Secured Claims

Subtotal
(Total of this page) $

TOTAL
(Use only on last page) $

(Report total also on Summary of Schedules)

In re _____   Case No. _____
                    Debtor   (If known)

SCHEDULE E-CREDITORS HOLDING UNSECURED PRIORITY CLAIMS

A complete list of claims entitled to priority, listed separately by type of priority, is to be set forth on the sheets provided. Only holders of unsecured claims entitled to priority should be listed in this schedule. In the boxes provided on the attached sheets, state the name and mailing address, including zip code, and account number, if any, of all entities holding priority claims against the debtor or the property of the debtor, as of the date of the filing of the petition.

If any entity other than a spouse in a joint case may be jointly liable on a claim, place an "X" in the column labeled "Codebtor," include the entity on the appropriate schedule of creditors, and complete Schedule H-Codebtors. If a joint petition is filed, state whether husband, wife, both of them, or the marital community may be liable on each claim by placing an "H", "W", "J", or "C" in the column labeled "Husband, Wife, Joint, or Community."

If the claim is contingent, place an "X" in the column labeled "Contingent." If the claim is unliquidated, place an "X" in the column labeled "Unliquidated." If the claim is disputed, place an "X" in the column labeled "Disputed." (You may need to place an "X" in more than one of these three columns.)

Report the total of all claims listed on each sheet in the box labeled "Subtotal" on each sheet. Report the total of all claims listed on this Schedule E in the box labeled "Total" on the last sheet of the completed schedule. Repeat this total also on the Summary of Schedules.

❑   Check this box if **debtor** has no **creditors** holding **unsecured priority claims to report** on **this** Schedule E.

TYPES OF PRIORITY CLAIMS (Check the appropriate box(es) below if claims in that category are listed on the attached sheets)

❑   **Extensions of credit in an involuntary case**
       Claims arising in the ordinary course of the debtor's business or financial affairs after the commencement of the case but before the earlier Of the appointment of a trustee or the order for relief. 11 U.S.C. § 507(a)(2).

❑   **Wages, salaries, and commissions**
       Wages, salaries, and commissions, including vacation, severance, and sick leave pay owing to employees and commissions owing to qualifying independent sales representatives up to $4000* per person, earned within 90 days immediately preceding the filing of the original petition, or the cessation of business, whichever occurred first, to the extent provided in 11 U.S.C. § 507(a)(3).

❑   **Contributions to employee benefit plans**
       Money owed to employee benefit plans for services rendered within 180 days immediately preceding the filing of the original petition, or the cessation of business, whichever occurred first, to the extent provided in 11 U.S.C. § 507(a)(4).

❑   **Certain farmers and fishermen**
       Claims of certain farmers and fishermen, up to a maximum of $4000* per farmer or fisherman, against the debtor, as provided in 1 1 U.S.C. § 507(a)(5).

❑   **Deposits by individuals**
       Claims of individuals up to a maximum of $1800* for deposits for the purchase, lease, or rental of property or services for personal, family, or household use, that were not delivered or provided. 11 U.S.C. § 507(a)(6).

❑   **Alimony, Maintenance, or Support**
       Claims of a spouse, former spouse, or child of the debtor for alimony, maintenance, or support, to the extent provided in 1 1 U.S.C. § 507(a)(7).

❑   **Taxes and Certain Other Debts Owed to Governmental Units**
       Taxes, customs, duties, and penalties owing to federal, state, and local governmental units as set forth in 1 1 U.S.C. § 507(a)(8).

❑   **Commitments to Maintain the Capital of an Insured Depository Institution**
       Claims based on commitments to the FDIC, RTC, Director of the Office of Thrift Supervision, Comptroller of the Currency, or Board of Governors of the Federal Reserve system, or their predecessors or successors, to maintain the capital of an insured depository institution. 1 1 U.S.C. § 507 (a)(9).

* Amounts are subject to adjustment on April 1, 1998, and every three years thereafter with respect to cases commenced on or after the date of adjustment.

_____ continuation sheets attached

In re _____   Case No. _____
           Debtor   (If known)

SCHEDULE E-CREDITORS HOLDING UNSECURED PRIORITY CLAIMS
(Continuation Sheet)

CREDITOR'S NAME AND MAILING ADDRESS INCLUDING ZIP CODE	CODEBTOR	HUSBAND, WIFE, JOINT, OR COMMUNITY	DATE CLAIM WAS INCURRED AND CONSIDERATION FOR CLAIM	CONTINGENT	UNLIQUIDATED	DISPUTED	TOTAL AMOUNT OF CLAIM	AMOUNT ENTITLED TO PRIORITY
Account No.								
Account No.								
Account No.								
Account No.								
Account No.								
Account No.								

Sheet no. ____ of ____ Continuation sheets attached
to Schedule E - Creditors Holding Unsecured Priority Claims

Subtotal (Total of this page) $ _____

TOTAL (Use only on last page) $ _____

(Report total also on Summary of Schedules)

In re _____   Case No. _____
                    Debtor   (If known)

SCHEDULE F-CREDITORS HOLDING UNSECURED NONPRIORITY CLAIMS

State the name, mailing address, including zip code, and account number, if any, of all entities holding unsecured claims without priority against the debtor or the property of the debtor as of the date of filing of the petition. Do not include claims listed in Schedules D and E. If all creditors will not fit on this page, use the continuation sheet provided.

If any entity other than a spouse in a joint case may be jointly liable on a claim, place an "X" in the column labeled "Codebtor," include the entity on the appropriate schedule of creditors, and complete Schedule H-Codebtors. If a joint petition is filed, state whether husband, wife, both of them, or the marital community may be liable on each claim by placing an "H", "W", "J", or "C" in the column labeled "Husband, Wife, Joint, or Community."

If the claim is contingent, place an "X" in the column labeled "Contingent." If the claim is unliquidated, place an "X" in the column labeled "Unliquidated." If the claim is disputed, place an "X" in the column labeled "Disputed." (You may need to place an "X" in more than one of these three columns.)

Report the total of all claims listed on this schedule in the box labeled "Total" on the last sheet of the completed schedule. Report this total also on the Summary of Schedules.

☐   Check this box if debtor has no creditors holding unsecured nonpriority claims to report on this Schedule F.

CREDITOR'S NAME AND MAILING ADDRESS INCLUDING ZIP CODE	CODEBTOR	HUSBAND, WIFE, JOINT, OR COMMUNITY	DATE CLAIM WAS INCURRED AND CONSIDERATION FOR CLAIM. IF CLAIM IS SUBJECT TO SETOFF, SO STATE.	CONTINGENT	UNLIQUIDATED	DISPUTED	AMOUNT OF CLAIM
Account No.							
Account No.							
Account No.							
Account No.							

_____ Continuation sheets attached

	Subtotal (Total of this page)	$
	TOTAL (Use only on last page)	$

(Report total also on Summary of Schedules)

In re _____   Case No. _____
                Debtor   (If known)

SCHEDULE F-CREDITORS HOLDING UNSECURED NONPRIORITY CLAIMS
(Continuation Sheet)

CREDITOR'S NAME AND MAILING ADDRESS INCLUDING ZIP CODE	CODEBTOR	HUSBAND, WIFE, JOINT, OR COMMUNITY	DATE CLAIM WAS INCURRED AND CONSIDERATION FOR CLAIM. IF CLAIM IS SUBJECT TO SETOFF, SO STATE.	CONTINGENT	UNLIQUIDATED	DISPUTED	AMOUNT OF CLAIM
Account No.							
Account No.							
Account No.							
Account No.							
Account No.							
Account No.							
				Subtotal (Total of this page)			$
				TOTAL (Use only on last page)			$

Sheet no. _____ of _____ Continuation sheets attached
to Schedule F - Creditors Holding Unsecured Nonpriority Claims

(Report total also on Summary of Schedules)

In re _____   Case No. _____
                    Debtor   (If known)

SCHEDULE G-EXECUTORY CONTRACTS AND UNEXPIRED LEASES

Describe all executory contracts of any nature and all unexpired leases of real personal property. Include any timeshare interests.

State nature of debtor's interest in contract, i.e., "Purchaser," "Agent," etc. State whether debtor is the lessor or lessee of a lease.

Provide the names and complete mailing addresses of all other parties to each lease or contract described.

NOTE: A party listed on this schedule will not receive notice of the filing of this case unless the party is also scheduled in the appropriate schedule of creditors.

❑   Check this box if debtor has no executory contracts or unexpired leases.

NAME AND MAILING ADDRESS, INCLUDING ZIP CODE, OF OTHER PARTIES TO LEASE OR CONTRACT.	DESCRIPTION OF CONTRACT OR LEASE AND NATURE OF DEBTOR'S INTEREST. STATE WHETHER LEASE IF FOR NONRESIDENTIAL REAL PROPERTY. STATE CONTRACT NUMBER OF ANY GOVERNMENT CONTRACT.

In re _____   Case No. _____
                    Debtor   (If known)

SCHEDULE H-CODEBTORS

Provide the information requested concerning any person or entity, other than a spouse in a joint case, that is also liable on any debts listed by debtor in the schedules of creditors. Include all guarantors and co-signers. In community property states, a married debtor not filing a joint case should report the name and address of the nondebtor spouse on this schedule. Include all names used by the nondebtor spouse during the six years

❑   Check this box if debtor has no codebtors.

NAME AND ADDRESS OF CODEBTOR	NAME AND ADDRESS OF CREDITOR

In re _____   Case No. _____
             Debtor   (If known)

SCHEDULE I-CURRENT INCOME OF INDIVIDUAL DEBTOR(S)

The column labeled "Spouse" must be completed in all cases filed by joint debtors and by a married debtor in a Chapter 12 or 13 case whether or not a joint petition is filed, unless the spouses are separated and a joint petition is not filed.

Debtor's Marital Status	DEPENDENTS OF DEBTOR AND SPOUSE		
	NAMES	AGE	RELATIONSHIP

Employment:	DEBTOR	SPOUSE
Occupation		
Name of Employer		
How long employed?		
Address of Employer		

	DEBTOR	SPOUSE
Income: (Estimate of average monthly income)		
Current monthly gross wages, salary, and commissions (pro rate if not paid monthly)	$ _____	$ _____
Estimated monthly overtime	$ _____	$ _____
SUBTOTAL OF MONTHLY WAGES	$ _____	$ _____
LESS PAYROLL DEDUCTIONS		
a. Payroll taxes and Social Security	$ _____	$ _____
b. Insurance	$ _____	$ _____
c. Union dues	$ _____	$ _____
d. Other (Specify: _____)	$ _____	$ _____
SUBTOTAL OF PAYROLL DEDUCTIONS	$ _____	$ _____
TOTAL NET MONTHLY TAKE HOME PAY	$ _____	$ _____
Regular income from operation of business or profession or farm (attach detailed statement)	$ _____	$ _____
Income from real property	$ _____	$ _____
Interest and dividends	$ _____	$ _____
Alimony, maintenance or support payments payable to the debtor for the debtor's use or that of dependents listed above	$ _____	$ _____
Social Security or other government assistance (Specify: _____)	$ _____	$ _____
Pension or retirement income	$ _____	$ _____
Other monthly income (Specify: _____)	$ _____	$ _____
TOTAL MONTHLY NON-WAGE INCOME	$ _____	$ _____

TOTAL COMBINED MONTHLY INCOME $ _____   (Report also on Summary of Schedules)

Describe any increase or decrease of more than 10% in any of the above categories anticipated to occur within the year following the filing of this document:

In re _____   Case No. _____
                    Debtor   (If known)

SCHEDULE J-CURRENT EXPENDITURES OF INDIVIDUAL DEBTOR(S)

Complete this schedule by estimating the average monthly expenses of the debtor and the debtor's family. Pro rate any payments made biweekly, quarterly, semi-annually, or annually to show monthly rate.

☐   Check this box if a joint petition is filed and debtor's spouse maintains a separate household. Complete a separate schedule of expenditures labeled "Spouse."

Rent or home mortgage payment (include lot rented for mobile home) $ _____
Are real estate taxes included? Yes _____   No _____
Is property insurance included? Yes _____   No _____
Utilities: Electricity and heating fuel $ _____
     Water and sewer $ _____
     Telephone $ _____
     Other (_____) $ _____
Home maintenance (repairs and upkeep) $ _____
Food $ _____
Clothing $ _____
Laundry and dry cleaning $ _____
Medical and dental expenses $ _____
Transportation (not including car payments) $ _____
Recreation, clubs and entertainment, newspapers, magazines, etc. $ _____
Charitable contributions $ _____
Insurance (not deducted from wages or included in home mortgage payments)
     Homeowner's or renter's $ _____
     Life $ _____
     Health $ _____
     Auto $ _____
     Other (_____) $ _____
Taxes (not deducted from wages or included in home mortgage payments)
(Specify: _____) $ _____
Installment payments: (In Chapter 12 and 13 cases, do not list payments to be included in the plan)
     Auto $ _____
     Other (_____) $ _____
     Other (_____) $ _____
Alimony, maintenance, and support paid to others $ _____
Payments for support of additional dependents not living at your home $ _____
Regular expenses from operation of business, profession, or farm (attach detailed statement) $ _____
Other (_____) $ _____
TOTAL MONTHLY EXPENSES (Report also on Summary of Schedules)

     $ _____

[FOR CHAPTER 12 AND CHAPTER 13 DEBTORS ONLY]
Provide the information requested below, including whether plan payments are to be made biweekly, monthly, annually, or at some other regular interval.

A. Total projected monthly income $ _____

B. Total projected monthly expenses $ _____

C. Excess income (A minus B) $ _____

D. Total amount to be paid into plan each _____ $ _____
                                    (interval)

In re _____ Case No. _____
           Debtor   (If known)

DECLARATION CONCERNING DEBTOR'S SCHEDULES

DECLARATION UNDER PENALTY OF PERJURY BY INDIVIDUAL DEBTOR

I declare under penalty of perjury that I have read the foregoing summary and schedules consisting of _____
sheets, and that they are true and correct to the best of my knowledge, information, and belief.   *(Total shown on summary page plus 1)*

Date _____ Signature _____
                                                         Debtor

Date _____ Signature _____
                                                     (Joint Debtor, if any)

                                         (If joint case, both spouses must sign.)

CERTIFICATION AND SIGNATURE OF NON-ATTORNEY BANKRUPTCY PETITION PREPARER (See 11 U.S.C. §110)

I certify that I am a bankruptcy petition preparer - as defined in 11 U.S.C. § 110, that I prepared this document for compensation, and that I have provided the debtor with a copy of this document.

_____ _____
Printed or Typed Name of Bankruptcy Petition Preparer   Social Security No.

_____

_____
Address

Names and Social Security numbers of all other individuals who prepared or assisted in preparing this document:

If more than one person prepared this document, attach additional signed sheets conforming to the appropriate Official Form for each person.

X _____ _____
Signature of Bankruptcy Petition Preparer   Date

A bankruptcy petition preparer's failure to comply with the provisions of title 11 and the Federal Rules of Bankruptcy Procedure may result in fines or imprisonment or both. 11 U.S.C. § 110, 18 U.S.C. § 156.

DECLARATION UNDER PENALTY OF PERJURY ON BEHALF OF CORPORATION OR PARTNERSHIP

I, the _____ (the president or other officer or an authorized agent of the corporation or an
authorized agent of the partnership] of the _____ (corporation or partnership) named as debtor
in this case, declare under penalty of perjury that I have read the foregoing summary and schedules, consisting of
_____ sheets, and that they are true and correct to the best of my knowledge, information, and belief.
(Total shown on summary page plus 1)

Date _____ Signature _____

                                         _____
                                     (Print or type name of individual signing on behalf of debtor]

[An individual signing on behalf of a partnership or corporation must indicate position or relationship to debtor.)

Penalty for making a false statement or concealing property: Fine of up to $500,000, imprisonment for up to 5 years, or both. 18 U.S.C. §§ 152 and 3571.

In re _____   Case No. _____
                    Debtor   (If known)

SUMMARY OF SCHEDULES

Indicate as to each schedule whether that schedule is attached and state the number of pages in each. Report the totals from Schedules A, B, D, E, F, I, and J in the boxes provided. Add the amounts from Schedules A and B to determine the total amount of the debtor's assets. Add the amounts from Schedules D, E, and F to determine the total amount of the debtor's liabilities.

NAME OF SCHEDULE	ATTACHED (YES/NO?)	# SHEETS	AMOUNTS SCHEDULED		
			ASSETS	DEBTS	OTHER
A: Real Property			$		
B: Personal Property			$		
C: Property Claimed as Exempt					
D: Creditors Holding Secured Claims				$	
E: Creditors with Unsecured Priority Claims				$	
F: Creditors with Unsecured Nonpriority Claims				$	
G: Executory Contracts and Unexpired Leases					
H: Codebtors					
I: Current Income of Individual Debtor(s)					$
J: Current Expenditures of Individual Debtor(s)					$
TOTAL # SHEETS ⇒ ALL SCHEDULES ⇒					
TOTAL ⇒ ASSETS ⇒			$		
TOTAL ⇒ DEBTS ⇒				$	

In re _____   Case No. _____

          Debtor   (If known)

SUPPLEMENTAL SHEET TO SCHEDULE _____

FORM 7. STATEMENT OF FINANCIAL AFFAIRS

UNITED STATES BANKRUPTCY COURT

_____ DISTRICT OF _____

In re _____   Case No. _____

Debtor   (If known)

STATEMENT OF FINANCIAL AFFAIRS

This statement is to be completed by every debtor. Spouses filing a joint petition may file a single statement on which the information for both spouses is combined. If the case is filed under Chapter 12 or Chapter 13, a married debtor must furnish information for both spouses whether or not a joint petition is filed, unless the spouses are separated and a joint petition is not filed. An individual debtor engaged in business as a sole proprietor, partner, family farmer, or self-employed professional, should provide the information requested on this statement concerning all such activities as well as the individual's personal affairs.

Questions 1-15 are to be completed by all debtors. Debtors that are or have been in business, as defined below, also must complete Questions 16-21. **Each question must be answered. If the answer to any question is "None," or the question is not applicable, mark the box labeled "None."** If additional space is needed for the answer to any question, use and attach a separate sheet properly identified with the case name, case number (if known), and the number of the question.

DEFINITIONS

"*In business*." A debtor is "in business" for the purpose of this form if the debtor is a corporation or partnership. An individual debtor is "in business" for the purpose of this form if the debtor is or has been, within the two years immediately preceding the filing of this bankruptcy case, any of the following: an officer, director, managing executive, or person in control of a corporation; a partner, other than a limited partner, of a partnership; a sole proprietor or self-employed.

"*Insider*." The term "insider" includes but is not limited to: relatives of the debtor; general partners of the debtor and their relatives; corporations of which the debtor is an officer, director, or person in control; officers, directors, and any person in control of a corporate debtor and their relatives; affiliates of the debtor and insiders of such affiliates; any managing agent of the debtor. 11 U.S.C. § 101(30).

1. Income from employment or operation of business

None

☐

State the gross amount of income the debtor has received from employment, trade, or profession, or from operation of the debtor's business from the beginning of this calendar year to the date this case was commenced. State also the gross amounts received during the **two years** immediately preceding this calendar year. (A debtor that maintains, or has maintained, financial records on the basis of a fiscal rather than a calendar year may report fiscal year income. Identify the beginning and ending dates of the debtor's fiscal year.) If a joint petition is filed, state income for each spouse separately. (Married debtors filing under Chapter 12 or Chapter 13 must state income of both spouses whether or not a joint petition is filed, unless the spouses are separated and a joint petition is not filed.)

AMOUNT   SOURCE (If more than one)

_____

2. Income other than from employment or operation of business

None

☐

State the amount of income received by the debtor other than from employment, trade, profession, or operation of the debtor's business during the **two years** immediately preceding the commencement of this case. Give particulars. If a joint petition is filed, state income for each spouse separately. (Married debtors filing under Chapter 12 or Chapter 13 must state income for each spouse whether or not a joint petition is filed, unless the spouses are separated and a joint petition is not filed.)

AMOUNT	SOURCE

3. Payments to creditors

None

☐

a. List all payments on loans, installment purchases of goods or services, and other debts, aggregating more than $600 to any creditor, made within **90 days** immediately preceding the commencement of this case. (Married debtors filing under Chapter 12 or Chapter 13 must include payments by either or both spouses whether not a joint petition is filed, unless the spouses are separated and a joint petition is not filed.)

NAME AND ADDRESS OF CREDITOR	DATES OF PAYMENTS	AMOUNT PAID	AMOUNT STILL OWING

None

☐

b. List all payments made within **one year** immediately preceding the commencement of this case, to or for the benefit of, creditors who are or **were** insiders. (Married debtors filing under Chapter 12 or Chapter 13 must include payments by either or both spouses whether or not a joint petition is filed, unless the spouses are separated and a joint petition is not filed.)

NAME AND ADDRESS OF CREDITOR RELATIONSHIP TO DEBTOR	DATES OF PAYMENTS	AMOUNT PAID	AMOUNT STILL OWING

4. Suits, executions, garnishments and attachments

None
☐

a. List all suits to which the debtor is or was a party within **one year** immediately preceding the filing of this bankruptcy case. (Married debtors filing under Chapter 12 or Chapter 13 must include information concerning either or both spouses whether or not a joint petition is filed, unless the spouses are separated and a joint petition is not filed.)

CAPTION OF SUIT AND CASE NUMBER	NATURE OF PROCEEDING	COURT AND LOCATION	STATUS OR DISPOSITION

None
☐

b. Describe all property that has been attached, garnished or seized under any legal or equitable process within **one year** immediately preceding the commencement of this case. (Married debtors filing under Chapter 12 or Chapter 13 must include information concerning property of either or both spouses whether or not a joint petition is filed, unless the spouses are separated and a joint petition is not filed.)

NAME AND ADDRESS OF PERSON FOR WHOSE BENEFIT PROPERTY WAS SEIZED	DATE OF SEIZURE	DESCRIPTION AND VALUE OF PROPERTY

5. Repossessions, foreclosures and returns

None
☐

List all property that has been repossessed by a creditor, sold at a foreclosure sale, transferred through a deed in lieu of foreclosure or returned to the seller, within **one year** immediately preceding the commencement of this case. (Married debtors filing under Chapter 12 or Chapter 13 must include information concerning property of either or both spouses whether or not a joint petition is filed, unless the spouses are separated and a joint petition is not filed.)

NAME AND ADDRESS OF CREDITOR OR SELLER	DATE OF REPOSSESSION, FORECLOSURE SALE, TRANSFER OR RETURN	DESCRIPTION AND VALUE OF PROPERTY

6. Assignments and receiverships

None
☐

a. Describe any assignment of property for the benefit of creditors made within **120 days** immediately preceding the commencement of this case. (Married debtors filing under Chapter 12 or Chapter 13 must include any assignment by either or both spouses whether or not a joint petition is filed, unless the spouses are separated and a joint petition is not filed.)

NAME AND ADDRESS OF ASSIGNEE	DATE OF ASSIGNMENT	TERMS OF ASSIGNMENT OR SETTLEMENT

None
☐

b. List all property which has been in the hands of a custodian, receiver, or court-appointed official within **one year** immediately preceding the commencement of this case. (Married debtors filing under Chapter 12 or Chapter 13 must include information concerning property of either or both spouses whether or not a joint petition is filed, unless the spouses are separated and a joint petition is not filed.)

NAME AND ADDRESS OF CUSTODIAN	NAME AND LOCATION OF COURT; CASE TITLE & NUMBER	DATE OF ORDER	DESCRIPTION AND VALUE OF PROPERTY

7. Gifts

None
☐

List all gifts or charitable contributions made within **one year** immediately preceding the commencement of this case except ordinary and usual gifts to family members aggregating less than $200 in value per individual family member and charitable contributions aggregating less than $100 per recipient. (Married debtors filing under Chapter 12 or Chapter 13 must include gifts or contributions by either or both spouses whether or not a joint petition is filed, unless the spouses are separated and a joint petition is not filed.)

NAME AND ADDRESS OF PERSON OR ORGANIZATION	RELATIONSHIP TO DEBTOR, IF ANY	DATE OF GIFT	DESCRIPTION AND VALUE OF GIFT

8. Losses

None
❑

List all losses from fire, theft, other casualty or gambling within **one year** immediately preceding the commencement of this case **or since the commencement of this case.** (Married debtors filing under Chapter 12 or Chapter 13 must include losses by either or both spouses whether or not a joint petition is filed, unless the spouses are separated and a joint petition is not filed.)

DESCRIPTION AND VALUE OF PROPERTY	DESCRIPTION OF CIRCUMSTANCES AND, IF LOSS WAS COVERED IN WHOLE OR IN PART BY INSURANCE, GIVE PARTICULARS	DATE OF LOSS

9. Payments related to debt counseling or bankruptcy

None
❑

List all payments made or property transferred by or on behalf of the debtor to any person, including attorneys, for consultation concerning debt consolidation, relief under the bankruptcy law or preparation of a petition in bankruptcy within **one year** immediately preceding the commencement of this case.

NAME AND ADDRESS OF PAYEE	DATE OF PAYMENT NAME OF PAYOR IF OTHER THAN DEBTOR	AMOUNT OF MONEY OR DESCRIPTION AND VALUE OF PROPERTY

10. Other transfers

None
❑

a. List all other property, other than property transferred in the ordinary course of the business or financial affairs of the debtor, transferred either absolutely or as security within **one year** immediately preceding the commencement of this case. (Married debtors filing under Chapter 12 or Chapter 13 must include transfers by either or both spouses whether or not a joint petition is filed, unless the spouses are separated and a joint petition is not filed.)

NAME AND ADDRESS OF TRANSFEREE; RELATIONSHIP TO DEBTOR	DATE	DESCRIBE PROPERTY TRANSFERRED AND VALUE RECEIVED

11. Closed financial accounts

None
❑

List all financial accounts and instruments held in the name of the debtor or for the benefit of the debtor which were closed, sold, or otherwise transferred within **one year** immediately preceding the commencement of this case. Include checking, savings, or other financial accounts, certificates of deposit, or other instruments; shares and share accounts held in banks, credit unions, pension funds, cooperatives, associations, brokerage houses and other financial institutions. (Married debtors filing under Chapter 12 or Chapter 13 must include information concerning accounts or instruments held by or for either or both spouses whether or not a joint petition is filed, unless the spouses are separated and a joint petition is not filed.)

NAME AND ADDRESS OF INSTITUTION	TYPE AND NUMBER OF ACCOUNT AND AMOUNT OF FINAL BALANCE	AMOUNT AND DATE OF SALE OR CLOSING

12. Safe deposit boxes

None
❑

List each safe deposit or other box or depository in which the debtor has or had securities, cash, or other valuables within **one year** immediately preceding the commencement of this case. (Married debtors filing under Chapter 12 or Chapter 13 must include boxes or depositories of either or both spouses whether or not a joint petition is filed, unless the spouses are separated and a joint petition is not filed.)

NAME AND ADDRESS OF BANK OR OTHER DEPOSITORY	NAMES AND ADDRESSES OF THOSE WITH ACCESS TO BOX OR DEPOSITORY	DESCRIPTION OF CONTENTS	DATE OF TRANSFER OR SURRENDER, IF ANY

13. Setoff

None
❑

List all setoffs made by any creditor, including a bank, against a debt or deposit of the debtor within **90 days** preceding the commencement of this case. (Married debtors filing under Chapter 12 or Chapter 13 must include information concerning either or both spouses whether or not a joint petition is filed, unless the spouses are separated and a joint petition is not filed.)

NAME AND ADDRESS OF CREDITOR	DATE OF SETOFF	AMOUNT OF SETOFF

14. Property held for another person

None ☐

List all property owned by another person that the debtor holds or controls.

NAME AND ADDRESS OF OWNER	DESCRIPTION AND VALUE OF PROPERTY	LOCATION OF PROPERTY

15. Prior address of debtor

None ☐

If the debtor has moved within the **two years** immediately preceding the commencement of this case, list all premises which the debtor occupied during that period and vacated prior to the commencement of this case. If a joint petition is filed, report also any separate address of either spouse.

ADDRESS	NAME USED	DATES OF OCCUPANCY

The following questions are to be completed by every debtor that is a corporation or partnership and by any individual debtor who is or has been, within the two years immediately preceding the commencement of this case, any of the following: an officer, director, managing executive, or owner of more than 5 percent of the voting securities of a corporation; a partner, other than a limited partner, of a partnership; a sole proprietor or otherwise self-employed.

*(An individual or joint DEBTOR should complete this portion of the statement **only** if the debtor is or has been in business, as defined above, within the two years immediately preceding the commencement of this case.)*

16. Nature, location and name of business

None
❏

a. If the debtor is an individual, list the names and addresses of all businesses in which the debtor was an officer, director, partner, or managing executive of a corporation, partnership, sole proprietorship, or was a self-employed professional within the **two years** immediately preceding the commencement of this case, or in which the debtor owned 5 percent or more of the voting or equity securities, within the **two years** immediately preceding the commencement of this case.

b. If the debtor is a partnership, list the names and addresses of all businesses in which the debtor was a partner or owned 5 percent or more of the voting securities, within the **two years** immediately preceding the commencement of this case.

c. If the debtor is a corporation, list the names and addresses of all businesses in which the debtor was a partner or owned 5 percent or more of the voting securities, within the **two years** immediately preceding the commencement of this case.

NAME	ADDRESS	NATURE OF BUSINESS	BEGINNING AND ENDING DATES OF OPERATION

17. Books, records and financial statements

None
❏

a. List all bookkeepers and accountants who within the **six years** immediately preceding the filing of this bankruptcy case kept or supervised the keeping of books of account and records of the debtor.

NAME AND ADDRESS	DATES SERVICES RENDERED

None
❏

b. List all firms or individuals who within the **two years** immediately preceding the filing of this bankruptcy case have audited the books of account and records, or prepared a financial statement of the debtor.

NAME AND ADDRESS	DATES SERVICES RENDERED

None ❑   **c.** List all firms or individuals who at the time of the commencement of this case were in possession of the books of account and records of the debtor. If any of the books of account and records are not available, explain.

NAME   ADDRESS

None ❑   **d.** List all financial institutions, creditors and other parties, including mercantile and trade agencies, to whom a financial statement was issued within the **two years** immediately preceding the commencement of this case by the debtor.

NAME AND ADDRESS   DATE ISSUED

18. Inventories

None ❑   **a.** List the dates of the last two inventories taken of your property, the name of the person who supervised the taking of each inventory, and the dollar amount and basis of each inventory.

DATE OF INVENTORY	INVENTORY SUPERVISOR	DOLLAR AMOUNT OF INVENTORY (Specify cost, market or other basis)

None ❑   **b.** List the name and address of the person having possession of the records of each of the two inventories reported in a., above.

DATE OF INVENTORY	NAME AND ADDRESSES OF CUSTODIAN OF INVENTORY RECORDS

19. Current partners, officers, directors and shareholders

None
❏

a. If the debtor is a partnership, list the nature and percentage of partnership interest of each member of the partnership.

NAME AND ADDRESS	NATURE OF INTEREST	PERCENTAGE OF INTEREST

None
❏

b. If the debtor is a corporation, list all officers and directors of the corporation, and each stockholder who directly or indirectly owns, controls, or holds 5 percent or more of the voting securities of the corporation.

NAME AND ADDRESS	TITLE	NATURE AND PERCENTAGE OF STOCK OWNERSHIP

20. Former partners, officers, directors and shareholders

None
❏

a. If the debtor is a partnership, list each member who withdrew from the partnership within **one year** immediately preceding the commencement of this case.

NAME	ADDRESS	DATE OF WITHDRAWAL

None
❑

b. If the debtor is a corporation, list all officers or directors whose relationship with the corporation terminated within **one year** immediately preceding the commencement of this case.

NAME AND ADDRESS	TITLE	DATE OF TERMINATION

21. Withdrawals from a partnership or distributions by a corporation

None
❑

If the debtor is a partnership or corporation, list all withdrawals or distributions credited or given to an insider, including compensation in any form, bonuses, loans, stock redemptions, options exercised and any other perquisite during **one year** immediately preceding the commencement of this case.

NAME AND ADDRESS OF RECIPIENT; RELATIONSHIP TO DEBTOR	DATE AND PURPOSE OF WITHDRAWAL	AMOUNT OF MONEY OR DESCRIPTION AND VALUE OF PROPERTY

[If completed by an individual or individual and spouse]

I declare under penalty of perjury that I have read the answers contained in the foregoing statement of financial affairs and any attachments thereto and that they are true and correct.

Date _____   Signature of Debtor _____

Date _____   Signature of Joint Debtor (if any) _____

CERTIFICATION AND SIGNATURE OF NON-ATTORNEY BANKRUPTCY PETITION PREPARER (See 11 U.S.C. § 110)

I certify that I am a bankruptcy petition preparer as defined in 1 1 U.S.C. § 1 10, that I prepared this document for compensation, and that I have provided the debtor with a copy of this document.

_____   _____
Printed or Typed Name of Bankruptcy Petition Preparer   Social Security No.

_____

_____
Address

Names and Social Security numbers of all other individuals who prepared or assisted in preparing this document:

If more than one person prepared this document, attach additional signed sheets conforming to the appropriate Official Form for each person.

X_____   _____
Signature of Bankruptcy Petition Preparer   Date

A bankruptcy petition preparer's failure to comply with the provisions of title 11 and the Federal Rules of Bankruptcy may result in fine or imprisonment or both. 11 U.S.C. §110, 18 U.S.C. §156.

[If completed on behalf of a partnership or corporation]

I declare under penalty of perjury that I have read the answers contained in the foregoing statement of financial affairs and any attachments thereto and that they are true and correct to the best of my knowledge, information and belief.

Date _____   Signature _____

_____
Print Name and Title

[An individual signing on behalf of a partnership or corporation must indicate position or relationship to debtor.]

Penalty for presenting fraudulent claim.- Fine of up to $500,00 or imprisonment for up to 5 years, or both. 18 U.S.C. §§ 152 and 3571

FORM 8. CHAPTER 7 INDIVIDUAL DEBTOR'S STATEMENT OF INTENTION

UNITED STATES BANKRUPTCY COURT
_____ DISTRICT OF _____

In re _____   Case No. _____
                        Debtor   (If known)

1. I, the debtor, have filed a schedule of assets and liabilities which includes consumer debts secured by property of the estate.

2. My intention with respect to the property of the estate which secures those consumer debts is as follows:

   a. *Property to be surrendered.*

   Description of Property   Creditor's Name

   1. _____
   2. _____
   3. _____

   b. *Property to be retained. [Check applicable statement of debtor's intention concerning reaffirmation, redemption or lien avoidance.]*

Description of property	Creditor's name	Debt will be reaffirmed pursuant to § 524(c)	Property is claimed as exempt and will be redeemed pursuant to § 722	Lien will be avoided pursuant to § 522(f) and property will be be claimed as exempt
1. _____	_____	_____	_____	_____
2. _____	_____	_____	_____	_____
3. _____	_____	_____	_____	_____
4. _____	_____	_____	_____	_____
5. _____	_____	_____	_____	_____

3. I understand that § 521(2)(B) of the Bankruptcy Code requires that I perform the above stated intentions within 45 days of the filing of this statement with the court or within such additional time as the court, for cause, within such 45-day period fixes.

Date: _____   _____
                                                                        Signature of Debtor

---

CERTIFICATION AND SIGNATURE OF NON-ATTORNEY BANKRUPTCY PETITION PREPARER (See 11 U.S.C. § 110)

I certify that I am a bankruptcy petition preparer as defined in 11 U.S.C. § 110, that I prepared this document for compensation, and that I have provided the debtor with a copy of this document.

_____   _____
Printed or Typed Name of Bankruptcy Petition Preparer   Social Security No.

_____

Address

Names and Social Security numbers of all other individuals who prepared or assisted in preparing this document:

If more than one person prepared this document, attach additional signed sheets conforming to the appropriate Official Form for each person.

X_____   _____
Signature of Bankruptcy Petition Preparer   Date

A bankruptcy petition preparer's failure to comply with the provisions of title 11 and the Federal Rules of Bankruptcy may result in fine or imprisonment or both. 11 U.S.C. §110, 18 U.S.C. §156.

FORM 3. APPLICATION TO PAY FILING FEE IN INSTALLMENTS

UNITED STATES BANKRUPTCY COURT

_____ DISTRICT OF _____

In re _____   Case No. _____

Debtor   (If known)

Chapter _____

APPLICATION TO PAY FILING FEE IN INSTALLMENTS

In accordance with Federal Rules of Bankruptcy Procedure 1006, application is made for permission to pay the filing fee on the following terms:

$ _____ with the filing of the petition, and the balance of

$ _____ in _____ installments, as follows:

$ _____ on or before _____

$ _____ on or before _____

$ _____ on or before _____

$ _____ on or before _____

I certify that I am unable to pay the filing fee except in installments. I further certify that I have not paid any money or transferred any property to an attorney or any other person for services in connection with this case or in connection with any other pending bankruptcy case and I will not make any payment or transfer of property for services in connection with the case until the filing fee is paid in full.

Date: _____

_____

Applicant

_____

Attorney for Applicant

CERTIFICATION AND SIGNATURE OF NON-ATTORNEY BANKRUPTCY PETITION PREPARER (See 11 U.S.C. § 110)

I certify that I am a bankruptcy petition preparer as defined in 1 1 U.S.C. § 1 10, that I prepared this document for compensation, and that I have provided the debtor with a copy of this document.

_____   _____

Printed or Typed Name of Bankruptcy Petition Preparer   Social Security No.

_____

_____

Address

Names and Social Security numbers of all other individuals who prepared or assisted in preparing this document:

If more than one person prepared this document, attach additional signed sheets conforming to the appropriate Official Form for each person.

X_____   _____

Signature of Bankruptcy Petition Preparer   Date

A bankruptcy petition preparer's failure to comply with the provisions of title 11 and the Federal Rules of Bankruptcy may result in fine or imprisonment or both. 11 U.S.C. §110, 18 U.S.C. §156.

ORDER

IT IS ORDERED that the debtor pay the filing fee in installments on the terms set forth in the foregoing application.

IT IS FURTHER ORDERED that until the filing fee is paid in full the debtor shall not pay, and no person shall accept, any money for services in connection with this case, and the debtor shall not relinquish, and no person shall accept, any property as payment for services in connection with this case.

BY THE COURT

Date: _____   _____

United States Bankruptcy Judge

United States Bankruptcy Court

_____ District of _____

Jn re _____   Case No. _____
                     Debtor   (If known)

VERIFICATION OF CREDITOR MATRIX

The above named debtor(s) in this case, declare under penalty of perjury that the information set forth in the attached list of creditors, consisting of _____ pages, is true and correct to the best of my (our) information and belief.

Dated: _____

_____   _____
Signature of Debtor   Signature of Joint Debtor (if any)

United States Bankruptcy Court

_____ District of _____

In re _____   Case No. _____
                    Debtor(s)   (If known)

COVER SHEET and INFORMATION SUMMARY

Presented to the court are the original and one copy of the following documents:

- ❑ Voluntary Petition
- ❑ Schedule A-Real Property
- ❑ Schedule B-Personal Property
- ❑ Schedule C-Property Claimed as Exempt
- ❑ Schedule D-Creditors Holding Secured Claims
- ❑ Schedule E-Creditors Holding Unsecured Priority Claims
- ❑ Schedule F-Creditors Holding Unsecured Nonpriority Claims
- ❑ Schedule G-Executory Contracts and Unexpired Leases
- ❑ Schedule H-Codebtors
- ❑ Schedule I-Current Income of Individual Debtor(s)
- ❑ Schedule J-Current Expenditures of Individual Debtor(s)
- ❑ Declaration Concerning Debtor's Schedules
- ❑ Summary of Schedules
- ❑ Statement of Financial Affairs
- ❑ Individual Debtor's Statement of Intention
- ❑ Application to Pay Filing Fee in Installments
- ❑ Creditor Mailing List Matrix
- ❑ Verification of Creditor Mailing List

NAME OF DEBTOR(S) _____
                         Last   First   Middle

Spouse (if Joint Petition) _____
                         Last   First   Middle

Social Security #   (Debtor) _____   (Spouse) _____
EIN # (if applicable)   (Debtor) _____   (Spouse) _____
A/K/A (if applicable)   (Debtor) _____   (Spouse) _____
D/B/A (if applicable)   (Debtor) _____   (Spouse) _____
Address of Debtor(s)   _____
                         Number   Street   Apt. #

                         _____
                         City   County   State ·   Zip

Check all applicable boxes:
- ▢ Voluntary Chapter 7   ▢ Business   ▢ Filing fees paid in installments   ▢ Joint Petition
- ▢ Pro-Se Petition   ▢ Non-Business   ▢ Filing fees paid in full   ▢ Individual Petition

Obligations, assets, and number of creditors of Debtor(s) as scheduled:
Priority: $ _____ .00   Unsecured: $ _____ .00
Secured: $ _____ .00   TOTAL ASSETS: $ _____ .00
Number of Creditors: _____

The above named debtor(s) in this case, declare under penalty of perjury that the information set forth in this summary and the attached documents, consisting of _____ pages, is true and correct to the best of my (our) information and belief.

Dated: _____

_____   _____
Signature of Debtor   Signature of Joint Debtor (if any)

United States Bankruptcy Court

_____ District of _____

In re _____   Case No. _____
                        Debtor   (If known)

PROOF OF SERVICE BY MAIL

I, _____, declare that I am over the age of 18 years and not a party to this

bankruptcy. I reside in the County of _____, and the State of _____.

My address is _____.

On the _____ day of _____, 19 ____, I served the following listed parties a copy of **Official Bankruptcy Form #8,**

Chapter 7 Individual Debtor's Statement of Intention of the debtor in this case, by placing a true and correct copy of it in a sealed

envelope with correct first-class postage fully prepaid, and depositing it in the United States mail at the U.S. Post Office located at

_____ addressed exactly as follows:

I declare under penalty of perjury that the foregoing is true and correct.

Signed and dated on the _____ day of _____, 19 ____.

_____
Signature

Appendix B

State and Federal Bankruptcy Exemptions

On the following pages, you will find an alphabetical state-by-state listing of state bankruptcy exemptions. In addition, at the end of this appendix, you will find a listing for federal bankruptcy exemptions and federal non-bankruptcy exemptions. In all states, you can use both the state and federal non-bankruptcy exemptions. In addition, residents of Arkansas, Connecticut, the District of Columbia, Hawaii, Massachusetts, Michigan, Minnesota, New Jersey, New Mexico, Pennsylvania, Rhode Island, South Carolina, Texas, Vermont, Washington, and Wisconsin have a choice. They may choose to use either their state exemptions *and* the federal non-bankruptcy exemptions *or* they may choose to use only the federal bankruptcy exemptions on listed on page 237. If residents of these states choose to use the federal bankruptcy exemptions, they may not use either the state exemptions or the federal non-bankruptcy exemptions. The first item in each listing will explain whether you can use the state exemptions and federal non-bankruptcy exemptions only or choose between those and the federal bankruptcy exemptions. California residents may choose between 2 different state exemption systems and may use the federal non-bankruptcy exemptions with either state system.

You should read through the entire listing for your state. Using your completed Schedule A (Real Property) and B (Personal Property), determine which of your property falls into any of the categories. On a separate worksheet, list the property which you feel is exempt under your state's laws. Then do the same for the federal non-bankruptcy exemptions. If your state does not allow a choice, fill in the property which you have determined is exempt on your *Schedule C: Property Claimed as Exempt* (using the instructions in Chapter 4).

If your state allows a choice, make another listing for the federal bankruptcy exemptions. Now, compare the state/federal non-bankruptcy exemption list with the federal bankruptcy exemption list. Decide which exemption list allows you to retain the most property and list that property on *Schedule C*. In general, all of your property is either personal property or real estate. *Real estate* includes all land and the buildings or improvements which are permanently attached to the land. All of the rest of your property is considered personal property. *Personal property* can be divided further into two categories: *tangible property* (property you can see and touch, such as artwork or a car) and *intangible property* (property which represents some type of ownership, such as stocks, bonds, copyrights, etc). If you are unclear of the meaning of the language in the statute, check the **Glossary of Bankruptcy Terms** at the end of this book for explanations. In general, each of the listings will indicate exemptions under the following general categories:

Benefits: Here will be listed various governmental benefits which are exempt from bankruptcy. This may include worker's compensation, unemployment payments, welfare payments, veteran's benefits and other government benefits. Private benefits are listed under either **Insurance** or **Pensions**.

Insurance: Under this listing you will find any insurance-related property, including the cash value of your insurance policies, private annuity and disability proceeds, and various other insurance-based assets.

Miscellaneous: This listing includes those types of property which are not listed elsewhere. This category most often includes property of a business partnership and exemption amounts which may be applied to any property (whether real estate or personal property).

Pensions: Here are listed those items of property which are related to retirement. Various pensions, IRA's, KEOGH's and other retirement plans are included. Also listed are certain profit-sharing plans which are exempt.

Personal Property: Here will be listed all of the personal property which is specifically exempt from bankruptcy. It is under this listing which you will most likely find property which you can keep after your bankruptcy. Every item listed as a state exemption (or federal if allowed) can be retained.

Real Estate: Listed here are the real estate exemptions. These may also be referred to as a *homestead* exemption. In general, these allow the exemption of a fixed value amount of the worth of your personal residence. In some states, this amount is very substantial and will allow you to retain your entire house. In other states, the actual size of the property determines the exemption.

Wages: Under this listing are both general wage exemptions and specific wage exemptions for certain professions. Generally, 75% of general wages are exempt from creditors. However, check your specific state listing.

NOTE for Spouses: Most states allow spouses who are filing jointly to each claim a complete set of exemptions. In other words, for joint filers, you can list exemptions for double the amounts which are shown under your state's listing. There are a few exceptions to this. Check your specific state's listings. If in doubt, claim double the exemption amount if filing jointly.

ALABAMA

Alabama residents may **not** use the Federal Bankruptcy Exemptions, but may use the Federal Non-Bankruptcy exemptions listed on p. 238 and the following state exemptions.

Benefits: Aid to aged, blind, disabled, families with dependent children (unlimited amount): Alabama Code 38-4-8;
    Coal miners pneumoconiosis benefits (unlimited amount): Alabama Code 25-5-179;
    Crime victims compensation (unlimited amount): Alabama Code 15-23-15(e);
    Southeast Asian War POW benefits (unlimited amount): Alabama Code 31-7-2;
    Unemployment compensation (unlimited amount): Alabama Code 25-4-140;
    Workers compensation (unlimited amount): Alabama Code 25-5-86(b).

Insurance: Annuity proceeds (up to $250 per month): Alabama Code 27-14-32;
    Disability proceeds (up to an average of $250 per month): Alabama Code 27-14-31;
    Fraternal society benefits (unlimited amount): Alabama Code 27-34-27;
    Life insurance proceeds if beneficiary is insured's spouse or child (unlimited amount): Alabama Code 6-10-8, 27-14-29;
    Life insurance proceeds if policy prohibits use to pay creditors (unlimited amount): Alabama Code 27-15-26;
    Mutual aid association benefits (unlimited amount): Alabama Code 27-30-25.

Miscellaneous: Property of business partnership (unlimited amount): Alabama Code 10-8-72(b)(3).

Pensions: Judges (payments actually being received): Alabama Code 12-18-10(a-b),;
    Law enforcement officers (unlimited amount): Alabama Code 36-21-77;
    State employees (unlimited amount): Alabama Code 36-27-28;
    Teachers (unlimited amount): Alabama Code 16-25-23.

Personal Property: Any personal property not listed below, except life insurance (up to $3,000 total): Alabama Code 6-10-6;
    Arms, uniforms, equipment required for military use (unlimited amount): Alabama Code 31-2-78.
    Books (unlimited amount): Alabama Code 6-10-6;
    Burial lot (unlimited amount): Alabama Code 6-10-5;
    Church pew (unlimited amount): Alabama Code 6-10-5;
    Clothing needed (unlimited amount): Alabama Code 6-10-6;
    Crops (unlimited amount): Alabama Code 6-9-41;
    Family portraits or pictures (unlimited amount): Alabama Code 6-10-6.

Real Estate: Real property or mobile home (up to $5,000): Alabama Code 6-10-2; up to 160 acres; husband and wife may double the amount; must file homestead exemption with Probate Court to be effective: Alabama Code 6-10-2.

Wages: 75% of earned but unpaid wages (judge may allow more for low-income debtors): Alabama Code 6-10-7.

ALASKA

Alaska residents may **not** use the Federal Bankruptcy Exemptions, but may use the Federal Non-Bankruptcy exemptions listed on p. 238 and the following state exemptions. Amounts may be revised by the state in even-numbered years.

Benefits: Aid to aged, blind, disabled, and families with dependent children (unlimited amount): Alaska Statutes 45.25.210, 47.25.395, 47.25.550;
Alaska longevity bonus (unlimited amount): Alaska Statutes 9.38.015(a)(5);
Crime victims compensation (unlimited amount): Alaska Statutes 9.38.015(a)(4);
Federally exempt benefits (unlimited amount): Alaska Statutes 9.38.015(a)(6);
General relief assistance (unlimited amount): Alaska Statutes 47.25.210;
Permanent fund dividends (45% of amount): Alaska Statutes 43.23.065;
Tuition credits under an advance college tuition payment contract (unlimited amount): Alaska Statutes 9.38.015(a)(9);
Unemployment compensation (unlimited amount): Alaska Statutes 9.38.015(b), 23.20.405;
Workers compensation (unlimited amount): Alaska Statutes 23.30.160.

Insurance: Disability benefits (unlimited amount): Alaska Statutes 9.38.015(b), 9.38.030(e)(1), (5);
Fraternal society benefits (unlimited amount): Alaska Statutes 21.84.240;
Insurance proceeds or recoveries for personal injury or wrongful death (up to wage exemption amount): Alaska Statutes 9.38.030(e)(3), 9.38.050(a);
Life insurance or annuity contract loan (up to $10,000); Alaska Statutes 9.38.017, 9.38.025;
Life insurance proceeds if beneficiary is insured's spouse or dependent (up to wage exemption amount): Alaska Statutes 9.38.030(e)(4);
Medical, surgical or hospital benefits (unlimited amount): Alaska Statutes 9.38.015(a)(3).
Unmatured life insurance contract (unlimited amount; accrued dividend, interest or loan value up to $10,000, if debtor is the insured or one debtor is dependent upon)): Alaska Statutes 9.38.015.

Miscellaneous: Alimony (up to wage exemption amount): Alaska Statutes 9.38.030(e)(2);
Child support payments made by collection agency (unlimited amount): Alaska Statutes 9.38.015(b);
Liquor licenses (unlimited amount): Alaska Statutes 9.38.015(a)(7);
Permits for limited entry into Alaska Fisheries (unlimited amount): Alaska Statutes 9.38.015(a)(8);
Property of business partnership (unlimited amount): Alaska Statutes 9.38.100(b).

Pensions: Elected public officers (unpaid benefits only): Alaska Statutes 9.38.015(b);
Judicial employees (unpaid benefits only): Alaska Statutes 9.38.015(b);
Other pensions (up to wage exemption amount and only for payments being paid): Alaska Statutes 9.38.030(e)(5).
Public employees (unpaid benefits only): Alaska Statutes 9.38.015(b), 39.35.505;
Retirement benefits deposited more than 120 days before filing bankruptcy (unlimited amount): Alaska Statutes 9.38,017;
Teachers (unpaid benefits only): Alaska Statutes 9.38.015(b);

Personal Property: Books, clothing, family portraits, heirlooms, household goods, and musical instruments (up to $3,000 total): Alaska Statutes 9.38.020(a);
Building materials (unlimited amount): Alaska Statutes 34.35.105;
Burial plot (unlimited amount): Alaska Statutes 9.38.015(a)(1);
Health aids (unlimited amount): Alaska Statutes 9.38.015(a)(2);
Implements, books or tools of a trade (up to $2,800): Alaska Statutes 9.38.020(c);
Jewelry (up to $1,000): Alaska Statutes 9.38.020(b);
Motor vehicle (up to $3,000; vehicle's market value cannot exceed $20,000): Alaska Statutes 9.38.020(e);
Pets (up to $1,000); Alaska Statutes 9.38.020(d);
Proceeds for lost, damaged or destroyed exempt property (up to exemption amount): Alaska Statutes 9.38,060.

Real Estate: Real property used as a residence (up to $54,000): Alaska Statutes 9.38.010.

Wages: If paid weekly, then net earnings up to $350, unless sole wage earner in household, then up to $550; if paid monthly or semi-monthly, then up to $1,400 in cash or liquid assets paid in any month, unless sole wage earner in household, then up to $2,200: Alaska Statutes 9.38.030(a)(b), 9.38.050(b).

ARIZONA

Arizona residents may **not** use the Federal Bankruptcy Exemptions, but may use the Federal Non-Bankruptcy exemptions listed on p. 238 and the following state exemptions. Wife and husband may double all exemption amounts, except real estate exemption.

Benefits: Unemployment compensation (unlimited amount): Arizona Revised Statutes 23-783;
   Welfare benefits (unlimited amount): Arizona Revised Statutes 46-208;
   Workers compensation (unlimited amount): Arizona Revised Statutes 23-1068.

Insurance: Fraternal society benefits (unlimited amount): Arizona Revised Statutes 20-881;
   Group life insurance policy or proceeds (unlimited amount): Arizona Revised Statutes 20-1132;
   Health, accident or disability benefits (unlimited amount): Arizona Revised Statutes 33-1126(A)(3);
   Life insurance cash value (up to $1,000 per dependent; $25,000 total): Arizona Revised Statutes 33-1126(A)(5);
   Life insurance proceeds (up to $20,000 if beneficiary is spouse or child): Arizona Revised Statutes 33-1126(A)(1); Husband and wife may double: Arizona Revised Statutes § 33-112 1.01.

Miscellaneous: Property of business partnership (unlimited amount): Arizona Revised Statutes 29-225.

Pensions: Board of regents members (unlimited amount): Arizona Revised Statutes 15-1628(I);
   Firefighters, police officers (unlimited amount): Arizona Revised Statutes 9-968, 9-931;
   Public safety personnel (unlimited amount): Arizona Revised Statutes 38-850(C);
   Rangers (unlimited amount): Arizona Revised Statutes 41-955; State employees: Arizona Revised Statutes 38-762.
   Retirement benefits deposited more than 120 days before filing bankruptcy (unlimited amount): Arizona Revised Statutes 33-1126(B).

Personal Property: Appliances, furniture, household goods, paintings (up to $4000 total for all listed): Arizona Revised Statutes 33-1123;
   Arms, uniforms and equipment required for military use (unlimited amount): Arizona Revised Statutes 33-1130(3);
   Bank deposit (up to $150 in one account; must file notice with bank): Arizona Revised Statutes 33-1126(A)(7);
   Bible; bicycle; sewing machine; typewriter; burial plot; rifle, pistol or shotgun (up to $500 total): Arizona Revised Statutes 33-1125;
   Books (up to $250); clothing (up to $500); wedding and engagement rings (up to $1,000); watch (up to $ 100); pets, horses, milk cows and poultry (up to $500); musical instruments (up to $250): Arizona Revised Statutes 33-1125;
   Farm machinery and equipment, utensils, seed, feed, grain and animals (up to $2,500 total): Arizona Revised Statutes 33-1130(2);
   Food and fuel (amount to last 6 months): Arizona Revised Statutes 33-1124;
   Health aids (unlimited amount): Arizona Revised Statutes 33-1125;
   Motor vehicle (up to $1,500; up to $4,000, if disabled): 33-1125(8);
   Prepaid rent or security deposit (up to $1,000 or 1 1/2 times rent, whichever is less, instead of real estate exemption): Arizona Revised Statutes 33-1126(C)
   Proceeds for sold or damaged exempt property (up to exemption amount): Arizona Revised Statutes 33-1126(A)(4), (6).
   Tools, equipment, instruments and books, except vehicle driven to work (up to $2,500): Arizona Revised Statutes 33-1130(1); Teaching aids of teacher (unlimited amount): Arizona Revised Statutes 33-1127.

Real Estate: Real estate, apartment, or mobile home used as residence (up to $100,000); sale proceeds are exempt for 18 months or until new home purchased, whichever occurs first; must record homestead declaration: Arizona Revised Statutes 33-1101;33-1102.

Wages: Minor child's earnings, unless debt is for child (unlimited amount): Arizona Revised Statutes 33-1126(A)(2);
   75% of earned but unpaid wages or pension payments (judge may allow more for low-income debtors): Arizona Revised Statutes 33-1131.

ARKANSAS

Arkansas residents **may use either** the Federal Bankruptcy Exemptions on p. 237 or the state exemptions listed below. If state exemptions are used, then Federal Non-Bankruptcy exemptions listed on p. 238 may also be used.

Benefits: Aid to aged, blind, disabled, and families with dependent children (unlimited amount): Arkansas Code Annotated 20-76-430;

Crime victims compensation unless for injury incurred during the crime (unlimited amount): Arkansas Code Annotated 16-90-716(e);

Unemployment compensation (unlimited amount): Arkansas Code Annotated 11-10-109;

Workers compensation (unlimited amount): Arkansas Code Annotated 11-9-110.

Insurance: Annuity contract (unlimited amount): Arkansas Code Annotated 23-79-134;

Disability benefits (unlimited amount): Arkansas Code Annotated 23-79-133;

Fraternal society benefits (unlimited amount): Arkansas Code Annotated 23-74-403;

Group life insurance (unlimited amount): Arkansas Code Annotated 23-79-132;

Life, health, accident or disability cash value or proceeds paid or due (limited to $500 personal property exemption provided by §§ 9-1 and 9-2 of the Arkansas Constitution): Arkansas Code Annotated 16-66-209;

Life insurance proceeds if policy prohibits proceeds from being used to pay creditors (unlimited amount): Arkansas Code Annotated 23-79-131;

Life insurance proceeds if beneficiary is not the insured (unlimited amount): Arkansas Code Annotated 23-79-131;

Mutual life or disability benefits (up to $1,000): Arkansas Code Annotated 23-72-114;

Stipulated insurance premiums (unlimited amount): Arkansas Code Annotated 23-71-112.

Miscellaneous: Any property (up to $800 if single; up to $1,250 if married): Arkansas Code Annotated 16-66-218(a)(1);

Property of business partnership (unlimited amount): Arkansas Code Annotated 4-42-502.

Pensions: Disabled firefighters (unlimited amount): Arkansas Code Annotated 24-11-814;

Disabled police officers (unlimited amount): Arkansas Code Annotated 24-11-417;

Firefighters (unlimited amount): Arkansas Code Annotated 24-10-616;

IRA deposits (up to $20,000 if deposited at least 1 year before filing for bankruptcy): Arkansas Code Annotated 16-66-218(b)(16);

Police officers (unlimited amount): Arkansas Code Annotated 24-10-616;

School employees (unlimited amount): Arkansas Code Annotated 24-7-715;

State police officers (unlimited amount): Arkansas Code Annotated 24-6-202, 24-6-205, 24-6-223.

Personal Property: Any personal property (up to $500 if married or head of household; otherwise up to $200): Arkansas Constitution 9-1,9-2; Arkansas Code Annotated 16-66-218(b)(1)(2).

Burial plot (up to 5 acres, instead of real estate option #2): Arkansas Code Annotated 16-66-207, 16-66-218(a)(1);

Clothing (unlimited amount): Arkansas Constitution 9-1, 9-2;

Implements, books and tools of a trade (up to $750): Arkansas Code Annotated 16-66-218(a)(4).

Motor vehicle (up to $1,200): Arkansas Code Annotated 16-66-218(a)(2);

Wedding bands (unlimited amount, diamond cannot exceed 1/2 carat): Arkansas Code Annotated 16-66-218(a)(3).

Real Estate: Real or personal property used as residence (only if head of family; unlimited value for up to 1/4 acre in city, town, village, or 80 acres elsewhere. If property is between 1/4 - 1 acre in city, town or village, or 80-160 acres elsewhere, up to $2,500; no homestead may exceed 1 acre in city, town or village, or 160 acres elsewhere: Arkansas Constitution 9-3, 9-4, 9-5; Arkansas Code Annotated 16-66-210, 16-66-218(b)(3);

Wages: Earned but unpaid wages due for 60 days (up to $500 if married or head of household; or up to $200 otherwise: Arkansas Code Annotated 16-66-208, 16-66-218(b)(6).

CALIFORNIA

California residents may **not** use the Federal Bankruptcy Exemptions, but may use the Federal Non-Bankruptcy exemptions listed on p. 238 and one of the following state exemption options only.

California OPTION #1

Benefits: Aid to aged, blind, disabled, families with dependent children (unlimited amount): California Code of Civil Procedure 704.170;
Financial aid to students (unlimited amount): California Code of Civil Procedure 704.190;
Relocation benefits (unlimited amount): California Code of Civil Procedure 704.180;
Unemployment benefits (unlimited amount): California Code of Civil Procedure 704.120;
Union benefits due to labor dispute (unlimited amount): California Code of Civil Procedure 704.120(b)(5);
Workers compensation (unlimited amount): California Code of Civil Procedure 704.160.

Insurance: Disability or health benefits (unlimited amount): California Code of Civil Procedure 704.130;
Fidelity bonds (unlimited amount): California Code of Civil Procedure - Labor 404;
Fraternal unemployment benefits (unlimited amount): California Code of Civil Procedure 704.120;
Homeowners insurance proceeds up to 6 months after receipt (up to real estate exemption amount): California Code of Civil Procedure 704.720(b);
Life insurance proceeds if policy prohibits proceeds from being used to pay creditors (unlimited amount): California Code of Civil Procedure Insurance 10132, 10170, 10171;
Matured life insurance benefits (amount needed for support): California Code of Civil Procedure 704.100(c);
Unmatured life insurance policy loan value (up to $4,000 - husband and wife may double): California Code of Civil Procedure 704.100(b).

Miscellaneous: Business or professional licenses, except liquor licenses (unlimited amount): California Code of Civil Procedure 695.060, 708.630;
Inmate's trust funds (up to $1,000): California Code of Civil Procedure 704.090;
Property of business partnership (unlimited amount): California Code of Civil Procedure Corporations 15025.

Pensions: County employees, firefighters, and peace officers (unlimited amount): California Code of Civil Procedure-Government 31452, 31913, 32210;
Public and private retirement benefits (unlimited amount): California Code of Civil Procedure 704.110, 704.115, Government 21201.

Personal Property: Appliances, clothing, food, and furnishings (amount needed): California Code of Civil Procedure 704.020;
Bank deposits from Social Security (up to $500; or $750 for husband and wife): California Code of Civil Procedure 704.080;
Building materials to repair or improve home (up to $1,000): California Code of Civil Procedure 704.030;
Burial plot; health aids (unlimited amount): California Code of Civil Procedure 704.050; 704.200;
Jewelry, heirlooms or art (up to $2,500 total): California Code of Civil Procedure 704.040;
Motor vehicles or auto insurance proceeds if vehicle lost, damaged or destroyed (up to $1,200): California Code of Civil Procedure 704.010;
Personal injury causes of action or recovery (amount needed for support): California Code of Civil Procedure 704.140;
Books, equipment, furnishings, materials, motor vehicle if not claimed otherwise, tools, uniforms, vessel (up to $2,500 total; up to $5,000 total for both spouses): California Code of Civil Procedure 704.060.
Wrongful death causes of action or recovery (amount needed for support): California Code of Civil Procedure 704.150.

Real Estate: Real or personal property used as residence (up to $50,000 if single and not disabled; up to $75,000 for families if no other member has a homestead; up to $100,000 if (a) 65 or older, or physically or mentally disabled (b) 55 or older, single, earn under $15,000 and creditors seek to force the sale of your home; or (c) 55 or older, married, earn under $20,000, and creditors seek to force the sale of your home); proceeds from sale of home exempt for 6 months: California Code of Civil Procedure 704.710, 704.720, and 704.730.

Wages: Public employee vacation credits (unlimited amount): California Code of Civil Procedure 704.113;
75% of wages paid within 30 days of filing for bankruptcy: California Code of Civil Procedure 704.070.

CALIFORNIA

California residents may **not** use the Federal Bankruptcy Exemptions, but may use the Federal Non-Bankruptcy exemptions listed on p. 238 and one of the following state exemption options. They must choose one exemption option only. Married couples may not double any exemptions under Option #2.

California OPTION #2

Benefits: Crime victims compensation (unlimited amount): California Code of Civil Procedure 703.140(b)(11)(A);
   Public assistance (unlimited amount): California Code of Civil Procedure 703.140(b)(10)(A);
   Social security (unlimited amount): California Code of Civil Procedure 703.140(b)(10)(A);
   Unemployment compensation (unlimited amount): California Code of Civil Procedure 703.140(b)(10)(A);
   Veterans benefits (unlimited amount): California Code of Civil Procedure 703.140(b)(10)(B).

Insurance: Disability benefits (unlimited amount): California Code of Civil Procedure 703.140(b)(10)(C);
   Life insurance proceeds (amount needed for support): California Code of Civil Procedure 703.140(b)(11)(C);
   Unmatured life insurance contract (up to $4000): California Code of Civil Procedure 703.140(b)(8);
   Unmatured life insurance policy other than credit (unlimited amount): California Code of Civil Procedure
      703.140(b)(7).

Miscellaneous: Alimony and child support (amount needed for support): California Code of Civil Procedure
      703.140(b)(10)(D);
   Any property (up to $400): California Code of Civil Procedure 703.140 (b)(5);
   Unused portion of real estate or burial exemption; can be used with any property: California Code of Civil
      Procedure 703.140 (b)(5).

Pensions: Retirement benefits (amount needed for support): California Code of Civil Procedure 703.140(b)(10)(E).

Personal Property: Animals, crops, appliances, furnishings, household goods, books, musical instruments and
      clothing (up to $200 per item): California Code of Civil Procedure 703.140(b)(3);
   Burial plot (up to $7,500, instead of real estate exemption): California Code of Civil Procedure 703.140;(b)(1)
   Health aids (unlimited amount): California Code of Civil Procedure 703.140 (b)(9);
   Jewelry (up to $500): California Code of Civil Procedure 703.140 (b)(4);
   Motor vehicle (up to $1,200): California Code of Civil Procedure 703.140 (b)(2);
   Personal injury recoveries (up to $7,500; but not pain and suffering or pecuniary loss): California Code of Civil
      Procedure 703.140(b)(11)(D, E);
   Implements, books and tools of a trade (up to $750): California Code of Civil Procedure 703.140 (b) (6).
   Wrongful death recoveries (amount needed for support): California Code of Civil Procedure 703.140(b)(11)(B).

Real Estate: Real or personal property, including co-op, used as residence (up to $7,500); unused portion of real estate
      exemption may be applied to any property: California Code of Civil Procedure 703.140 (b)(1).

Wages: No exemption.

California Residents: Please note that as this book went to press, passage of a revision of the California bankruptcy exemptions in the California Legislature was imminent. California Senate Bill 832, which would significantly increase the exemption amounts available to California Residents, appeared certain to become law. This legislation would double the monetary amounts for all California Option #1 and #2 exemptions with the following exceptions: the Option #1 real estate exemption and inmate trust fund exemption would remain unchanged. The Option #1 Social Security bank account deposit exemption would increase to $2,000 for individuals and $3,000 for couples. You are advised to check with you local librarian or law librarian to determine the current status of California law regarding bankruptcy exemptions.

COLORADO

Colorado residents may **not** use the Federal Bankruptcy Exemptions, but may use the Federal Non-Bankruptcy exemptions listed on p. 238 and the following state exemptions.

Benefits: Aid to aged, blind, disabled, and families with dependent children (unlimited amount): Colorado Revised Statutes 26-2-131;
Crime victims compensation (unlimited amount): Colorado Revised Statutes 13-54-102(1)(q), 24-4.1-114;
Unemployment compensation (unlimited amount): Colorado Revised Statutes 8-80-103;
Veterans benefits if war veteran (unlimited amount): Colorado Revised Statutes 13-54-102(1)(h);
Workers compensation (unlimited amount) Colorado Revised Statutes 8-42-124.

Insurance: Disability benefits (up to $200 per month; entire amount if received as a lump sum): Colorado Revised Statutes 10-8-114;
Fraternal society benefits (unlimited amount) Colorado Revised Statutes 10-14-122;
Group life insurance policy or proceeds (unlimited amount) Colorado Revised Statutes 10-7-205;
Homeowners insurance proceeds for 1 year after received (up to real estate exemption amount): Colorado Revised Statutes 38-41-209;
Life insurance cash value or proceeds (up to $5,000): Colorado Revised Statutes 13-54-102(1)(1);
Life insurance proceeds if policy prohibits proceeds from being used to pay creditors (unlimited amount): Colorado Revised Statutes 10-7-106.

Miscellaneous: Property of a business partnership (unlimited amount): Colorado Revised Statutes 7-60-125.

Pensions: Firefighters (unlimited amount): Colorado Revised Statutes 31-30-412,31-30-518;
Police officers (unlimited amount): Colorado Revised Statutes 31-30-313,31-30-616;
Public employees (unlimited amount): Colorado Revised Statutes 24-51-212;
Retirement benefits, including IRAs (unlimited amount): Colorado Revised Statutes 13-54-102(1)(s);
Teachers (unlimited amount): Colorado Revised Statutes 22-64-120;
Veterans (unlimited amount): Colorado Revised Statutes 13-54-102(1)(h),13-54-104.

Personal Property: Appliances or household goods (up to $1,500): Colorado Revised Statutes 13-54-102(1)(e);
Burial plot (unlimited amount): Colorado Revised Statutes 13-54-102(1)(d);
Clothing (up to $750): Colorado Revised Statutes 13-54-102(1)(a);
Food and fuel (up to $300): Colorado Revised Statutes 13-54-102(1)(0;
Health aids (unlimited amount): Colorado Revised Statutes 13-54-102(1)(p);
Horses, mules, machinery, and tools of farmer (up to $2,000 total): Colorado Revised Statutes 13-54-102(1)(g);
Jewelry (up to $500): Colorado Revised Statutes 13-54-102(1)(b);
Library of professional, supplies, machines, tools, equipment or books (up to $1,500 total): Colorado Revised Statutes 13-54102(1)(i)(k);
Livestock and poultry of farmer (up to $3,000): Colorado Revised Statutes 13-54-102(1)(g).
Motor vehicles used for work (up to $1,000; up to $3000 if used to get medical care, or if elderly or disabled): Colorado Revised Statutes 13-54-102(j)(1)(11);
Personal injury recoveries, unless debt is related to injury (unlimited amount): Colorado Revised Statutes 13-54-102(1)(n);
Pictures and books (up to $750): Colorado Revised Statutes 13-54-102(1)(c);
Proceeds for damaged exempt property (up to exemption amount): Colorado Revised Statutes 13-54-102(1)(m);
Security deposit (unlimited amount): Colorado Revised Statutes 13-54-102(1)(r).

Real Estate: Real property, mobile home or manufactured home (up to $30,000); proceeds from sale exempt for 1 year after received; must file exemption with county: Colorado Revised Statutes 38-41-201, 38-41-201.6, 38-41-203, 38-41-207;
House trailer or motor coach used as residence (up to $3,500): Colorado Revised Statutes 13-54-102(1)(o)(l);
Mobile home used as residence (up to $6,000): Colorado Revised Statutes 13-54-102(1)(o)(ll).

Wages:75% of earned but unpaid wages or pension payments (judge may allow more for low-income debtors): Colorado Revised Statutes 13-54-104.

CONNECTICUT

Connecticut residents **may use** either the Federal Bankruptcy Exemptions on p. 237 or the state exemptions listed below. If state exemptions are used, then Federal Non-Bankruptcy exemptions listed on p. 238 may also be used.

Benefits: Aid to aged, blind, disabled, and families with dependent children (unlimited amount): Connecticut General Statutes Annotated 52-352b(d);
Crime victims compensation (unlimited amount): Connecticut General Statutes Annotated 52-352b(o), 54-213;
Social security (unlimited amount): Connecticut General Statutes Annotated 52-352b(g);
Unemployment compensation (unlimited amount): Connecticut General Statutes Annotated 31-272(c), 52-352b(g);
Veterans benefits (unlimited amount): Connecticut General Statutes Annotated 27-140(1), 52-352b(g);
Wages from earnings incentive program (unlimited amount): Connecticut General Statutes Annotated 52-352b(d);
Workers compensation (unlimited amount): Connecticut General Statutes Annotated 52-352b(g).

Insurance: Disability benefits paid by association (unlimited amount): Connecticut General Statutes Annotated 52-352b(p);
Fraternal society benefits (unlimited amount): Connecticut General Statutes Annotated 38a-637;
Health or disability benefits (unlimited amount): Connecticut General Statutes Annotated 52-352b(e);
Life insurance proceeds if policy prohibits proceeds from being used to pay creditors (unlimited amount): Connecticut General Statutes Annotated 38a-454;
Life insurance proceeds (unlimited amount): Connecticut General Statutes Annotated 38a-453
Unmatured life insurance policy loan value (up to $4,000): Connecticut General Statutes Annotated 52-352b(s).

Miscellaneous: Alimony (up to amount of wage exemption): Connecticut General Statutes Annotated 52-352b(n);
Any property (up to $1,000): Connecticut General Statutes Annotated 52-352b(r)
Child support (unlimited amount): Connecticut General Statutes Annotated 52-352b(h);
Farm partnership animals and livestock feed (amount reasonably required to run farm where at least 50% of partners are members of same family: Connecticut General Statutes Annotated 52-352d;
Property of business partnership (unlimited amount): Connecticut General Statutes Annotated 34-63.

Pensions: Municipal employees (unlimited amount): Connecticut General Statutes Annotated 7-446;
Probate judges and employees (unlimited amount): Connecticut General Statutes Annotated 45-29o;
Retirement benefits (amounts being received): Connecticut General Statutes Annotated 52-352b(m);
State employees (unlimited amount): Connecticut General Statutes Annotated 5-171, 5-192w;
Teachers (unlimited amount): Connecticut General Statutes Annotated 10-183q.

Personal Property: Appliances, food, clothing, furniture and bedding (amounts needed): Connecticut General Statutes Annotated 52-352b(a);
Arms, equipment, uniforms, or musical instruments required for military use (unlimited amount): Connecticut General Statutes Annotated 52-352b(i);
Burial plot (unlimited amount): Connecticut General Statutes Annotated 52-352b(c);
Health aids (unlimited amount): Connecticut General Statutes Annotated 52-352b(f);
Motor vehicle (up to $1,500): Connecticut General Statutes Annotated 52-352bo);
Proceeds for damaged exempt property (up to exemption amount): Connecticut General Statutes Annotated 52-352b(q);
Security deposits for residence (unlimited amount): Connecticut General Statutes Annotated 52-352b(1);
Tools, books, instruments and farm animals (amounts needed): Connecticut General Statutes Annotated 52-352b(b).
Wedding and engagement rings (unlimited amount): Connecticut General Statutes Annotated 52-352b(k).

Real Estate: Real property, including mobile or manufactured home (up to $75,000): Connecticut General Statutes Annotated 52-352b(t).

Wages: 75% of earned but unpaid wages (judge may allow more for low-income debtors): Connecticut General Statutes Annotated 52-36la(o).

DELAWARE

Delaware residents may **not** use the Federal Bankruptcy Exemptions, but may use the Federal Non-Bankruptcy exemptions listed on p. 238 and the following state exemptions. Wife and husband may double exemption amounts. Total exemptions are limited to $5,000 if single and $10,000 for a husband and wife: Delaware Code Annotated 10-4914.

Benefits: Aid to aged, blind, disabled, and families with dependent children, general assistance (up to exemption limit): Delaware Code Annotated 31-513, 31-2309;
Unemployment compensation (up to exemption limit): Delaware Code Annotated 19-3374;
Workers compensation (up to exemption limit): Delaware Code Annotated 19-2355.

Insurance: Annuity contract proceeds (up to $350 per month): Delaware Code Annotated 18-2728;
Fraternal society benefits (up to exemption limit): Delaware Code Annotated 18-6118;
Group life insurance policy or proceeds (up to exemption limit): Delaware Code Annotated 18-2727;
Health or disability benefits (up to exemption limit): Delaware Code Annotated 18-2726;
Life insurance proceeds if policy prohibits proceeds from being used to pay creditors (up to exemption limit): Delaware Code Annotated 18-2729;
Life insurance proceeds (up to exemption limit): Delaware Code Annotated 18-2725.

Miscellaneous: Property of business partnership (up to exemption limit): Delaware Code Annotated 6-1525.

Pensions: Kent County employees (up to exemption limit): Delaware Code Annotated 9-4316;
Police officers (up to exemption limit): Delaware Code Annotated 11-8803;
State employees (up to exemption limit): Delaware Code Annotated 29-5503;
Volunteer firefighters (up to exemption limit): Delaware Code Annotated 16-6653.

Personal Property: Any personal property, except tools of a trade, if debtor is head of family (up to $500): Delaware Code Annotated 10-4903.
Bible, books and family pictures (up to exemption limit): Delaware Code Annotated 10-4902(a);
Burial plot (up to exemption limit): Delaware Code Annotated 10-4902(a);
Church pew or seat in public place of worship (up to exemption limit): Delaware Code Annotated 10-4902(a);
Clothing, includes jewelry (up to exemption limit): Delaware Code Annotated 10-4902(a);
Household goods: Delaware Code Annotated 10-4914(b);
Pianos and leased organs (up to exemption limit): Delaware Code Annotated 10-4902(d);
Sewing machines (up to exemption limit): Delaware Code Annotated 10-4902(c);
Tools, implements and fixtures (up to $75 in New Castle and Sussex Counties; up to $50 in Kent County): Delaware Code Annotated 10-4902(b).

Real Estate: No exemption.

Wages: 85% of earned but unpaid wages: Delaware Code Annotated 10-4913.

DISTRICT OF COLUMBIA

District of Columbia residents **may use either** the Federal Bankruptcy Exemptions on p. 237 or the state exemptions listed below. If district exemptions are used, then Federal Non-Bankruptcy exemptions on p. 238 may also be used.

Benefits: Aid to aged, blind, disabled, families with dependent children, and general assistance (unlimited amount): District of Columbia Code 3-215.1;
   Crime victims compensation (unlimited amount): District of Columbia Code 3-407;
   Unemployment compensation (unlimited amount): District of Columbia Code 46-119;
   Workers compensation (unlimited amount): District of Columbia Code 36-317.

Insurance: Disability benefits (unlimited amount): District of Columbia Code 35-522;
   Fraternal society benefits (unlimited amount): District of Columbia Code 35-1211;
   Group life insurance policy or proceeds (unlimited amount): District of Columbia Code 35-523;
   Life insurance proceeds if policy prohibits proceeds from being used to pay creditors (unlimited amount): District of Columbia Code 35-525;
   Life insurance proceeds (unlimited amount): District of Columbia Code 35-521;
   Other insurance proceeds (up to $60 per month, for 2 months; if head of family, then up to $200 per month): District of Columbia Code 15-503.

Miscellaneous: Property of business partnership (unlimited amount): District of Columbia Code 41-124.

Pensions: Judges (unlimited amount): District of Columbia Code 11-1570(d);
   Public school teachers (unlimited amount): District of Columbia Code 31-1217,31-1238.

Personal Property: Beds, bedding, radios, cooking utensils, stoves, furniture, furnishings and sewing machines (up to $300 total): District of Columbia Code 5-501(a)(2);
   Books and family pictures (up to $400): District of Columbia Code 15-501(a)(8);
   Business inventory and materials (up to $200): District of Columbia Code 15-501 (a) (5).
   Clothing (up to $300): District of Columbia Code 15-501(a)(1), 15-503(b);
   Cooperative association holdings (up to $50): District of Columbia Code 29-1128;
   Food and fuel (amount to last 3 months): District of Columbia Code 15-501 (a) (3), (4);
   Library, furniture, tools of professional or artist (up to $300): District of Columbia Code 15-501(a)(6);
   Mechanic's tools; tools of a trade or business (up to $200): District of Columbia Code 15-501 (a) (5), 15-503 (b);
   Motor vehicle, wagon and harness (up to $500): District of Columbia Code 15-501(a)(7);
   Residential condominium deposit (unlimited amount): District of Columbia Code 45-1869.
   Seal and documents of notary public (unlimited amount): District of Columbia Code 1-806.

Real Estate: No exemption.

Wages: 75% of earned but unpaid wages or pension payments (judge may allow more for low-income debtors): District of Columbia Code 16-572;
   Non-wage earnings for 60 days (up to $60 per month; if head of family, then up to $200 per month): District of Columbia Code 15-503.

FLORIDA

Florida residents may **not** use the Federal Bankruptcy Exemptions, but may use the Federal Non-Bankruptcy exemptions listed on p. 238 and the following state exemptions.

Benefits: Crime victims compensation unless for injury incurred during the crime (unlimited amount): Florida Statutes Annotated 960.14;
Public assistance (unlimited amount): Florida Statutes Annotated 222.201;
Social security (unlimited amount): Florida Statutes Annotated 222.201;
Unemployment compensation (unlimited amount): Florida Statutes Annotated 222.201, 443.051(2),(3);
Veterans benefits (unlimited amount): Florida Statutes Annotated 222.201, 744.626;
Workers compensation (unlimited amount): Florida Statutes Annotated 440.22.

Insurance: Annuity contract proceeds (unlimited amount): Florida Statutes Annotated 222.14;
Death benefits if not payable to the deceased's estate (unlimited amount): Florida Statutes Annotated 222.13;
Disability or illness benefits (unlimited amount): Florida Statutes Annotated 222.18;
Fraternal society benefits, if received before 10/1/96 (unlimited amount): Florida Statutes Annotated 632.619;
Life insurance cash surrender value (unlimited amount): Florida Statutes Annotated 222.14.

Miscellaneous: Alimony, child support (amount needed for support): Florida Statutes Annotated 222.201;
Damages to employees for injuries in hazardous occupations (unlimited amount): Florida Statutes Annotated 769.05;
Property of business partnership (unlimited amount): Florida Statutes Annotated 620.68.

Pensions: County officers or employees (unlimited amount): Florida Statutes Annotated 122.15;
Federal employee pension payments (amounts needed for support and received at least 3 months before filing for bankruptcy): Florida Statutes Annotated 222.21
Firefighters (unlimited amount): Florida Statutes Annotated 175.241;
Highway patrol officers (unlimited amount): Florida Statutes Annotated 321.22;
Police officers (unlimited amount): Florida Statutes Annotated 185.25;
Retirement benefits (unlimited amount): Florida Statutes Annotated 222.21(2);
State officers or employees (unlimited amount): Florida Statutes Annotated 121.131;
Teachers (unlimited amount): Florida Statutes Annotated 238.15.

Personal Property: Any personal property (up to $1,000; husband and wife may double) Florida Constitution 10-4; Florida Statutes Annotated 222.06;
Health aids (unlimited amount): Florida Statutes Annotated 222.11;
Motor vehicle (up to $1,000): Florida Statutes Annotated 222.11.

Real Estate: Real or personal property used as residence including mobile or modular home (unlimited value; property cannot exceed 1/2 acre in municipality or 160 contiguous acres elsewhere); must file exemption in Circuit Court: Florida Constitution 10-4; Florida Statutes Annotated 222.01, 222.02, 222.03, 222.05.

Wages: 100% of wages for heads of family (up to $500 per week either unpaid or paid and deposited into bank account for up to 6 months): Florida Statutes Annotated 222.11.

GEORGIA

Georgia residents may **not** use the Federal Bankruptcy Exemptions, but may use the Federal Non-Bankruptcy exemptions listed on p. 238 and the following state exemptions.

Benefits: Aid to aged, blind, or disabled (unlimited amount): Code of Georgia Annotated 49-4-35, 49-4-58, 49-4-84; Crime victims compensation (unlimited amount): Code of Georgia Annotated 44-13-100(a)(11)(A); Local public assistance (unlimited amount): Code of Georgia Annotated 44-13-100(a)(2)(A); Social security (unlimited amount): Code of Georgia Annotated 44-13-100(a)(2)(A); Unemployment compensation (unlimited amount): Code of Georgia Annotated 44-13-100(a)(2)(A); Veterans benefits (unlimited amount): Code of Georgia Annotated 44-13-100(a)(2)(B); Workers compensation (unlimited amount): Code of Georgia Annotated 34-9-84.

Insurance: Annuity contract benefits (unlimited amount): Code of Georgia Annotated 33-28-7; Disability or health benefits (up to $250 per month): Code of Georgia Annotated 3-29-15; Fraternal society benefits (unlimited amount): Code of Georgia Annotated 33-15-20; Group insurance (unlimited amount): Code of Georgia Annotated 33-30-10; Industrial life insurance if policy needed for support (unlimited amount): Code of Georgia Annotated 33-26-5; Life insurance proceeds if policy needed for support (unlimited amount): Code of Georgia Annotated 44-13-100(a)(11)(C); Unmatured life insurance contract (unlimited amount): Code of Georgia Annotated 44-13-100(a)(8) Unmatured life insurance dividends, interest, loan value or cash value (up to $2,000): Code of Georgia Annotated 44-13-100(a)(9).

Miscellaneous: Alimony or child support (amount needed for support): Code of Georgia Annotated 44-13-100(a)(2)(D). Any property (up to $400 plus any unused portion of real estate exemption): Code of Georgia Annotated 44-13-100(a)(6).

Pensions: Any pensions or retirement benefits (unlimited amount): Code of Georgia Annotated 18-4-22, 44-13-100(a)(2)(E), 44-13-100(a)(2.1)(C). Employees of non-profit corporations (unlimited amount): Code of Georgia Annotated 44-13-100(a)(2.1)(B); Public employees (unlimited amount): Code of Georgia Annotated 44-13-100(a)(2.1)(A), 47-2-332;

Personal Property: Animals, appliances, books, clothing, crops, furnishings, household goods, musical instruments (up to $200 per item and up to $3,500 total): Code of Georgia Annotated 4-13-100(a)(4); Burial plot (if taken instead of real estate exemption): Code of Georgia Annotated 44-13-100(a)(1); Health aids (unlimited amount): Code of Georgia Annotated 44-13-100(a)(10); Implements, books or tools of a trade (up to $500): Code of Georgia Annotated 44-13-100(a)(7). Jewelry (up to $500): Code of Georgia Annotated 44-13-100(a)(5); Lost future earnings (amount needed for support): Code of Georgia Annotated 44-13-100(a)(11)(E); Motor vehicles (up to $1000): Code of Georgia Annotated 44-13-100(a)(3); Personal injury recoveries (up to $7,500, but not for pain and suffering): Code of Georgia Annotated 44-13-100(a)(11)(C); Wrongful death recoveries (amount needed for support): Code of Georgia Annotated 44-13-100(a)(11)(B);

Real Estate: Real or personal property used as residence (up to $5,000; unused portion of real estate exemption may be used with any property): Code of Georgia Annotated 4-13-100(a)(1), 4-13-100(a)(6);

Wages: 75% of earned but unpaid wages (judge may allow more for low-income debtors): Code of Georgia Annotated 18-4-20, 18-4-21

HAWAII

Hawaii residents **may use either** the Federal Bankruptcy Exemptions on p. 237 or the state exemptions listed below. If state exemptions are used, then Federal Non-Bankruptcy exemptions on p. 238 may also be used.

Benefits: Public assistance for work done in home or workshop (unlimited amount): Hawaii Revised Statutes 20-346-33;
    Unemployment compensation (unlimited amount): Hawaii Revised Statutes 21-383-163;
    Unemployment work relief funds (up to $60 per month): Hawaii Revised Statutes 36-653-4;
    Workers compensation (unlimited amount): Hawaii Revised Statutes 21-386-57.

Insurance: Annuity contract if beneficiary is insured's spouse, child or parent (unlimited amount): Hawaii Revised Statutes 24-431:10-232(b)
    Disability benefits (unlimited amount): Hawaii Revised Statutes 24-431:10-231;
    Fraternal society benefits (unlimited amount): Hawaii Revised Statutes 24-432:2-403;
    Group life insurance policy or proceeds (unlimited amount): Hawaii Revised Statutes 24-431:10-233;
    Life or health insurance policy for spouse or child (unlimited amount): Hawaii Revised Statutes 24-431:10-234;
    Life insurance proceeds if policy prohibits proceeds from being used to pay creditors (unlimited amount): Hawaii Revised Statutes 24-431:10-D:112.

Miscellaneous: Property of business partnership (unlimited amount): Hawaii Revised Statutes 23-425-125.

Pensions: Public officers and employees (unlimited amount): Hawaii Revised Statutes 7-88-91, 36-653-3
    Firefighters (unlimited amount): Hawaii Revised Statutes 7-88-169;
    Police officers (unlimited amount): Hawaii Revised Statutes 7-88-169;
    Retirement benefits paid in at least 3 years before filing for bankruptcy (unlimited amount): Hawaii Revised Statutes 36-651-124.

Personal Property: Appliances and furnishings (amounts needed for support): Hawaii Revised Statutes 36-651-121(1);
    Books (unlimited amount): Hawaii Revised Statutes 36-651-121(1);
    Burial plot and tombstones (unlimited amount): Hawaii Revised Statutes 36-651-121(4);
    Clothing (unlimited amount): Hawaii Revised Statutes 36-651-121(1);
    Jewelry (up to $1,000): Hawaii Revised Statutes 36-651-121(1);
    Motor vehicle (up to $1,000): Hawaii Revised Statutes 36-651-121(2);
    Proceeds from sold or damaged exempt property within last 6 months (up to exemption amount): Hawaii Revised Statutes 36-651-121(5);
    Tools, books, uniforms, furnishings, fishing equipment, motor vehicle and other personal property (amount needed for work): Hawaii Revised Statutes 6-651-121(3).

Real Estate: Real estate down payments for home in state project (unlimited amount): Hawaii Revised Statutes 20-359-104.
    Real estate if used as a residence (up to 1 acre and up to $30,000 for head of family or if over 65; otherwise up to $20,000); sale proceeds exempt for 6 months: Hawaii Revised Statutes 6-651-91, 36-651-92, 36-651-96;

Wages: Prisoner's wages (unlimited amount): Hawaii Revised Statutes 20-353-22.
    Unpaid wages due for work of past 31 days; wages due for over 31 days, then 95% of 1st $100, 90% of 2nd $100, and 80% of remainder: Hawaii Revised Statutes 36-651-121(6), 36-652-1;

IDAHO

Idaho residents may **not** use the Federal Bankruptcy Exemptions, but may use the Federal Non-Bankruptcy exemptions listed on p. 238 and the following state exemptions.

Benefits: Aid to aged, blind, disabled, families with dependent children (unlimited amount): Idaho Code 56-223;
Federal, state or local public assistance (unlimited amount): Idaho Code 11-603(4);
General assistance (unlimited amount): Idaho Code 56-223;
Social security (unlimited amount): Idaho Code 11-603(3);
Unemployment compensation (unlimited amount): Idaho Code 11-603(6);
Veterans benefits (unlimited amount): Idaho Code 11-603(3);
Workers compensation (unlimited amount): Idaho Code 72-802.

Insurance: Annuity proceeds (up to $350 per month): Idaho Code 41-1836;
Death or disability benefits (unlimited amount): Idaho Code 11-604(1)(a), 41-1834;
Fraternal society benefits (unlimited amount): Idaho Code 41-3218;
Group life insurance benefits (unlimited amount): Idaho Code 41-1835;
Homeowners insurance proceeds (up to amount of real estate exemption): Idaho Code 55-1008;
Life insurance proceeds if policy prohibits proceeds from being used to pay creditors (unlimited amount): Idaho Code 41-1930;
Life insurance proceeds for beneficiary other than the insured (unlimited amount): Idaho Code 11-604(d), 41-1833;
Medical, surgical or hospital care benefits (unlimited amount): Idaho Code 11-603(5).

Miscellaneous: Alimony or child support (amount needed for support): Idaho Code 11-604(1)(b);
Liquor licenses (unlimited amount): Idaho Code 23-514;
Motor vehicle financial responsibility deposits: Idaho Code 49-1525;
Property of business partnership (unlimited amount): Idaho Code 53-325.

Pensions: Any pension (amount needed for support): Idaho Code 11-604(1)(e);
Firefighters (unlimited amount): Idaho Code 72-1422;
Police officers (unlimited amount): Idaho Code 50-1517;
Public employees (unlimited amount): Idaho Code 59-1317;
Retirement benefits (unlimited amount): Idaho Code 55-1011.

Personal Property: Appliances, books, clothing, family portraits, 1 firearm, furnishings, musical instruments, pets, and sentimental heirlooms (up to $500 per item, and up to $4,000 total): Idaho Code 1-605(1);
Arms, uniforms and equipment required for peace officer, national guard or military personnel (unlimited amount): Idaho Code 1-605(5);
Building materials (unlimited amount): Idaho Code 45-514;
Burial plot (unlimited amount): Idaho Code 11-603(1)
Crops on up to 50 acres (up to $1,000): Idaho Code 11-605(6);
Health aids (unlimited amount): Idaho Code 11-603(2);
Implements, books and tools of a trade (up to $1,000): Idaho Code 11-605(3).
Jewelry (up to $250): Idaho Code 11-605(2);
Motor vehicle (up to $1,500): Idaho Code 11-605(3);
Personal injury recoveries (unlimited amount): Idaho Code 11-604(1)(c)
Proceeds for damaged exempt property within last 3 months (up to amount of exemption): Idaho Code 11-606;
Water rights (up to 160 inches): Idaho Code 11-605(6);
Wrongful death recoveries (unlimited amount): Idaho Code 11-604(1)(c).

Real Estate: Real property or mobile home used as residence (up to $50,000); proceeds from sale are exempt for 6 months; must record homestead exemption: Idaho Code 55-1003, 55-1004, 55-1113.

Wages: 75% of earned but unpaid wages or pension payments (judge may allow more for low-income debtors): Idaho Code 11-207.

ILLINOIS

Illinois residents may **not** use the Federal Bankruptcy Exemptions, but may use the Federal Non-Bankruptcy exemptions listed on p. 238 and the following state exemptions. Wife and husband may double the real estate exemption.

Benefits: Aid to aged, blind, disabled, families with dependent children (unlimited amount): Illinois Annotated Statutes 305-5/11-3;
Crime victims compensation (unlimited amount): Illinois Annotated Statutes 735-5/12-1001(h)(1);
Social security (unlimited amount): Illinois Annotated Statutes 735-5/12-1001(g)(1);
Unemployment compensation (unlimited amount): Illinois Annotated Statutes 735-5/12-1001(g)(1),(3);
Veterans benefits (unlimited amount): Illinois Annotated Statutes 735-5/12-1001(g)(2);
Workers compensation (unlimited amount): Illinois Annotated Statutes 820-305/21;
Workers occupational disease compensation (unlimited amount): Illinois Annotated Statutes 820-310/21.

Insurance: Annuity or life insurance proceeds or cash value if beneficiary is insured's child, parent, spouse or other dependent (unlimited amount): Illinois Annotated Statutes 215-5/238;
Fraternal society benefits (unlimited amount): Illinois Annotated Statutes 215-5/299.1a;
Health or disability benefits (unlimited amount): Illinois Annotated Statutes 735-5/12-1001(g)(3);
Homeowners insurance proceeds (up to $7,500): Illinois Annotated Statutes 735-5/12-907;
Life insurance policy if beneficiary is insured's spouse or child (unlimited amount): Illinois Annotated Statutes 735-5/12-1001(0;
Life insurance proceeds if policy prohibits proceeds from being used to pay creditors (unlimited amount): Illinois Annotated Statutes 215-5/238;
Life insurance proceeds (amount needed for support): Illinois Annotated Statutes 735-5/12-1001(f)(g)(3).

Miscellaneous: Alimony and child support (needed for support): Illinois Annotated Statutes 735-5/12-1001(g)(4);
Any property (up to $2,000): Illinois Annotated Statutes 735-5/12-1001(b).
Property of a business partnership (unlimited amount): Illinois Annotated Statutes 805-205/25.

Pensions: Civil service employees (unlimited amount): Illinois Annotated Statutes 40-5/11-223;
Correction employees (unlimited amount): Illinois Annotated Statutes 40-5/19-117;
Firefighters, disabled firefighters; and widows and children of firefighters (unlimited amount): Illinois Annotated Statutes 40-5/4-135, 40-5/6-213; 40-5/22-230;
General assembly members (unlimited amount): Illinois Annotated Statutes 40-5/2-154;
Judges (unlimited amount): Illinois Annotated Statutes 40-5/18-161;
Park employees (unlimited amount): Illinois Annotated Statutes 40-5/12-190;
Police officers (unlimited amount): Illinois Annotated Statutes 40-5/3-144.1, 40-5/5-218;
Public, public library, municipal, county, and state employees (unlimited amount): Illinois Annotated Statutes 40-5/7-217(a), 40-5/8-244, 40-5/9-228, 40-5/14-147, 40-5/19-218, 735-5/12-1006;
Retirement benefits (unlimited amount): Illinois Annotated Statutes 735-5/12-1006;
Sanitation district employees (unlimited amount): Illinois Annotated Statutes 40-5/13-808;
State university employees (unlimited amount): Illinois Annotated Statutes 40-5/15-185;
Teachers (unlimited amount): Illinois Annotated Statutes 40-5/16-190, 40-5/17-151.

Personal Property: Bible, family pictures, and schoolbooks (unlimited amount); clothing (amount needed): Illinois Annotated Statutes 735-5/12-1001(a):
Health aids (unlimited amount): Illinois Annotated Statutes 735-5/12-1001(e);
Implements, books and tools of a trade (up to $750): Illinois Annotated Statutes 735-5/12-1001(d);
Motor vehicle (up to $1,200 per person): Illinois Annotated Statutes 735-5/12-1001(c);
Personal injury recoveries (up to $7,500): Illinois Annotated Statutes 735-5/12-1001(g)(4);
Proceeds from sale of exempt property (up to exemption amount): Illinois Annotated Statutes 735-5/12-1001;
Wrongful death recoveries (unlimited amount): Illinois Annotated Statutes 735-5/12-1001(h)(2).

Real Estate: Real or personal property used as a residence including a farm, building, condominium, co-op or mobile home (up to $7,500); proceeds from sale are exempt for up to 1 year from sale; must file exemption with county: Illinois Annotated Statutes 735-5/12-901, 735-5/12-902, 735-5/12-906.

Wages: 85% of earned but unpaid wages; judge may allow more for low-income debtors: Illinois Annotated Statutes 740-170/4.

INDIANA

Indiana residents may **not** use the Federal Bankruptcy Exemptions, but may use the Federal Non-Bankruptcy exemptions listed on p. 238 and the following state exemptions. Wife and husband may double the real estate exemption.

Benefits: Crime victims compensation except for treatment of injury incurred during the crime (unlimited amount): Indiana Statutes Annotated 2-18-6-36;
Unemployment compensation (unlimited amount): Indiana Statutes Annotated 22-4-33-3;
Workers compensation (unlimited amount): Indiana Statutes Annotated 22-3-2-17.

Insurance: Fraternal society benefits (unlimited amount): Indiana Statutes Annotated 27-11-6-3;
Group life insurance policy (unlimited amount): Indiana Statutes Annotated 27-1-12-29;
Life insurance policy, proceeds or cash value if beneficiary is insured's spouse or dependent (unlimited amount): Indiana Statutes Annotated 27-1-12-14;
Life insurance proceeds if policy prohibits proceeds to be used to pay creditors (unlimited amount): Indiana Statutes Annotated 27-2-5-1;
Mutual life or accident insurance proceeds (unlimited amount): Indiana Statutes Annotated 27-8-3-23.

Miscellaneous: Property of a business partnership (unlimited amount): Indiana Statutes Annotated 23-4-1-25
Any real estate or tangible personal property (up to $4,000): Indiana Statutes Annotated 34-2-28-1(a)(2).

Pensions: Firefighters (unlimited amount): Indiana Statutes Annotated 36-8-7-22, 36-8-8-17;
Police officers (only unpaid benefits): Indiana Statutes Annotated 10-1-2-9, 36-8-8-17;
Public employees (unlimited amount): Indiana Statutes Annotated 5-10.3-8-9;
Retirement benefits (unlimited amount): Indiana Statutes Annotated 34-2-28-1(a)(6);
Sheriffs (only unpaid benefits): Indiana Statutes Annotated 36-8-10-19;
State teachers (unlimited amount): Indiana Statutes Annotated 21-6.1-5-17.

Personal Property: Any intangible personal property, except money which is owed to debtor (up to $100): Indiana Statutes Annotated 34-2-28-1(a)(3);
Health aids (unlimited amount): Indiana Statutes Annotated 34-2-28-1(a)(4);
National guard uniforms, arms and equipment (unlimited amount): Indiana Statutes Annotated 10-2-6-3.

Real Estate: Real estate or personal property used as residence (up to $7,500; residence plus personal property exemption, not including health aids, cannot exceed $10,000 total): Indiana Statutes Annotated 34-28-1(c).

Wages: 75% of earned but unpaid wages (judge may allow more for low-income debtors): Indiana Statutes Annotated 24-4.5-5-105.

IOWA

Iowa residents may **not** use the Federal Bankruptcy Exemptions, but may use the Federal Non-Bankruptcy exemptions listed on p. 238 and the following state exemptions.

Benefits: Adopted child assistance (unlimited amount): Iowa Code Annotated 627.19;
Aid to Families with Dependent Children (unlimited amount): Iowa Code Annotated 627.6(8)(a);
Local public assistance (unlimited amount) Iowa Code Annotated 627.6(8)(a);
Social security (unlimited amount) Iowa Code Annotated 627.6(8)(a);
Unemployment compensation (unlimited amount) Iowa Code Annotated 627.6(8)(a);
Veterans benefits (unlimited amount) Iowa Code Annotated 627.6(8)(b);
Workers compensation (unlimited amount) Iowa Code Annotated 627.13.

Insurance: Accident, disability, health, illness, or life insurance proceeds (up to $15,000, if paid to a surviving spouse, child or other dependent): Iowa Code Annotated 27.6(6);
Employee group insurance policy or proceeds (unlimited amount) Iowa Code Annotated 509.12;
Life insurance cash value or proceeds (up to $10,000, if acquired within 2 years of filing for bankruptcy, and if paid to spouse, child or other dependent): Iowa Code Annotated 627.6(6);
Life insurance proceeds if policy prohibits proceeds from being used to pay creditors (unlimited amount) Iowa Code Annotated 508.32.

Miscellaneous: Alimony or child support (amount needed for support): Iowa Code Annotated 627.6(8)(d);
Liquor licenses (unlimited amount): Iowa Code Annotated 123.38;
Property of a business partnership (unlimited amount): Iowa Code Annotated 544.25.

Pensions: Disabled firefighters or police officers (payments being received): Iowa Code Annotated 410.11;
Federal government pensions (payments being received): Iowa Code Annotated 627.8
Firefighters (unlimited amount): Iowa Code Annotated 411.13;
Other pensions (payments being received): Iowa Code Annotated 627.6(8)(e).
Peace officers (unlimited amount): Iowa Code Annotated 97A.12;
Police officers (unlimited amount): Iowa Code Annotated 411.13;
Public employees (unlimited amount): Iowa Code Annotated 97B.39;

Personal Property: Any personal property, including cash (up to $100): Iowa Code Annotated 627.6(13).
Appliances, furnishings and household goods (up to $2,000 total): Iowa Code Annotated 627.6(5);
Bibles, books, paintings, pictures, and portraits (up to $1,000 total): Iowa Code Annotated 627.6(3);
Burial plot (up to 1 acre): Iowa Code Annotated 627.6(4);
Clothing, engagement, or wedding rings (up to $1,000 plus receptacles to hold clothing): Iowa Code Annotated 627.6(1)
Farm equipment, including livestock and feed (up to $10,000): Iowa Code Annotated 627.6(11)
Health aids (unlimited amount): Iowa Code Annotated 627.6(7);
Motor vehicle, musical instruments, and tax refund (up to $5,000 total; only up to $1,000 may be from tax refund): Iowa Code Annotated 627.6(9);
Musket, rifle, or shotgun (unlimited amount): Iowa Code Annotated 627.6(2);
Non-farm business books, equipment, and tools (up to $10,000): Iowa Code Annotated 627.6(10).

Real Estate: Real property or an apartment used as a residence (unlimited value; property cannot exceed 1/2 acre in town or city, or 40 acres elsewhere): Iowa Code Annotated 99A.18, 561.2, 561.16.

Wages: 75% of earned but unpaid wages or pension payments (judge may allow more for low-income debtors): Iowa Code Annotated 642.21.

KANSAS

Kansas residents may **not** use the Federal Bankruptcy Exemptions, but may use the Federal Non-Bankruptcy exemptions listed on p. 238 and the following state exemptions.

Benefits: Aid to families with dependent children, general assistance, welfare (unlimited amount): Kansas Statutes Annotated 39-717;
Crime victims compensation (unlimited amount): Kansas Statutes Annotated 74-7313(d);
Unemployment compensation (unlimited amount): Kansas Statutes Annotated 44-718(c);
Workers compensation (unlimited amount): Kansas Statutes Annotated 44-514.

Insurance: Fraternal life insurance benefits (unlimited amount): Kansas Statutes Annotated 40-414(a);
Life insurance cash value if bankruptcy filed at least 1 year after policy issued (unlimited amount): Kansas Statutes Annotated 40-414(b)
Life insurance proceeds if policy prohibits proceeds from being used to pay creditors (unlimited amount): Kansas Statutes Annotated 40-414(a).

Miscellaneous: Liquor licenses (unlimited amount): Kansas Statutes Annotated 41-326;
Property of a business partnership (unlimited amount): Kansas Statutes Annotated 56-325.

Pensions: Elected and appointed officials in cities with populations between 120,000 and 200,000 (unlimited amount): Kansas Statutes Annotated 13-14,102
Federal government pension payments paid within 3 months of filing for bankruptcy (unlimited amount): Kansas Statutes Annotated 602308(a);
Firefighters (unlimited amount): Kansas Statutes Annotated 12-5005(e), 14-10alO;
Judges (unlimited amount): Kansas Statutes Annotated 20-2618;
Police officers (unlimited amount): Kansas Statutes Annotated 12-5005(e), 13-14alO;
Public employees (unlimited amount): Kansas Statutes Annotated 74-4923,74-49,105;
Retirement benefits (unlimited amount): Kansas Statutes Annotated 60-2308(b);
State highway patrol officers (unlimited amount): Kansas Statutes Annotated 74-4978g;
State school employees (unlimited amount): Kansas Statutes Annotated 72-5526.

Personal Property: Books, documents, furniture, instruments, equipment, breeding stock, seed, grain and livestock used in farm business (up to $7,500 total): Kansas Statutes Annotated 60-2304(c);
Burial plot or crypt (unlimited amount): Kansas Statutes Annotated 60-2304(d);
Clothing (amount to last 1 year): Kansas Statutes Annotated 60-2304(a);
Food and fuel (amount to last 1 year): Kansas Statutes Annotated 60-2304(a);
Funeral plan prepayments (unlimited amount): Kansas Statutes Annotated 16-310(d);
Household furnishings and equipment (unlimited amount): Kansas Statutes Annotated 60-2304(a)
Jewelry (up to $1,000): Kansas Statutes Annotated 60-2304(b);
Motor vehicle (up to $20,000; if equipped for disabled person, then unlimited amount): Kansas Statutes Annotated 60-2304(c);
National Guard uniforms, arms and equipment (unlimited amount): Kansas Statutes Annotated 48-245.

Real Estate: Real property or mobile home used as residence (unlimited value, up to 1 acre in town or city, or 160 acres on farm): Kansas Statutes Annotated 60-2301, Kansas Constitution 15-9.

Wages: 75% of earned but unpaid wages (judge may allow more for low-income debtors): Kansas Statutes Annotated 60-2310.

KENTUCKY

Kentucky residents may **not** use the Federal Bankruptcy Exemptions, but may use the Federal Non-Bankruptcy exemptions listed on p. 238 and the following state exemptions.

Benefits: Aid to aged, blind, disabled, and families with dependent children (unlimited amount): Kentucky Revised Statutes 205.220;
Crime victims compensation (unlimited amount): Kentucky Revised Statutes 427.150(2)(a);
Unemployment compensation (unlimited amount): Kentucky Revised Statutes 341.470;
Workers compensation (unlimited amount): Kentucky Revised Statutes 342.180.

Insurance: Annuity contract proceeds (up to $350 per month): Kentucky Revised Statutes 304.14-330;
Cooperative life or casualty insurance benefits (unlimited amount): Kentucky Revised Statutes 427.110(1);
Fraternal society benefits (unlimited amount): Kentucky Revised Statutes 427.110(2);
Group life insurance proceeds (unlimited amount): Kentucky Revised Statutes 304.14-320;
Health or disability benefits (unlimited amount): Kentucky Revised Statutes 304.14-310;
Life insurance policy if beneficiary is a married woman (unlimited amount): Kentucky Revised Statutes 304.14-340;
Life insurance proceeds if policy prohibits proceeds from being used to pay creditors (unlimited amount): Kentucky Revised Statutes 304.14-350;
Life insurance proceeds or cash value if beneficiary is someone other than insured (unlimited amount): Kentucky Revised Statutes 304.14-300.

Miscellaneous: Alimony or child support (amount needed for support): Kentucky Revised Statutes 427.150(1);
Any property: real estate or personal property (up to $,1000): Kentucky Revised Statutes 427.160.
Property of a business partnership (unlimited amount): Kentucky Revised Statutes 362.270.

Pensions: Firefighters and police officers (unlimited amount): Kentucky Revised Statutes 67A.620, 95.878, 427.120, 427.125;
State employees (unlimited amount): Kentucky Revised Statutes 61.690;
Teachers (unlimited amount): Kentucky Revised Statutes 161.700
Urban county government employees (unlimited amount): Kentucky Revised Statutes 67A.350;
Other pensions (unlimited amount): Kentucky Revised Statutes 427.150(2)(e).

Personal Property: Burial plot (up to $5,000; instead of real estate exemption): Kentucky Revised Statutes 427.060;
Clothing, jewelry, or furnishings (up to $3,000 total): Kentucky Revised Statutes 427.010(1);
Health aids (unlimited amount): Kentucky Revised Statutes 427.010(1);
Library, equipment, instruments and furnishings of minister, attorney, physician, surgeon, chiropractor, veterinarian or dentist (up to $1,000): Kentucky Revised Statutes 427.040;
Lost earnings payments (amount needed for support): Kentucky Revised Statutes 427.150(2)(d);
Medical expenses benefits received under Kentucky motor vehicle reparation law (unlimited amount): Kentucky Revised Statutes 304.39-260
Motor vehicle of mechanic, mechanical or electrical equipment servicer, minister, attorney, physician, surgeon, chiropractor, veterinarian or dentist (up to $2,500): Kentucky Revised Statutes 427,030
Motor vehicle (up to $2,500): Kentucky Revised Statutes 427.010(1);
Personal injury recoveries (up to $7,500; not including pain and suffering or pecuniary loss): Kentucky Revised Statutes 427.150(2)(c);
Tools of a non-farmer (up to $300): Kentucky Revised Statutes 427.30;
Tools, equipment, livestock and poultry of a farmer (up to $3,000): Kentucky Revised Statutes 427.010(1);
Wrongful death recoveries (unlimited amount): Kentucky Revised Statutes 427.150(2)(b);

Real Estate: Real or personal property used as residence (up to $5,000); proceeds from sale are also exempt: Kentucky Revised Statutes 427.060, 427.090

Wages: 75% of earned but unpaid wages; (judge may allow more for low-income debtors): Kentucky Revised Statutes 427.010(2),(3).

LOUISIANA

Louisiana residents may **not** use the Federal Bankruptcy Exemptions, but may use the Federal Non-Bankruptcy exemptions listed on p. 238 and the following state exemptions.

Benefits: Aid to aged, blind, disabled, and families with dependent children (unlimited amount): Louisiana Revised Statutes Annotated 46:111;
Crime victims compensation (unlimited amount): Louisiana Revised Statutes Annotated 46:1811;
Unemployment compensation (unlimited amount): Louisiana Revised Statutes Annotated 23:1693;
Workers compensation (unlimited amount): Louisiana Revised Statutes Annotated 23:1205.

Insurance: Fraternal society benefits (unlimited amount): Louisiana Revised Statutes Annotated 22:558;
Group insurance policies or proceeds (unlimited amount): Louisiana Revised Statutes Annotated 22:649;
Health, accident, or disability proceeds (unlimited amount): Louisiana Revised Statutes Annotated 22:646;
Life insurance proceeds (unlimited amount, unless policy was issued within 9 months of bankruptcy filing, then exempt only up to $35,000): Louisiana Revised Statutes Annotated 22:647.

Miscellaneous: Property of a minor child (unlimited amount): Louisiana Revised Statutes Annotated 13:3881A(3), Louisiana Civil Code 223.

Pensions: Gratuitous payments to an employee or heirs (unlimited amount): Louisiana Revised Statutes Annotated 20:33(2);
Retirement benefits (unlimited amount if contribution was made over 1 year before bankruptcy filed): Louisiana Revised Statutes Annotated 13:3881D(1), 20:33(4).

Personal Property: Arms, bedding, chinaware, clothing, cow (1), family portraits, freezer, glassware, heating and cooling equipment, household pets, linens and bedroom furniture, living room and dining room furniture, military equipment, musical instruments, poultry, pressing irons, refrigerator, sewing machine, silverware (if non-sterling), stove, utensils, washer and dryer: Louisiana Revised Statutes Annotated 13:388 1A(4);
Cemetery plot and monuments (unlimited amount): Louisiana Revised Statutes Annotated 8:313
Engagement and wedding rings (up to $5,000): Louisiana Revised Statutes Annotated 13:3881A(5);
Tools, instruments, books, pickup truck (up to 3 tons), auto (non-luxury), or utility trailer (amount needed for work): Louisiana Revised Statutes Annotated 3:3881A(2).

Real Estate: Real estate used as residence (up to $15,000 and up to 160 acres); spouse or child of deceased owner may claim homestead exemption: Louisiana Revised Statutes Annotated 20:1.

Wages: 75% of earned but unpaid wages (judge may allow more for low-income debtors): Louisiana Revised Statutes Annotated 13:3881A(1).

MAINE

Maine residents may **not** use the Federal Bankruptcy Exemptions, but may use the Federal Non-Bankruptcy exemptions listed on p. 238 and the following state exemptions.

Benefits: Aid to families with dependent children (unlimited amount): Maine Revised Statutes Annotated 22-3753; Crime victims compensation (unlimited amount): Maine Revised Statutes Annotated 14-4422(14)A; Social security (unlimited amount): Maine Revised Statutes Annotated 14-4422(13)A; Unemployment compensation (unlimited amount): Maine Revised Statutes Annotated 14-4422(13)A, C; Veterans benefits (unlimited amount): Maine Revised Statutes Annotated 14-4422(13)B; Workers compensation (unlimited amount): Maine Revised Statutes Annotated 39-67.

Insurance: Annuity proceeds (up to $450 per month): Maine Revised Statutes Annotated 24-A-2431; Disability or health insurance proceeds (unlimited amount): Maine Revised Statutes Annotated 14-4422(13)A, C; 24-A-2429; Fraternal society benefits (unlimited amount): Maine Revised Statutes Annotated 24-A-4118; Group health or life insurance policy or proceeds (unlimited amount): Maine Revised Statutes Annotated 24-A-2430; Life, endowment, annuity or accident policy or proceeds (unlimited amount): Maine Revised Statutes Annotated 14-4422(14)C, 24-A-2428; Life insurance policy, proceeds, or loan value (up to $4,000): Maine Revised Statutes Annotated 14-4422(11) Unmatured life insurance policy, except credit insurance policy (unlimited amount): Maine Revised Statutes Annotated 14-4422(10).

Miscellaneous: Alimony/child support (amount needed for support): Maine Revised Statutes Annotated 14-4422(13)D; Any additional property (up to $400): Maine Revised Statutes Annotated 14-4422(15). Property of a business partnership (unlimited amount): Maine Revised Statutes Annotated 31-305.

Pensions: Judges, legislators, state employees (unlimited amount): Maine Revised Statutes Annotated 3-703, 4-1203; 5-17054. Retirement benefits (unlimited amount): Maine Revised Statutes Annotated 14-4422(13)E.

Personal Property: Animals, appliances, books, clothing, crops, furnishings, household goods, musical instruments (up to $200 per item): Maine Revised Statutes Annotated 14-4422(3); Boat used in commercial fishing (up to 5 tons): Maine Revised Statutes Annotated 14-4422(9); Burial plot (instead of real estate exemption): Maine Revised Statutes Annotated 14-4422(1) Business books, materials and stock (up to $5,000): Maine Revised Statutes Annotated 14-4422(5); Cooking or heating stove or furnaces and fuel (unlimited amount and up to 10 cords of wood, 5 tons of coal or 1000 gallons of petroleum): Maine Revised Statutes Annotated 14-4422(6)A-C; Food (amount to last 6 months): Maine Revised Statutes Annotated 14-4422(7)A; Health aids (unlimited amount): Maine Revised Statutes Annotated 14-4422(12) Jewelry (up to $750; no limit for wedding/engagement ring: Maine Revised Statutes Annotated 14-4422(4); Lost earnings payments (unlimited amount): Maine Revised Statutes Annotated 14-4422(14)E; Military uniforms, arms, and equipment (unlimited amount): Maine Revised Statutes Annotated 37-B-262 Motor vehicle (up to $2,500): Maine Revised Statutes Annotated 14-4422(2); Personal injury recoveries (up to $12,500, but not pain and suffering): Maine Revised Statutes Annotated 14-4422(14)D; Tools, seeds, fertilizer, and equipment (amount to raise and harvest food for 1 season) and farm implements needed to harvest and raise crops (1 of each type): Maine Revised Statutes Annotated 14-4422(7-8); Unused portion of real estate exemption up to $6,000 may be used for animals, appliances, books, clothing, crops, furnishings, household goods, musical instruments, personal injury recoveries, and tools of a trade: Maine Revised Statutes Annotated 14 4422(15); Wrongful death recoveries (unlimited amount): Maine Revised Statutes Annotated 14-4422(14)B.

Real Estate: Real or personal property (including co-op) used as residence (up to $12,500; up to $60,000 if debtor is over age 60 or physically or mentally disabled); joint debtors may double exemption amount: Maine Revised Statutes Annotated 4-4422(1).

Wages: None.

MARYLAND

Maryland residents may **not** use the Federal Bankruptcy Exemptions, but may use the Federal Non-Bankruptcy exemptions listed on p. 238 and the following state exemptions.

Benefits: Aid to families with dependent children and general assistance (unlimited amount): Annotated Code of Maryland 88A-73;

Crime victims compensation (unlimited amount): Annotated Code of Maryland 26A-13;

Unemployment compensation (unlimited amount): Annotated Code of Maryland-Labor and Employment 8-106;

Workers compensation (unlimited amount): Annotated Code of Maryland-Labor and Employment 9-732.

Insurance: Disability and health benefits, court awards and settlements (unlimited amount): Annotated Code of Maryland- Courts and Judicial Proceedings 11-504(b)(2)

Fraternal society benefits (unlimited amount): Annotated Code of Maryland 48A-328, Estates and Trusts 8-115;

Life insurance or annuity contract proceeds if beneficiary is insured's dependent, child or spouse (unlimited amount): Annotated Code of Maryland 48A-385, Estates and Trusts 8-115;

Medical benefits which are deducted from wages (unlimited amount): Annotated Code of Maryland-Commercial 15-601.1.

Miscellaneous: Any property, including a car or real estate (up to $5,500): Annotated Code of Maryland-Courts and Judicial Proceedings 11-504(b)(5), (f);

Property of a business partnership (unlimited amount): Annotated Code of Maryland-Corporation 9-502.

Pensions: Deceased Baltimore police officers (unpaid benefits only): Annotated Code of Maryland 73B-49;

State employees (unlimited amount): Annotated Code of Maryland 73B-17, 73B-125;

State police (unlimited amount): Annotated Code of Maryland 88B-60;

Retirement benefits; except IRA's (unlimited amount): Annotated Code of Maryland-Courts and Judicial Proceedings 11 -504(h);

Teachers (unlimited amount): Annotated Code of Maryland 73B-96, 73B-152.

Personal Property: Appliances, books, clothing, furnishings, household goods, and pets (up to $500 total): Annotated Code of Maryland Courts and Judicial Proceedings 11-504(b)(4);

Burial plot (unlimited amount): Annotated Code of Maryland 23-164

Clothing, books, tools, instruments, and appliances (up to $2,500): Annotated Code of Maryland- Courts and Judicial Proceedings 11-504(b)(1);

Health aids (unlimited amount): Annotated Code of Maryland-Courts and Judicial Proceedings 11-504(b)(3);

Lost future earnings recoveries (unlimited amount): Annotated Code of Maryland-Courts and Judicial Proceedings 11-504(b)(2).

Real Estate: None, specifically, but may use $5,500 exemption noted under Miscellaneous for real estate.

Wages: Earned but unpaid wages (up to the greater of 75% or $145 per week; except in Kent, Caroline, and Queen Anne's of Worcester Counties, up to the greater of 75% of actual wages or 30% of federal minimum wage): Annotated Code of Maryland Commercial 15-601.1.

MASSACHUSETTS

Massachusetts residents **may use either** the Federal Bankruptcy Exemptions on p. 237 or the state exemptions listed below. If state exemptions are used, then the Federal Non-Bankruptcy exemptions on p. 238 may also be used.

Benefits: Aid to families with dependent children (unlimited amount): Massachusetts General Laws Annotated 118-10; Aid to aged, disabled (unlimited amount): Massachusetts General Laws Annotated 235-34; Unemployment compensation (unlimited amount): Massachusetts General Laws Annotated 151A-36; Veterans benefits (unlimited amount): Massachusetts General Laws Annotated 115-5; Workers compensation (unlimited amount): Massachusetts General Laws Annotated 152-47.

Insurance: Disability benefits (up to $400 per week): Massachusetts General Laws Annotated 175-110A; Fraternal society benefits (unlimited amount): Massachusetts General Laws Annotated 176-22; Group annuity policy or proceeds (unlimited amount): Massachusetts General Laws Annotated 175-132C; Group life insurance policy (unlimited amount): Massachusetts General Laws Annotated 175-135; Life or endowment policy, proceeds or cash value (unlimited amount): Massachusetts General Laws Annotated 175-125; Life insurance annuity contract if contract states that it is exempt (unlimited amount): Massachusetts General Laws Annotated 175-125; Life insurance policy if beneficiary is married woman (unlimited amount): Massachusetts General Laws Annotated 175-126; Life insurance proceeds if policy prohibits proceeds from being used to pay creditors (unlimited amount): Massachusetts General Laws Annotated 175-119A; Medical malpractice self-insurance (unlimited amount): Massachusetts General Laws Annotated 175F-15.

Miscellaneous: Property of business partnership (unlimited): Massachusetts General Laws Annotated 108A-25.

Pensions: Private retirement benefits (unlimited amount): Massachusetts General Laws Annotated 32-41; Public employees (unlimited amount): Massachusetts General Laws Annotated 32-19; Retirement benefits (unlimited amount): Massachusetts General Laws Annotated 235-34A, 246-28; Savings bank employees (unlimited amount): Massachusetts General Laws Annotated 168-41, 168-44.

Personal Property: Arms, equipment and uniforms required for military use (unlimited amount): Massachusetts General Laws Annotated 235-34; Cash or bank deposits (up to $500): Massachusetts General Laws Annotated 235-34; 246-28A; Beds, bedding and heating unit (unlimited amount); clothing (amount needed): Massachusetts General Laws Annotated 235-34; Bibles and books (up to $200 total): Massachusetts General Laws Annotated 235-34; Boats, tackle and nets of a fisherman (up to $500 total): Massachusetts General Laws Annotated 235-34; Burial plots, tombs and church pew (unlimited amount): Massachusetts General Laws Annotated 235-34; Cash for fuel, heat, water or light (up to $75 per month): Massachusetts General Laws Annotated 235-34; Cash for rent (up to $200 per month; instead of real estate exemption): Massachusetts General Laws Annotated 235-34; Cooperative association shares (up to $100): Massachusetts General Laws Annotated 235-34; Cows (2), sheep (12), swine (2), hay (4 tons): Massachusetts General Laws Annotated 235-34; Food or cash for food (up to $300): Massachusetts General Laws Annotated 235-34 Furniture (up to $3,000): Massachusetts General Laws Annotated 235-34; Materials used in business (up to $500): Massachusetts General Laws Annotated 235-34; Motor vehicle (up to $750): Massachusetts General Laws Annotated 235-34; Sewing machine (up to $200): Massachusetts General Laws Annotated 235-34; Tools, implements and fixtures of business (up to $500 total): Massachusetts General Laws Annotated 235-34.

Real Estate: Property used as a residence (up to $100,000; if over 65 or disabled, then up to $200,000) must record homestead declaration before filing bankruptcy: Massachusetts General Laws Annotated 188-1, 188-1A, 188-2, 188-4.

Wages: Earned but unpaid wages (up to $125 per week): Massachusetts General Laws Annotated 246-28; Seaman's wages (unlimited amount): Massachusetts General Laws Annotated 246-32(7).

MICHIGAN

Michigan residents **may use either** the Federal Bankruptcy Exemptions on p. 237 or the state exemptions listed below. If state exemptions are used, then the Federal Non-Bankruptcy exemptions on p. 238 may also be used.

Benefits: Aid to families with dependent children (unlimited amount): Michigan Compiled Laws Annotated 330.1158a;
Crime victims compensation (unlimited amount): Michigan Compiled Laws Annotated 18.362;
Unemployment compensation (unlimited amount): Michigan Compiled Laws Annotated 421.30;
Veterans benefits for war veterans (unlimited amount): Michigan Compiled Laws Annotated 35.926, 35.977, 35.1027;
Welfare benefits (unlimited amount): Michigan Compiled Laws Annotated 400.63;
Workers compensation (unlimited amount): Michigan Compiled Laws Annotated 418.821.

Insurance: Disability, mutual life or health insurance benefits (unlimited amount): Michigan Compiled Laws Annotated 600.6023(1)(f);
Fraternal society benefits (unlimited amount): Michigan Compiled Laws Annotated 500.8181;
Life, endowment or annuity proceeds if policy prohibits proceeds from being used to pay creditors (unlimited amount): Michigan Compiled Laws Annotated 500.4054.

Miscellaneous: Property of a business partnership (unlimited amount): Michigan Compiled Laws Annotated 449.25.

Pensions: Firefighters (unlimited amount): Michigan Compiled Laws Annotated 38.559(6);
Police officers (unlimited amount): Michigan Compiled Laws Annotated 38.559(6);
Retirement benefits (unlimited amount): Michigan Compiled Laws Annotated 600.6023(1)(k);
IRAs (unlimited amount): Michigan Compiled Laws Annotated 600.6023(1)(1);
Judges (unlimited amount): Michigan Compiled Laws Annotated 38.826, 38.927;
Legislators (unlimited amount): Michigan Compiled Laws Annotated 38.1057;
Public school employees (unlimited amount): Michigan Compiled Laws Annotated 38.1346;
State employees (unlimited amount): Michigan Compiled Laws Annotated 38.40;

Personal Property: Arms and equipment required for military use (unlimited amount): Michigan Compiled Laws Annotated 600.6023(1)(a);
Appliances, books, furniture, household goods, and utensils (up to $1,000 total): Michigan Compiled Laws Annotated 600. 6023(1)(b);
Building and loan association shares (up to $1,000 par value; instead of real estate): Michigan Compiled Laws Annotated 600.6023(1)(g);
Burial plots or church pew (unlimited amount): Michigan Compiled Laws Annotated 600.6023(1)(c);
Clothing (unlimited amount): Michigan Compiled Laws Annotated 600.6023(1)(a);
Cows (2), hens (100), roosters (5), sheep (10), swine (5); feed to last 6 months (head of household only) : Michigan Compiled Laws Annotated 600.6023(1)(d);
Family pictures (unlimited amount): Michigan Compiled Laws Annotated 600.6023(1)(a);
Food and fuel (amount to last 6 months): Michigan Compiled Laws Annotated 600.6023(1)(a);
Tools, implements, materials, stock, apparatus, team, motor vehicle, horse and harness used in a business (up to $1,000 total): Michigan Compiled Laws Annotated 600.6023(1)(e).

Real Estate: Real estate (up to $3,500; up to 1 lot in town, village, city, or 40 acres elsewhere): Michigan Compiled Laws Annotated 559.214, 600.6023(1)(h),(i), 600.6023(3), 600.6027.

Wages: 60% of earned but unpaid wages (head of household only) otherwise 40%; head of household may keep at least $15 per week plus $2 per week per non-spouse dependent; others at least $10 per week: Michigan Compiled Laws Annotated 600.5311.

MINNESOTA

Minnesota residents **may use either** the Federal Bankruptcy Exemptions on p. 237 or the state exemptions listed below. If state exemptions are used, then Federal Non-Bankruptcy exemptions on p. 238 may also be used. Certain state exemptions are adjusted for inflation on July 1st of even-numbered years. The exemptions noted below are current as of July 1, 1994. Please check the specific statute if you are using this book after July 1, 1996: Minnesota Statutes Annotated Section 550.37(4)(a).

Benefits: Aid to families with dependent children, supplemental and general assistance, supplemental security income (unlimited amount): Minnesota Statutes Annotated 550.37-14;
Crime victims compensation (unlimited amount): Minnesota Statutes Annotated 611A.60;
Unemployment compensation (unlimited amount): Minnesota Statutes Annotated 268.17-2;
Veterans benefits (unlimited amount): Minnesota Statutes Annotated 550.38;
Workers compensation (unlimited amount): Minnesota Statutes Annotated 176.175.

Insurance: Accident or disability insurance proceeds (unlimited amount): Minnesota Statutes Annotated 550.39;
Fraternal society benefits (unlimited amount): Minnesota Statutes Annotated 64B.18;
Life insurance proceeds if beneficiary is spouse or child of insured (up to $20,000, plus $5,000 per dependent): Minnesota Statutes Annotated 550.37-10;
Police, fire or beneficiary association benefits (unlimited amount): Minnesota Statutes Annotated 550.37-11;
Unmatured life insurance contract dividends, interest or loan value (up to $4,000 if insured is debtor or dependent): Minnesota Statutes Annotated 550.37-23;

Miscellaneous: Property of a business partnership (unlimited amount) Minnesota Statutes Annotated 323.24.

Pensions: Retirement benefits and IRAs (up to $30,000 in present value): Minnesota Statutes Annotated 550.37-24;
Private retirement benefits (unpaid benefits only): Minnesota Statutes Annotated 181B.16;
Public employees (unlimited amount): Minnesota Statutes Annotated 353.15;
State employees (unlimited amount): Minnesota Statutes Annotated 352.96;
State troopers (unlimited amount): Minnesota Statutes Annotated 352B.071.

Personal Property: Appliances, furniture, phonographs, radio, and TV (up to $4,500 total): Minnesota Statutes Annotated 550.37-4(b);
Bible, books, and musical instruments (unlimited amount): Minnesota Statutes Annotated 550.37-2;
Burial plot and church pew seat (unlimited amount): Minnesota Statutes Annotated 550.37-3;
Clothing, food, utensils, watch (unlimited amount): Minnesota Statutes Annotated 550.37-4(a);
Farm machines, implements, livestock, farm produce and crops (up to $13,000 total; total farm tools and other tools exemption can not exceed $13,000): Minnesota Statutes Annotated 550.37-5;
Motor vehicle (up to $2,000; up to $20,000 if modified for disability): Minnesota Statutes Annotated 550.37-12(a);
Personal injury recoveries (unlimited amount): Minnesota Statutes Annotated 550.37-22;
Proceeds for damaged exempt property (up to exemption amount): Minnesota Statutes Annotated 550.37-9,16;
Teaching materials of public school teacher (unlimited amount): Minnesota Statutes Annotated 550.37-8;
Wrongful death recoveries (unlimited amount): Minnesota Statutes Annotated 550.37-22;
Tools, implements, machines, business furniture, stock in trade and library used in business (up to $5,000 total): Minnesota Statutes Annotated 550.37-6.

Real Estate: Real property, mobile home or manufactured home (unlimited value; up to 1/2 acre in city or 160 acres elsewhere): Minnesota Statutes Annotated 510.01, 510.02, 550.37-12.

Wages: Earned but unpaid wages (unlimited amount if paid within 6 months of returning to work and if debtor has ever received welfare: Minnesota Statutes Annotated 550.37-13;
Earnings of a minor child (unlimited amount): Minnesota Statutes Annotated 550.37-15;
Wages deposited into bank accounts for 20 days after deposit: Minnesota Statutes Annotated 550.37-13;
Wages of released inmates paid within 6 months of release (unlimited amount): Minnesota Statutes Annotated 550.37-14;
75% of earned but unpaid wages (judge may allow more for low-income debtors): Minnesota Statutes Annotated 571.922.

MISSISSIPPI

Mississippi residents may **not** use the Federal Bankruptcy Exemptions, but may use the Federal Non-Bankruptcy exemptions listed on p. 238 and the following state exemptions.

Benefits: Assistance to aged, blind, and disabled (unlimited amount): Mississippi Code 43-9-19, 43-3-71, 43-29-15;
Crime victims compensation (unlimited amount): Mississippi Code 99-41-23;
Social security (unlimited amount): Mississippi Code 25-11-129;
Unemployment compensation (unlimited amount): Mississippi Code 71-5-539;
Workers compensation (unlimited amount): Mississippi Code 71-3-43.

Insurance: Disability benefits (unlimited amount): Mississippi Code 85-3-1(b)(ii);
Fraternal society benefits (unlimited amount): Mississippi Code 83-29-39;
Homeowners insurance proceeds (up to $75,000): Mississippi Code 85-3-23;
Life insurance cash value (up to $50,000): Mississippi Code 85-3-11;
Life insurance proceeds if policy prohibits proceeds from being used to pay creditors (unlimited amount): Mississippi Code 83-7-5.

Miscellaneous: Property of a business partnership (unlimited amount): Mississippi Code 79-12-49.

Pensions: Firefighters (unlimited amount): Mississippi Code 21-29-257;
Highway patrol officers (unlimited amount): Mississippi Code 25-13-31;
IRAs (unlimited amount if deposited over 1 year before filing for bankruptcy): Mississippi Code 85-3-1(b)(iii);
Keoghs (unlimited amount if deposited over 1 year before filing for bankruptcy): Mississippi Code 85-3-1(b)(iii);
Private retirement benefits (unlimited amount to the extent they are tax-deferred): Mississippi Code 71-1-43;
Police officers (unlimited amount): Mississippi Code 21-29-257;
Public employees retirement and disability benefits (unlimited amount): Mississippi Code 25-11-129;
Retirement benefits (unlimited amount if deposited over 1 year before filing for bankruptcy): Mississippi Code 85-3-1(b)(iii);
State employees (unlimited amount): Mississippi Code 25-14-5;
Teachers (unlimited amount): Mississippi Code 25-11-201(i)(d).

Personal Property: Tangible personal property of any type (up to $10,000): Mississippi Code 85-3-1(a);
Personal injury recoveries (up to $10,000): Mississippi Code 85-3-17;
Proceeds from sale of exempt property (up to exemption amount): Mississippi Code 85-3-1(b)(i).

Real Estate: Property used as residence (up to $75,000 and up to 160 acres): Mississippi Code 85-3-1(b)(i), 85-3-21;
Proceeds from the sale of residence (up to exemption amount): Mississippi Code 85-3-23.

Wages: Earned but unpaid wages owed for 30 days; after 30 days, 75% of wages due (judge may allow more for low-income debtors): Mississippi Code 85-3-4.

MISSOURI

Missouri residents may **not** use the Federal Bankruptcy Exemptions, but may use the Federal Non-Bankruptcy exemptions listed on p. 238 and the following state exemptions.

Benefits: Aid to families with dependent children (unlimited amount): Missouri Annotated Statutes 513.430(10)(a);
Social security (unlimited amount): Missouri Annotated Statutes 513.430(10)(a);
Unemployment compensation (unlimited amount): Missouri Annotated Statutes 288.380(10)(1), 513.430(10)(c);
Veterans benefits (unlimited amount): Missouri Annotated Statutes 513.430(10)(b);
Workers compensation (unlimited amount): Missouri Annotated Statutes 287.260.

Insurance: Disability or illness benefits (unlimited amount): Missouri Annotated Statutes 513.430(10)(c);
Fraternal society benefits (up to $5,000 if purchased over 6 months before filing for bankruptcy: Missouri Annotated Statutes 513.430(8);
Insurance premium proceeds (unlimited amount): Missouri Annotated Statutes 377.090;
Life insurance dividends, loan value or interest (up to $5,000 if purchased over 6 months before filing for bankruptcy): Missouri Annotated Statutes 513.430(8);
Life insurance proceeds if policy owned by a woman and insures her husband (unlimited amount): Missouri Annotated Statutes 376.530;
Life insurance proceeds if policy owned by unmarried woman and insures her father or brother (unlimited amount): Missouri Annotated Statutes 376.550;
Stipulated insurance premiums (unlimited amount): Missouri Annotated Statutes 377.330;
Unmatured life insurance policy (unlimited amount): Missouri Annotated Statutes 513.430(7).

Miscellaneous: Alimony or child support (up to $500 per month): Missouri Annotated Statutes 513.430(10)(d);
Any property (up to $1,250 + $250 per child if head of family, otherwise up to $400): Missouri Annotated Statutes 513.430(3), 513.440;
Property of a business partnership (unlimited amount): Missouri Annotated Statutes 358.250.

Pensions: Employees of cities with 100,000 or more people (unlimited amount): Missouri Annotated Statutes 71.207;
Firefighters (unlimited amount): Missouri Annotated Statutes 87.090, 87.365, 87.485;
Highway and transportation employees (unlimited amount): Missouri Annotated Statutes 104.250;
Police department employees (unlimited amount): Missouri Annotated Statutes 86.190, 86.353, 86.493, 86.780;
Public officers and employees (unlimited amount): Missouri Annotated Statutes 70.695;
Retirement benefits (amount needed for support and only payments being received): Missouri Annotated Statutes 513.430(10)(e);
State employees (unlimited amount): Missouri Annotated Statutes 104.540;
Teachers (unlimited amount): Missouri Annotated Statutes 169.090.

Personal Property: Animals, appliances, books, clothing, crops, furnishings, household goods, and musical instruments (up to $1,000 total): Missouri Annotated Statutes 413.430(1);
Burial grounds (up to 1 acre): Missouri Annotated Statutes 214.190;
Health aids (unlimited amount): Missouri Annotated Statutes 513.430(9);
Implements, books, and tools of a trade (up to $2,000): Missouri Annotated Statutes 513.430(4);
Jewelry (up to $500): Missouri Annotated Statutes 513.430(2);
Motor vehicle (up to $1,000): Missouri Annotated Statutes 513.430(5);
Wrongful death recoveries (unlimited amount): Missouri Annotated Statutes 513.430(11).

Real Estate: Real property (up to $8,000) or mobile home (up to $1,000); joint owners may not double: Missouri Annotated Statutes 513.430(6), 513.475.

Wages: 75% of earned but unpaid wages (90% if head of family and judge may allow more for low-income debtors): Missouri Annotated Statutes 525.030;
Wages of servant or common laborer (up to $90): Missouri Annotated Statutes 513.470.

MONTANA

Montana residents may **not** use the Federal Bankruptcy Exemptions, but may use the Federal Non-Bankruptcy exemptions listed on p. 238 and the following state exemptions.

Benefits: Aid to aged, blind, disabled, and families with dependent children (unlimited amount): Montana Code Annotated 53-2-607;
Crime victims compensation (unlimited amount): Montana Code Annotated 53-9-129;
Local public assistance (unlimited amount): Montana Code Annotated 25-13-608(1)(b);
Silicosis benefits (unlimited amount): Montana Code Annotated 39-73-110;
Social security (unlimited amount): Montana Code Annotated 25-13-608(1)(b);
Unemployment compensation (unlimited amount): Montana Code Annotated 31-2-106(2),39-51-3105;
Veterans benefits (unlimited amount): Montana Code Annotated 25-13-608(1)(c);
Workers compensation (unlimited amount): Montana Code Annotated 39-71-743.

Insurance: Annuity contract proceeds (up to $350 per month): Montana Code Annotated 33-15-514;
Disability or illness proceeds or benefits (unlimited amount): Montana Code Annotated 25-13-608(1)(d), 33-15-513;
Fraternal society benefits (unlimited amount): Montana Code Annotated 33-7-522;
Group life insurance policy or proceeds (unlimited amount): Montana Code Annotated 33-15-512;
Hail insurance benefits (unlimited amount): Montana Code Annotated 80-2-245;
Life insurance proceeds if policy prohibits proceeds from being used to pay creditors (unlimited amount): Montana Code Annotated 33-20-120;
Medical, surgical or hospital care benefits (unlimited amount): Montana Code Annotated 25-13-608(1)(e);
Unmatured life insurance contracts (up to $4,000): Montana Code Annotated 25-13-609(4).

Miscellaneous: Alimony or child support (unlimited amount): Montana Code Annotated 25-13-608(1)(f);
Property of a business partnership (unlimited amount): Montana Code Annotated 35-10-502.

Pensions: Firefighters (unlimited amount): Montana Code Annotated 19-11-612(1),19-13-1004;
Game wardens (unlimited amount): Montana Code Annotated 19-8-805(2);
Highway patrol officers (unlimited amount): Montana Code Annotated 19-6-705(2);
Judges (unlimited amount): Montana Code Annotated 19-5-704;
Police officers (unlimited amount): Montana Code Annotated 19-9-1006, 19-10-504(1);
Public employees (unlimited amount): Montana Code Annotated 19-3-105(1);
Retirement benefits (unlimited amount; amount in excess of 15% of debtor's yearly income must have been deposited over 1 year before filing for bankruptcy): Montana Code Annotated 31-2-106;
Sheriffs (unlimited amount): Montana Code Annotated 19-7-705(2);
Teachers (unlimited amount): Montana Code Annotated 19-4-706(2);
University system employees (unlimited amount): Montana Code Annotated 19-21-212;

Personal Property: Animals, appliances, books, clothing, crops, firearms, household furnishings, jewelry, musical instruments, and sporting goods (up to $600 per item, $4,500 total): Montana Code Annotated 5-13-609(1);
Arms, equipment required for military use (unlimited amount): Montana Code Annotated 25-13-613(b);
Burial plot (unlimited amount): Montana Code Annotated 25-13-608(1)(g);
Cooperative association shares (up to $500): Montana Code Annotated 35-15-404;
Health aids (unlimited amount): Montana Code Annotated 25-13-608(1)(a);
Implements, books and tools of a trade (up to $3,000: Montana Code Annotated 25-13-609(3);
Motor vehicle (up to $1,200): Montana Code Annotated 25-13-609(2);
Proceeds for damaged or lost exempt property for 6 months after received (up to exemption amount): Montana Code Annotated 25-13-610;

Real Estate: Real property or mobile home used as a residence (up to $40,000; and up to 1 acre in city, town or village and up to 320 acres elsewhere); proceeds from sale, condemnation or insurance are exempt for 18 months; must record homestead declaration before filing for bankruptcy: Montana Code Annotated 70-32-104, 70-32-105, 70-32-201, 70-32-216.

Wages: 75% of earned but unpaid wages (judge may allow more for low-income debtors): Montana Code Annotated 25-13-614.

NEBRASKA

Nebraska residents may **not** use the Federal Bankruptcy Exemptions, but may use the Federal Non-Bankruptcy exemptions listed on p. 238 and the following state exemptions.

Benefits: Aid to aged, blind, disabled, and families with dependent children (unlimited amount): Revised Statutes of Nebraska 68-1013;
Unemployment compensation (unlimited amount): Revised Statutes of Nebraska 48-647;
Workers compensation (unlimited amount): Revised Statutes of Nebraska 48-149.

Insurance: Fraternal society benefits (up to $10,000 loan value): Revised Statutes of Nebraska 44-1089;
Life insurance or annuity contract proceeds (up to $10,000 loan value: Revised Statutes of Nebraska 44-371.

Miscellaneous: Property of a business partnership: Revised Statutes of Nebraska 67-325.

Pensions: County employees (unlimited amount): Revised Statutes of Nebraska 23-2322;
Military disability benefits (up to $2,000): Revised Statutes of Nebraska 25-1559;
Retirement benefits (amount needed for support): Revised Statutes of Nebraska 25-1563.01;
School employees (unlimited amount): Revised Statutes of Nebraska 79-1060, 79-1552;
State employees (unlimited amount): Revised Statutes of Nebraska 84-1324.

Personal Property: Any personal property, except wages (up to $2,500 if taken instead of real estate exemption): Revised Statutes of Nebraska 25-1552;
Burial plot, crypts, lots, tombs, vaults(unlimited amount): Revised Statutes of Nebraska 12-517, 12-605;
Clothing (amount needed): Revised Statutes of Nebraska 25-1556;
Equipment or tools (up to $1,500): Revised Statutes of Nebraska 25-1556;
Food and fuel (amount to last 6 months): Revised Statutes of Nebraska 25-1556;
Furniture and kitchen utensils (up to $1,500): Revised Statutes of Nebraska 25-1556;
Perpetual care funds (unlimited amount): Revised Statutes of Nebraska 12-511;
Personal injury recoveries (unlimited amount): Revised Statutes of Nebraska 25-1563.02;
Personal possessions (unlimited amount): Revised Statutes of Nebraska 25-1556.

Real Estate: Real estate used as residence (up to $10,000 and up to 2 lots in city or village, 160 acres elsewhere); sale proceeds exempt for 6 months after sale: Revised Statutes of Nebraska 40-101, 40-111, 40-113.

Wages: Earned but unpaid wages or pension payments (85% for head of family; 75% for others; judge may allow more for low-income debtors): Revised Statutes of Nebraska 25-1558.

NEVADA

Nevada residents may **not** use the Federal Bankruptcy Exemptions, but may use the Federal Non-Bankruptcy exemptions listed on p. 238 and the following state exemptions.

Benefits: Aid to aged, blind, disabled, and families with dependent children (unlimited amount): Nevada Revised Statutes Annotated 422.291;
Industrial insurance (workers compensation) (unlimited amount): Nevada Revised Statutes Annotated 616.550;
Unemployment compensation (unlimited amount): Nevada Revised Statutes Annotated 612.710;
Vocational rehabilitation benefits (unlimited amount): Nevada Revised Statutes Annotated 615.270.

Insurance: Annuity contract proceeds (up to $350 per month): Nevada Revised Statutes Annotated 687B.290;
Fraternal society benefits (unlimited amount): Nevada Revised Statutes Annotated 695A.220;
Group life or health policy or proceeds (unlimited amount): Nevada Revised Statutes Annotated 687B.280;
Health proceeds (unlimited amount): Nevada Revised Statutes Annotated 687B.270;
Life insurance policy or proceeds (unlimited): Nevada Revised Statutes Annotated 21.090(1)(k);
Life insurance proceeds if debtor is not the insured (unlimited amount): Nevada Revised Statutes Annotated 687B.260.

Miscellaneous: Property of a business partnership (unlimited amount): Nevada Revised Statutes Annotated 87.250.

Pensions: Public employees (unlimited amount): Nevada Revised Statutes Annotated 286.670;
Retirement benefits (up to $100,000): Nevada Revised Statutes Annotated 21.090(1)(q).

Personal Property: Appliances, furniture, home and yard equipment, and household goods (up to $3000 total): Nevada Revised Statutes Annotated 21.090(1)(b);
Arms, uniforms and equipment required for military use (unlimited amount): Nevada Revised Statutes Annotated 21.090(1)(j);
Books (up to $1,500): Nevada Revised Statutes Annotated 21.090(1)(a);
Cabin or dwelling of miner or prospector; cars and equipment for mining and mining claim (up to $4,500): Nevada Revised Statutes Annotated 121.090(1)(e);
Farm trucks, stock, tools, equipment and seed (up to $4,500): Nevada Revised Statutes Annotated 21.090(1)(c);
Funeral service money held in trust (unlimited amount): Nevada Revised Statutes Annotated 689.700;
Geological specimens, art curiosities or paleontological remains (up to $4,500, if catalogued and numbered): Nevada Revised Statutes Annotated 21.100
Gun (1 only): Nevada Revised Statutes Annotated 21.090(1)(i);
Health aids (unlimited amount): Nevada Revised Statutes Annotated 21.090(1)(p);
Keepsakes and pictures (unlimited amount): Nevada Revised Statutes Annotated 21.090(1)(a);
Library, equipment, supplies, tools and materials for business (up to $4,500): Nevada Revised Statutes Annotated 21.090(1)(d);
Motor vehicle (up to $1,500; unlimited amount if equipped for disabled person: Nevada Revised Statutes Annotated 21.090(1)(f), (o).

Real Estate: Real property or mobile home used as a residence (up to $125,000; husband and wife may not double); must record homestead declaration before filing for bankruptcy: Nevada Revised Statutes Annotated 21.090(1)(m), 115.010, 115.020.

Wages: 75% of earned but unpaid wages (judge may allow more for low-income debtors): Nevada Revised Statutes Annotated 21.090(1)(g).

NEW HAMPSHIRE

New Hampshire residents may **not** use the Federal Bankruptcy Exemptions, but may use the Federal Non-Bankruptcy exemptions listed on p. 238 and the following state exemptions.

Benefits: Aid to aged, blind, disabled, families with dependent children (unlimited amount): New Hampshire Revised Statutes Annotated 167:25;
Unemployment compensation (unlimited amount): New Hampshire Revised Statutes Annotated 282A:159;
Workers compensation (unlimited amount): New Hampshire Revised Statutes Annotated 281A:52.

Insurance: Firefighters insurance (unlimited amount): New Hampshire Revised Statutes Annotated 402:69;
Fraternal society benefits (unlimited amount): New Hampshire Revised Statutes Annotated 418:24;
Homeowners insurance proceeds (up to $5,000): New Hampshire Revised Statutes Annotated 512:21(VIII).

Miscellaneous: Child support (unlimited amount): New Hampshire Revised Statutes Annotated 161-C-11;
Jury and witness fees (unlimited amount): New Hampshire Revised Statutes Annotated 512:21(VI);
Property of a business partnership (unlimited amount): New Hampshire Revised Statutes Annotated 304A-25.

Pensions: Federal pension (unpaid benefits only): New Hampshire Revised Statutes Annotated 512:21(IV);
Firefighters (unlimited amount): New Hampshire Revised Statutes Annotated 102:23;
Police officers (unlimited amount): New Hampshire Revised Statutes Annotated 103:18;
Public employees (unlimited amount): New Hampshire Revised Statutes Annotated 100A.26.

Personal Property: Auto (up to $1,000): New Hampshire Revised Statutes Annotated 511:2(XVI);
Beds, bedding, and cooking utensils (amount needed): New Hampshire Revised Statutes Annotated 511:2(II);
Bibles and books (up to $800): New Hampshire Revised Statutes Annotated 511:2(VIII);
Burial plot or lot, or church pew (unlimited amount): New Hampshire Revised Statutes Annotated 511:2(XIV), 511:2(XV);
Clothing (amount needed): New Hampshire Revised Statutes Annotated 511:2(1);
Cooking and heating stoves, refrigerator (unlimited amount): New Hampshire Revised Statutes Annotated 511:2(IV);
Cow (1), sheep and fleece (6); hay (4 tons): New Hampshire Revised Statutes Annotated 511:2 (XI), (XII);
Food and fuel (up to $400): New Hampshire Revised Statutes Annotated 511:2(VI);
Fowl (up to $300): New Hampshire Revised Statutes Annotated 511:2(XIII);
Furniture (up to $2,000): New Hampshire Revised Statutes Annotated 511:2(III);
Jewelry (up to $500): New Hampshire Revised Statutes Annotated 511:2(XVII);
Pork (one, if already slaughtered): New Hampshire Revised Statutes Annotated 511:2(X);
Proceeds for lost or destroyed exempt property (up to exemption amount): New Hampshire Revised Statutes Annotated 512:21(VIII);
Sewing machine (unlimited amount): New Hampshire Revised Statutes Annotated 511:2 (V);
Tools of a trade (up to $1,200): New Hampshire Revised Statutes Annotated 511:2(IX);
Uniforms, arms and equipment required for military use (unlimited amount): New Hampshire Revised Statutes Annotated 511:2(VII);
Yoke of oxen or horse (one if needed for farming): New Hampshire Revised Statutes Annotated 511:2(XII).

Real Estate: Real property or manufactured housing, if located on land owned by debtor (up to $30,000): New Hampshire Revised Statutes Annotated 480:1.

Wages: Earned but unpaid wage (judge decides amount of exemption): New Hampshire Revised Statutes Annotated 512:21(II);
Earned but unpaid wages of spouse (unlimited amount): New Hampshire Revised Statutes Annotated 512:21 (III);
Wages of a minor child (unlimited amount): New Hampshire Revised Statutes Annotated 512:21 (III).

NEW JERSEY

New Jersey residents **may use either** the Federal Bankruptcy Exemptions on p. 237 or the state exemptions listed below. If state exemptions are used, then the Federal Non-Bankruptcy exemptions on p. 238 may also be used.

Benefits: Aid to aged, and permanent disability assistance (unlimited amount): New Jersey Statutes Annotated 44:7-35;
Crime victims compensation (unlimited amount): New Jersey Statutes Annotated 52:4B-30;
Unemployment compensation (unlimited amount): New Jersey Statutes Annotated 43:21-53;
Workers compensation (unlimited amount): New Jersey Statutes Annotated 34:15-29.

Insurance: Annuity contract proceeds (up to $500 per month): New Jersey Statutes Annotated 17B:24-7;
Civil defense workers disability, death, medical, and hospital benefits (unlimited amount): New Jersey Statutes Annotated App. A:9-57.6;
Fraternal society benefits (unlimited amount): New Jersey Statutes Annotated 17:44A-19;
Group life or health policy or proceeds (unlimited amount): New Jersey Statutes Annotated 17B:24-9;
Health or disability benefits (unlimited amount): New Jersey Statutes Annotated 17:18-12, 17B:24-8;
Life insurance proceeds if policy prohibits proceeds from being used to pay creditors (unlimited amount): New Jersey Statutes Annotated 17B:24-10;
Life insurance proceeds if debtor is not the insured (unlimited amount): New Jersey Statutes Annotated 17B:24-6b;
Military disability or death benefits (unlimited amount): New Jersey Statutes Annotated 38A:4-8.

Miscellaneous: Property of a business partnership (unlimited amount): New Jersey Statutes Annotated 42:1-25.

Pensions: Alcohol beverage control officers (unlimited amount): New Jersey Statutes Annotated 43:8A-20;
City board of health employees (unlimited amount): New Jersey Statutes Annotated 43:18-12;
Civil defense workers (unlimited amount): New Jersey Statutes Annotated App. A:9-57.6;
County employees (unlimited amount): New Jersey Statutes Annotated 43:10-57, 43:10-105;
Firefighters (unlimited amount): New Jersey Statutes Annotated 43:16-7;
Judges (unlimited amount): New Jersey Statutes Annotated 43:6A-41;
Municipal employees (unlimited amount): New Jersey Statutes Annotated 43:13-44;
Police officers (unlimited amount): New Jersey Statutes Annotated 43:16-7;
Prison employees (unlimited amount): New Jersey Statutes Annotated 43:7-13;
Public employees (unlimited amount): New Jersey Statutes Annotated 43:15A-53;
Retirement benefits (unlimited amount): New Jersey Statutes Annotated 43:13-9;
School district employees (unlimited amount): New Jersey Statutes Annotated 18A:66-116;
State police (unlimited amount): New Jersey Statutes Annotated 53:5A-45;
Street and water department employees (unlimited amount): New Jersey Statutes Annotated 43:19-17;
Teachers (unlimited amount): New Jersey Statutes Annotated 18A:66-51;
Traffic officers (unlimited amount): New Jersey Statutes Annotated 43:16A-17.

Personal Property: Any personal property or stock in corporation (up to $1,000 total): New Jersey Statutes Annotated 2A:17-19;
Burial plots (unlimited amount): New Jersey Statutes Annotated 8A:5-10;
Clothing (unlimited amount): New Jersey Statutes Annotated 2A:17-19;
Furniture and household goods (up to $1,000): New Jersey Statutes Annotated 2A:26-4.

Real Estate: None.

Wages: 90% of earned but unpaid wages (if income under $7,500; if income over $7,500, judge decides wage exemption amount): New Jersey Statutes Annotated 2A:17-56;
Military wages or allowances (unlimited amount): New Jersey Statutes Annotated 38A:4-8.

NEW MEXICO

New Mexico residents **may use either** the Federal Bankruptcy Exemptions on p. 237 or the state exemptions listed below. If state exemptions are used, then the Federal Non-Bankruptcy exemptions on p. 238 may also be used.

Benefits: Aid to families with dependent children and general assistance (unlimited amount): New Mexico Statutes Annotated 27-2-21;
Crime victims compensation if paid before 7/l/93 (unlimited amount): New Mexico Statutes Annotated 31-22-15;
Occupational disease disability benefits (unlimited amount): New Mexico Statutes Annotated 52-3-37;
Unemployment compensation (unlimited amount): New Mexico Statutes Annotated 51-1-37;
Workers compensation (unlimited amount): New Mexico Statutes Annotated 52-1-52.

Insurance: Benevolent association benefits (up to $5,000): New Mexico Statutes Annotated 42-10-4;
Fraternal society benefits (unlimited amount): New Mexico Statutes Annotated 59A-44-18;
Life, accident, health or annuity benefits or cash value, if beneficiary is a New Mexican citizen (unlimited amount): New Mexico Statutes Annotated 42-10-3.

Miscellaneous: Any property (up to $2,000, if taken instead of real estate exemption): New Mexico Statutes Annotated 42-10-10;
Ownership in an unincorporated association (unlimited amount): New Mexico Statutes Annotated 53-10-2;
Property of a business partnership (unlimited amount): New Mexico Statutes Annotated 54-1-25.

Pensions: Pension or retirement benefits (unlimited amount): New Mexico Statutes Annotated 42-10-1, 42-10-2;
Public school employees (unlimited amount): New Mexico Statutes Annotated 22-11-42A.

Personal Property: Any personal property (up to $500): New Mexico Statutes Annotated 42-10-1;
Books, furniture, and health equipment (unlimited amount): New Mexico Statutes Annotated 42-10-1, 42-10-2;
Books, implement and tools of a trade (up to $1,500): New Mexico Statutes Annotated 42-10-1, 42-10-2;
Building materials (unlimited amount): New Mexico Statutes Annotated 48-2-15;
Clothing (unlimited amount): New Mexico Statutes Annotated 42-10-1, 42-10-2;
Cooperative association shares (minimum amount needed to be member): New Mexico Statutes Annotated 53-4-28;
Health aids (unlimited amount): New Mexico Statutes Annotated 42-10-1;
Jewelry (up to $2,500): New Mexico Statutes Annotated 42-10-1, 42-10-2;
Materials, tools, and machinery to drill, complete, operate or repair oil line, gas well or pipeline (unlimited amount): New Mexico Statutes Annotated 70-4-12;
Motor vehicle (up to $4,000): New Mexico Statutes Annotated 42-10-1, 42-10-2.

Real Estate: Real property (up to $30,000 if married, widowed or are supporting another; joint owners may double): New Mexico Statutes Annotated 2-10-9.

Wages: 75% of earned but unpaid wages (judge may allow more for low-income debtors): New Mexico Statutes Annotated 35-12-7.

NEW YORK

New York residents may **not** use the Federal Bankruptcy Exemptions, but may use the Federal Non-Bankruptcy exemptions listed on p. 238 and the following state exemptions.

Benefits: Aid to aged, blind, disabled, families with dependent children (unlimited amount): Consolidated Laws of New York: Debtor and Creditor 282(2)(c);
Crime victims compensation (unlimited amount): Consolidated Laws of New York: Debtor and Creditor 282(3)(i);
Unemployment compensation, local public assistance and social security (unlimited amount): Consolidated Laws of New York: Debtor and Creditor 282(2)(a);
Veterans benefits (unlimited amount): Consolidated Laws of New York: Debtor and Creditor 282(2)(b);
Workers compensation (unlimited amount): Consolidated Laws of New York: Debtor and Creditor 282(2)(c).

Insurance: Annuity contract benefits (unlimited amount, unless purchased within 6 months of filing for bankruptcy and not tax-deferred, then up to $5,000): Insurance 3212(d), Debtor and Creditor 283(1);
Disability or illness benefits (up to $400 per month): Consolidated Laws of New York, Insurance 3212(c);
Life insurance proceeds if policy prohibits proceeds from being used to pay creditors (unlimited amount): Consolidated Laws of New York: Estates, Powers and Trusts 7-1.5(a)(2);
Life insurance proceeds if beneficiary is the spouse of the insured (unlimited amount): Consolidated Laws of New York: Insurance 3212(b)(2).

Miscellaneous: Alimony and child support (amount needed for support): Consolidated Laws of New York: Debtor and Creditor 282(2)(d);
Property of a business partnership (unlimited amount): Consolidated Laws of New York: Partnership 51;
Trust fund principal and 90% of income: Consolidated Laws of New York, Civil Practice Law and Rules 5205(c),(d).

Pensions: Public retirement benefits (unlimited amount): Consolidated Laws of New York: Insurance 4607;
Retirement benefits, IRAs, and Keoghs (amount needed for support): Consolidated Laws of New York: Debtor and Creditor 282(2)(e), Civil Practice Law and Rules 5205(c);
State employees (unlimited amount): Consolidated Laws of New York: Retirement and Social Security 110.

Personal Property: Bible, books (up to $50), church pew or seat, clothing, cooking utensils, crockery, food (amount to last 60 days), furniture, pet (with food to last 60 days; up to $450), pictures, radio, refrigerator, schoolbooks, sewing machine, stoves and fuel to last 60 days, tableware, TV, watch (up to $35), wedding ring (up to $5,000 total, with additional limits as noted): Consolidated Laws of New York, Civil Practice Law and Rules 5205(1)-(6); Debtor and Creditor 283(1);
Burial plot (up to 1/4 acre): Consolidated Laws of New York, Civil Practice Law and Rules 5206(f);
Cash (the lesser of either $2,500 or $5,000 as an annuity; to be taken instead of real estate): Consolidated Laws of New York: Debtor and Creditor 283(2);
Farm machinery, team with food for 60 days, business furniture, books and instruments (up to $600 total): Consolidated Laws of New York, Civil Practice Law and Rules 5205(a)(7);
Health aids (unlimited amount): Consolidated Laws of New York, Civil Practice Law and Rules 5205(h);
Lost earnings recoveries (amount needed for support): Consolidated Laws of New York: Debtor and Creditor 282(3)(iv);
Motor vehicle (up to $2,400): Consolidated Laws of New York: Debtor and Creditor 282(1);
Personal injury recoveries (up to $7,500): Consolidated Laws of New York: Debtor and Creditor 282(3)(iii);
Security deposits (unlimited amount): Consolidated Laws of New York, Civil Practice Law and Rules 5205(g);
Uniforms, arms and equipment required for military use (unlimited amount): Consolidated Laws of New York, Civil Practice Law and Rules 5205(e);
Wrongful death recoveries (amount needed for support): Consolidated Laws of New York: Debtor and Creditor 282(3)(ii).

Real Estate: Real property used as residence including co-op, condo, or mobile home (up to $10,000): Consolidated Laws of New York, Civil Practice Law and Rules 5206(a).

Wages: 90% of earned but unpaid wages (if received within 60 days of filing for bankruptcy): Consolidated Laws of New York, Civil Practice Law and Rules 5205(d),(e).

NORTH CAROLINA

North Carolina residents may **not** use the Federal Bankruptcy Exemptions, but may use the Federal Non-Bankruptcy exemptions listed on p. 238 and the following state exemptions.

Benefits: Aid to blind, families with dependent children, and special adult assistance (unlimited amount): General Statutes of North Carolina 108A-36, 111-18;
Crime victims compensation (unlimited amount): General Statutes of North Carolina 15B-17;
Unemployment compensation (unlimited amount): General Statutes of North Carolina 96-17;
Workers compensation (unlimited amount): General Statutes of North Carolina 97-21.

Insurance: Employee group life policy or proceeds (unlimited amount): General Statutes of North Carolina 58-58-165;
Fraternal society benefits (unlimited amount): General Statutes of North Carolina 58-24-85;
Life insurance policy or proceeds (unlimited amount): General Statutes of North Carolina 1C-1601(a)(6).

Miscellaneous: Any property (up to $3,500, if taken instead of real estate or burial plot exemption): General Statutes of North Carolina 1C-1601(a)(2);
Property of a business partnership (unlimited amount): General Statutes of North Carolina 59-55.

Pensions: Firefighters and rescue squad workers (unlimited amount): General Statutes of North Carolina 58-86-90;
Law enforcement officers (unlimited amount): General Statutes of North Carolina 143-166.30(g);
Legislators (unlimited amount): General Statutes of North Carolina 120-4.29;
Municipal, city, and county employees (unlimited amount): General Statutes of North Carolina 128-31;
Teachers and state employees (unlimited amount): General Statutes of North Carolina 135-9, 135-95.

Personal Property: Animals, appliances, books, clothing, crops, furnishings, household goods, musical instruments (up to $3,500 total, plus up to $750 additional per dependent, maximum 4 dependents): General Statutes of North Carolina 1C-1601(a)(4);
Burial plot (up to $10,000, if taken instead of real estate): General Statutes of North Carolina 1C-1601(a)(1);
Health aids (unlimited amount): General Statutes of North Carolina 1C-1601(a)(7);
Implements, books, and tools of a trade (up to $750): General Statutes of North Carolina 1C-1601(a)(5);
Motor vehicle (up to $1,500): General Statutes of North Carolina 1C-1601(a)(3);
Personal injury recoveries (unlimited amount): General Statutes of North Carolina 1C-1601(a)(8);
Wrongful death recoveries (unlimited amount): General Statutes of North Carolina 1C-1601(a)(8).

Real Estate: Real or personal property, including co-op, used as residence (up to $10,000): General Statutes of North Carolina 1C-1601(a)(1),(2).

Wages: Earned but unpaid wages (amount needed for support and if received 60 days before filing for bankruptcy): General Statutes of North Carolina 1-362.

NORTH DAKOTA

North Dakota residents may **not** use the Federal Bankruptcy Exemptions, but may use the Federal Non-Bankruptcy exemptions listed on p. 238 and the following state exemptions.

Benefits: Aid to families with dependent children (unlimited amount): North Dakota Century Code 28-22-19(3);
Crime victims compensation (unlimited amount): North Dakota Century Code 28-22-19(2);
Social security (unlimited amount): North Dakota Century Code 28-22-03.1(4)(c);
Unemployment compensation (unlimited amount): North Dakota Century Code 52-06-30;
Vietnam veterans bonus (unlimited amount): North Dakota Century Code 37-25-07;
Workers compensation (unlimited amount): North Dakota Century Code 65-05-29.

Insurance: Fraternal society benefits (unlimited amount): North Dakota Century Code 26.1-15.1-18, 26.1-33-40;
Life insurance proceeds payable to deceased's estate (unlimited amount): North Dakota Century Code 26.1-33-40;
Life insurance if beneficiary is insured's relative and policy was owned over 1 year before filing for bankruptcy (up to $100,000 per policy and up to $200,000 total life insurance and Retirement, IRA or KEOGH; unlimited life insurance if needed for support): North Dakota Century Code 28-22-03.1(3).

Miscellaneous: Property of a business partnership (unlimited amount): North Dakota Century Code 45-08-02.

Pensions: Disabled veterans benefits, except military retirement pay (unlimited amount): North Dakota Century Code 28-22-03.1(4)(d);
Retirement benefits, IRAs, and Keoghs (up to $100,000 per plan and up to $200,000 total life insurance and retirement, IRA, or KEOGH; unlimited if needed for support): North Dakota Century Code 28-22-03.1(3);
Public employees (unlimited amount): North Dakota Century Code 28-22-19(1).

Personal Property: Any personal property (up to $7,500, if taken instead of real estate exemption): North Dakota Century Code 28-22-03, 28-22-05.
Bible and books (up to $100): North Dakota Century Code 28-22-02(1);
Burial plots and church pew (unlimited amount): North Dakota Century Code 28-22-02(2),(3);
Crops (amount raised on debtor's land of up to 160 acres): North Dakota Century Code 28-22-02(8);
Food and fuel (amount to last 1 year): North Dakota Century Code 28-22-02(6);
Motor vehicle (up to $1,200): North Dakota Century Code 28-22-03.1(2);
Personal injury recoveries (up to $7,500; but not for pain and suffering): North Dakota Century Code 28-22-03.1(4)(b);
Pictures and clothing (unlimited amount): North Dakota Century Code 28-22-02(1)(5);
Wrongful death recoveries (up to $7,500): North Dakota Century Code 28-22-03.1(4)(a);
Note: Any non-head of household who does not claim a crops exemption may claim an additional $2,500 of any personal property: North Dakota Century Code 28-22-05;
Any head of household who does not claim a crops exemption may claim an additional $5,000 of any personal property **or** all of the following: North Dakota Century Code 28-22-03:
    Books and musical instruments (up to $1,500): North Dakota Century Code 28-22-04(1);
    Furniture and bedding (up to $1,000): North Dakota Century Code 28-22-04(2);
    Library and professional tools (up to $1,000): North Dakota Century Code 28-22-04(4);
    Livestock and farm implements (up to $4,500): North Dakota Century Code 28-22-04(3);
    Tools of a mechanic and business inventory (up to $1,000): North Dakota Century Code 28-22-04(4).

Real Estate: Real property, house trailer or mobile home used as a residence (up to $80,000); proceeds for sale of exempt real estate are exempt: North Dakota Century Code 28-22-02(10), 47-18-01.

Wages: 75% of earned but unpaid pensions or wages (judge may allow more for low-income debtors): North Dakota Century Code 32-09.1-03.

OHIO

Ohio residents may **not** use the Federal Bankruptcy Exemptions, but may use the Federal Non-Bankruptcy exemptions listed on p. 238 and the following state exemptions.

Benefits: Aid to families with dependent children (unlimited amount): Ohio Revised Code 2329.66(A)(9)(d), 5107.12;
Crime victims compensation (unlimited amount if received during 12 months before filing for bankruptcy): Ohio Revised Code 2329.66(A)(12)(a), 2743.66;
Disability assistance payments (unlimited amount): Ohio Revised Code 2329.66(A)(9)(f), 5115.07;
General assistance payments (unlimited amount): Ohio Revised Code 2329.66(A)(9)(e), 5113.03;
Tuition credit (unlimited amount): Ohio Revised Code 2329.66(A)(16);
Unemployment compensation (unlimited amount): Ohio Revised Code 2329.66(A)(9)(c), 4141.32;
Vocational rehabilitation benefits (unlimited amount): Ohio Revised Code 2329.66(A)(9)(a), 3304.19;
Workers compensation (unlimited amount): Ohio Revised Code 2329.66(A)(9)(b), 4123.67.

Insurance: Benevolent society benefits (up to $5,000): Ohio Revised Code 2329.63, 2329.66(A)(6)(a);
Disability benefits (up to $600 per month): Ohio Revised Code 2329.66(A)(6)(e), 3923.19;
Fraternal society benefits (unlimited amount): Ohio Revised Code 2329.66(A)(6)(d), 3921.18;
Group life insurance policy or proceeds (unlimited amount): Ohio Revised Code 2329.66(A)(6)(c), 3917.05;
Life, endowment or annuity contract benefits for spouse, child or dependent (unlimited amount): Ohio Revised Code 2329.66(A)(6)(b), 3911.10;
Life insurance proceeds for spouse (unlimited amount): Ohio Revised Code 3911.12;
Life insurance proceeds if policy prohibits proceeds from being used to pay creditors (unlimited amount): Ohio Revised Code 3911.14.

Miscellaneous: Alimony or child support (amount needed for support): Ohio Revised Code 2329.66(A)(11);
Any property: real estate or personal property (up to $400): Ohio Revised Code 2329.66(A)(17);
Property of a business partnership (unlimited amount): Ohio Revised Code 1775.24, 2329.66(A) (14).

Pensions: Firefighters and police officers pensions or death benefits (unlimited amount): Ohio Revised Code 742.47, 2329.66(A)(10)(a);
Public employees (unlimited amount): Ohio Revised Code 145.56;
Public school employees (unlimited amount): Ohio Revised Code 3307.71, 3309.66;
Retirement benefits, IRAs, and Keoghs (amount needed for support): Ohio Revised Code 2329.66(A)(10)(b),(c);
State highway patrol employees (unlimited amount): Ohio Revised Code 5505.22;
Volunteer firefighters dependents (unlimited amount): Ohio Revised Code 146.13.

Personal Property: Animals, appliances, books, crops, firearms, furnishings, household goods, hunting and fishing equipment, jewelry, and musical instruments (up to $200 per item) Refrigerator and stove (up to $300 each) [Note: 1 item of jewelry may be up to $400] and up to $1,500 total; $2,000 total if no real estate exemption is taken): Ohio Revised Code 2329.66(A)(3); 2329.66(A)(4)(b),(d); 2329.66(A)(c),(d);
Beds, bedding, and clothing (up to $200 per item): Ohio Revised Code 2329.66(A)(3);
Burial plot (unlimited amount): Ohio Revised Code 517.09, 2329.66(A)(8);
Bank deposits, cash, money due within 90 days, security deposits, and tax refunds (up to $400 total): Ohio Revised Code 2329.66()(4)(a);
Implements, books and tools of a trade (up to $750): Ohio Revised Code 2329.66(A)(5);
Health aids (unlimited amount): Ohio Revised Code 2329.66(A)(7);
Lost future earnings (amount needed for support if received during 12 months before filing for bankruptcy): Ohio Revised Code 2329.66(A)(12)(d);
Motor vehicle (to $ 1,000): Ohio Revised Code 2329.66(A)(2)(b);
Personal injury recoveries (up to $5,000 if received during 12 months before filing for bankruptcy; but not for pain and suffering): Ohio Revised Code 2329.66(A)(12)(c);
Wrongful death recoveries (amount needed for support if received during 12 months before filing: Ohio Revised Code 2329.66(A)(12)(b).

Real Estate: Real or personal property used as a residence (up to $5,000): Ohio Revised Code 2329.66(A)(1)(b).

Wages: 75% of earned but unpaid wages which are due for 30 days (judge may allow more for low-income debtors): Ohio Revised Code 2329.66(A)(13).

OKLAHOMA

Oklahoma residents may **not** use the Federal Bankruptcy Exemptions, but may use the Federal Non-Bankruptcy exemptions listed on p. 238 and the following state exemptions.

Benefits: Aid to families with dependent children (unlimited amount): Oklahoma Statutes Annotated 56-173;
Crime victims compensation (unlimited amount): Oklahoma Statutes Annotated 21-142.13;
Social security (unlimited amount): Oklahoma Statutes Annotated 56-173;
Unemployment compensation (unlimited amount): Oklahoma Statutes Annotated 40-2-303;
Workers compensation (unlimited amount): Oklahoma Statutes Annotated 85-48.

Insurance: Fraternal society benefits (unlimited amount): Oklahoma Statutes Annotated 36-2718.1;
Funeral benefits (if prepaid and placed in trust; unlimited amount): Oklahoma Statutes Annotated 36-6125;
Group life policy or proceeds (unlimited amount): Oklahoma Statutes Annotated 36-3632;
Limited stock insurance benefits (unlimited amount): Oklahoma Statutes Annotated 36-2510;
Mutual benefits (unlimited amount): Oklahoma Statutes Annotated 36-2410.

Miscellaneous: Alimony and child support (unlimited amount): Oklahoma Statutes Annotated 31-1(A)(19);
Property of a business partnership (unlimited amount): Oklahoma Statutes Annotated 54-225.

Pensions: County employees (unlimited amount): Oklahoma Statutes Annotated 19-959;
Disabled veterans (unlimited amount): Oklahoma Statutes Annotated 31-7;
Firefighters (unlimited amount): Oklahoma Statutes Annotated 11-49-126;
Law enforcement employees (unlimited amount): Oklahoma Statutes Annotated 47-2-303.3;
Police officers (unlimited amount): Oklahoma Statutes Annotated 11-50-124;
Public employees (unlimited amount): Oklahoma Statutes Annotated 74-923;
Retirement benefits (unlimited amount): Oklahoma Statutes Annotated 31-1(A)(20);
Tax exempt benefits (unlimited amount): Oklahoma Statutes Annotated 60-328;
Teachers (unlimited amount): Oklahoma Statutes Annotated 70-17-109.

Personal Property: Books, gun (1), pictures, and portraits (unlimited amount): Oklahoma Statutes Annotated 31-1(A)(7),(14);
Bridles and saddles (2 each total): Oklahoma Statutes Annotated 31-1(A)(12);
Burial plots (unlimited amount): Oklahoma Statutes Annotated 31-1(A)(4);
Chickens (100), dairy cows and calves under 6 months (5), hogs (10), horses (2), sheep (20); feed to last 1 year: Oklahoma Statutes Annotated 31-1(A)(10),(11),(15),(16);
Clothing (up to $4,000): Oklahoma Statutes Annotated 31-1(A)(8);
Farm implements, tools, books, and business equipment (up to $5,000 total): Oklahoma Statutes Annotated 31-1(A)(5), (6); 31-1(C);
Food (amount to last 1 year): Oklahoma Statutes Annotated 31-1(A)(17);
Furniture and health aids (unlimited amount): Oklahoma Statutes Annotated 31-1-(A)(3),(9);
Motor vehicle (up to $3,000): Oklahoma Statutes Annotated 31-1(A)(13);
Personal injury, wrongful death and workers compensation recoveries (up to $50,000 total; but not punitive damages): Oklahoma Statutes Annotated 31-1(A)(21);

Real Estate: Real property or manufactured home (unlimited value if up to 1/4 acre; if over 1/4 acre, up to $5,000 for up to 1 acre in city, town or village, or up to 160 acres elsewhere): Oklahoma Statutes Annotated 31-1(A)(1), 31-1(A)(2), 31-2.

Wages: 75% of wages earned in the 90 days before filing for bankruptcy (judge may allow more for hardship): Oklahoma Statutes Annotated 12-1171.1, 31-1(A)(18).

OREGON

Oregon residents may **not** use the Federal Bankruptcy Exemptions, but may use the Federal Non-Bankruptcy exemptions listed on p. 238 and the following state exemptions.

Benefits: Aid to aged, blind, disabled (unlimited amount): Oregon Revised Statutes 412.115, 412.610, 413.130;
Civil defense and disaster relief (unlimited amount): Oregon Revised Statutes 401.405;
Crime victims compensation (unlimited amount): Oregon Revised Statutes 23.160(1)(j)(A), 147.325;
General assistance (unlimited amount): Oregon Revised Statutes 411.760;
Inmates injury benefits (unlimited amount): Oregon Revised Statutes 655.530;
Medical assistance (unlimited amount): Oregon Revised Statutes 414.095;
Unemployment compensation (unlimited amount): Oregon Revised Statutes 657.855;
Vocational rehabilitation (unlimited amount): Oregon Revised Statutes 344.580;
Workers compensation (unlimited amount): Oregon Revised Statutes 656.234.

Insurance: Annuity contract benefits (up to $500 per month): Oregon Revised Statutes 743.049;
Fraternal society benefits (unlimited amount): Oregon Revised Statutes 748.207;
Group life policy or proceeds not payable to the insured (unlimited amount): Oregon Revised Statutes 743.047;
Health or disability proceeds (unlimited amount): Oregon Revised Statutes 743.050;
Life insurance proceeds or cash value debtor is not the insured (unlimited amount): Oregon Revised Statutes 743.046.

Miscellaneous: Alimony and child support (amount needed for support: Oregon Revised Statutes 23.160(1)(i);
Liquor licenses (unlimited amount): Oregon Revised Statutes 471.301(1);
Property of a business partnership (unlimited amount): Oregon Revised Statutes 68.420.

Pensions: Public officials and employees (unlimited amount): Oregon Revised Statutes 237.201;
Retirement benefits (unlimited amount): Oregon Revised Statutes 23.170;
School district employees (unlimited amount): Oregon Revised Statutes 239.261.

Personal Property: Any personal property not listed below (up to $400): Oregon Revised Statutes 23.160(1)(k);
Bank deposits (up to $7,500, if from exempt wages or pension): Oregon Revised Statutes 23.166;
Books, pictures, and musical instruments (up to $600 total): Oregon Revised Statutes 23.160(1)(a);
Burial plot (unlimited amount): Oregon Revised Statutes 65.870;
Clothing, jewelry and personal items (up to $1,800 total): Oregon Revised Statutes 23.160(1)(b);
Domestic animals and poultry with food to last 60 days (up to $1,000): Oregon Revised Statutes 23.160(1)(e);
Food and fuel (amount to last 60 days): Oregon Revised Statutes 23.160(1)(f);
Furniture, household items, radios, TVs, and utensils (up to $3,000 total: Oregon Revised Statutes 23.160(1)(f);
Health aids (unlimited amount): Oregon Revised Statutes 23.160(1)(h);
Lost future earnings payments (amount needed for support): Oregon Revised Statutes 23.160(1)(j)(C);
Motor vehicle (up to $1,700): Oregon Revised Statutes 23.160(1)(d);
Personal injury recoveries (up to $7,500, but not for pain and suffering): Oregon Revised Statutes 23.160(1)(j)(B);
Pistol, rifle, or shotgun (up to $1,000): Oregon Revised Statutes 23.200;
Proceeds from sale of exempt property (up to exemption amount): Oregon Revised Statutes 23.166;
Tools, business equipment, library, and team with food to last 60 days (up to $3,000): Oregon Revised Statutes 23.160(1)(c).

Real Estate: Real property, mobile home or houseboat used as a residence (up to $25,000; $33,000 for joint owners; and only $23,000 if mobile home is on rented land; $30,000 for joint mobile home owners on rented land; property may be up to 1 block in town or city or 160 acres elsewhere; sale proceeds are exempt for one year if held to purchase another home): Oregon Revised Statutes 23.164, 23.240, 23.250.

Wages: 75% of earned but unpaid wages (judge may allow more for low-income debtors): Oregon Revised Statutes 23.185;
Wages withheld in state employees bond savings accounts: Oregon Revised Statutes 292.070.

PENNSYLVANIA

Pennsylvania residents **may use either** the Federal Bankruptcy Exemptions on p. 237 or the state exemptions listed below. If state exemptions are used, then the Federal Non-Bankruptcy exemptions on p. 238 may also be used.

Benefits: Crime victims compensation (unlimited amount): Pennsylvania Consolidated Statutes Annotated 71-180-7.10;
    Unemployment compensation (unlimited amount): Pennsylvania Consolidated Statutes Annotated 42-8124(a)(10), 43-863;
    Veterans benefits (unlimited amount): Pennsylvania Consolidated Statutes Annotated 51-20012, 51-20098;
    Workers compensation (unlimited amount): Pennsylvania Consolidated Statutes Annotated 42-8124(c)(2).

Insurance: Accident or disability benefits (unlimited amount): Pennsylvania Consolidated Statutes Annotated 42-8124(c)(7);
    Fraternal society benefits (unlimited amount): Pennsylvania Consolidated Statutes Annotated 40-1141-403, 42-8124(c)(1),(8);
    Group life policy or proceeds (unlimited amount): Pennsylvania Consolidated Statutes Annotated 42-8124(c)(5);
    Insurance annuity policy, cash value or proceeds if beneficiary is insured's dependent, child or spouse (unlimited amount): Pennsylvania Consolidated Statutes Annotated 42-8124(c)(6);
    Insurance or annuity payments, if insured is beneficiary, (up to $100 per month): Pennsylvania Consolidated Statutes Annotated 42-8124(c)(3);
    Life insurance proceeds if policy prohibits proceeds from being used to pay creditors (unlimited amount): Pennsylvania Consolidated Statutes Annotated 42-8214(c)(4);
    No-fault automobile insurance proceeds (unlimited amount): Pennsylvania Consolidated Statutes Annotated 42-8124(c)(9).

Miscellaneous: Any property (up to $300): Pennsylvania Consolidated Statutes Annotated 42-8123;
    Property of a business partnership (unlimited amount): Pennsylvania Consolidated Statutes Annotated 15-8341.

Pensions: City employees (unlimited amount): Pennsylvania Consolidated Statutes Annotated 53-13445, 53-23572,53-39383;
    County employees (unlimited amount): Pennsylvania Consolidated Statutes Annotated 16-4716;
    Municipal employees (unlimited amount): Pennsylvania Consolidated Statutes Annotated 53-881.115;
    Police officers (unlimited amount): Pennsylvania Consolidated Statutes Annotated 53-764, 53-776, 53-23666;
    Public school employees (unlimited amount): Pennsylvania Consolidated Statutes Annotated 24-8533;
    State employees (unlimited amount): Pennsylvania Consolidated Statutes Annotated 71-5953;
    Private retirement benefits if deposited for over 1 year before filing for bankruptcy and if policy prohibits proceeds from being used to pay creditors (up to $15,000): Pennsylvania Consolidated Statutes Annotated 42-8124(b).

Personal Property: Bibles, schoolbooks, and sewing machines (unlimited amount): Pennsylvania Consolidated Statutes Annotated 42-8124(a)(2), (3);
    Clothing (unlimited amount): Pennsylvania Consolidated Statutes Annotated 42-8124(a)(1);
    Personal property located at a U. S. government international exhibit (unlimited amount): Pennsylvania Consolidated Statutes Annotated 42-8125;
    Uniform and equipment required for military use (unlimited amount): Pennsylvania Consolidated Statutes Annotated 42-8124(a)(4).

Real Estate: None.

Wages: Earned but unpaid wages (unlimited amount): Pennsylvania Consolidated Statutes Annotated 42-8127.

RHODE ISLAND

Rhode Island residents **may use either** the Federal Bankruptcy Exemptions on p. 237 or the state exemptions listed below. If state exemptions are used, then the Federal Non-Bankruptcy exemptions on p. 238 may also be used.

Benefits: Aid to aged, blind, disabled, families with dependent children, and general assistance (unlimited amount): General Laws of Rhode Island 40-6-14;
Disability benefits (unlimited amount): General Laws of Rhode Island 28-41-32;
Unemployment compensation (unlimited amount): General Laws of Rhode Island 28-44-58;
Veterans disability or death benefits (unlimited amount): General Laws of Rhode Island 30-7-9;
Workers compensation (unlimited amount): General Laws of Rhode Island 28-33-27.

Insurance: Accident or sickness proceeds or benefits (unlimited amount): General Laws of Rhode Island 27-18-24;
Fraternal society benefits (unlimited amount): General Laws of Rhode Island 27-25-18;
Life insurance proceeds if policy prohibits proceeds from being used to pay creditors (unlimited amount): General Laws of Rhode Island 27-4-12;
Temporary disability insurance (unlimited amount): General Laws of Rhode Island 28-41-32.

Miscellaneous: Property of business partnership: General Laws of Rhode Island 7-12-36.

Pensions: Firefighters (unlimited amount): General Laws of Rhode Island 9-26-5;
IRAs (unlimited amount): General Laws of Rhode Island 9-26-4(12);
Police officers (unlimited amount): General Laws of Rhode Island 9-26-5;
Private employees (unlimited amount): General Laws of Rhode Island 28-17-4;
Retirement benefits (unlimited amount): General Laws of Rhode Island 9-26-4(11);
State and municipal employees (unlimited amount): General Laws of Rhode Island 36-10-34.

Personal Property: Beds, bedding, furniture, household goods (up to $1,000 total): General Laws of Rhode Island 19-26-4(3);
Bibles and books (up to $300): General Laws of Rhode Island 9-26-4(4);
Burial plot (unlimited amount): General Laws of Rhode Island 9-26-4(5);
Clothing (amount needed) (unlimited amount): General Laws of Rhode Island 9-26-4(1);
Cooperative association holdings (up to $50): General Laws of Rhode Island 7-8-25;
Debt secured by promissory note (unlimited amount): General Laws of Rhode Island 9-26-4(7);
Library of a professional in practice (unlimited amount): General Laws of Rhode Island 9-26-4(2);
Tools used for work (up to $500): General Laws of Rhode Island 9-26-4(2).

Real Estate: None.

Wages: Earned but unpaid wages (up to $50): General Laws of Rhode Island 9-26-4(8)(C);
Earned but unpaid wages due military member on active duty (unlimited amount): General Laws of Rhode Island 30-7-9;
Earned but unpaid wages due seaman (unlimited amount): General Laws of Rhode Island 9-26-4(6);
Earned but unpaid wages if debtor received welfare during the year before filing for bankruptcy (unlimited amount): General Laws of Rhode Island 9-26-4(8)(B);
Earnings of a minor child (unlimited amount): General Laws of Rhode Island 9-26-4(9);
Wages of spouse (unlimited amount): General Laws of Rhode Island 9-26-4(9);
Wages to the needy if paid by a charitable organization (unlimited amount): General Laws of Rhode Island 9-26-4(8)(A).

SOUTH CAROLINA

South Carolina residents **may use either** the Federal Bankruptcy Exemptions on p. 237 or the state exemptions listed below. If state exemptions are used, then the Federal Non-Bankruptcy exemptions on p. 238 may also be used.

Benefits: Aid to aged, blind, disabled, families with dependent children, and general relief (unlimited amount): Code of Laws of South Carolina 43-5-190;
Crime victims compensation (unlimited amount): Code of Laws of South Carolina 15-41-30(11)(A), 16-3-1300;
Local public assistance (unlimited amount): Code of Laws of South Carolina 15-41-30(10)(A);
Social security (unlimited amount): Code of Laws of South Carolina 15-41-30(10)(A);
Unemployment compensation (unlimited amount): Code of Laws of South Carolina 15-41-30(10)(A);
Veterans benefits (unlimited amount): Code of Laws of South Carolina 15-41-30(10)(B);
Workers compensation (unlimited amount): Code of Laws of South Carolina 42-9-360.

Insurance: Disability or illness benefits (unlimited amount): Code of Laws of South Carolina 15-41-30(10C);
Fraternal society benefits (unlimited amount): Code of Laws of South Carolina 38-37-870;
Life insurance benefits if proceeds left with insurance company: Code of Laws of South Carolina 8-63-50;
Life insurance proceeds (up to $4,000): Code of Laws of South Carolina 15-41-30(8), 15-41-30(11)(C);
Unmatured life insurance contract (unlimited amount): Code of Laws of South Carolina 15-41-30(7).

Miscellaneous: Alimony and child support (unlimited amount): Code of Laws of South Carolina 15-41-30(10)(D);
Property of a business partnership (unlimited amount): Code of Laws of South Carolina 33-41-720;

Pensions: Firefighters (unlimited amount): Code of Laws of South Carolina 9-13-230;
General assembly members (unlimited amount): Code of Laws of South Carolina 9-9-180;
Judges, solicitors (unlimited amount): Code of Laws of South Carolina 9-8-190;
Police officers (unlimited amount): Code of Laws of South Carolina 9-11-270;
Public employees (unlimited amount): Code of Laws of South Carolina 9-1-1680;
Retirement benefits (unlimited amount): Code of Laws of South Carolina 15-41-30(10)(E).

Personal Property: Animals, appliances, books, clothing, crops, furnishings, household goods, musical instruments (up to $2,500): Code of Laws of South Carolina 15-41-30(3);
Burial plot (up to $5,000 if taken instead of real estate exemption): Code of Laws of South Carolina 15-41-30(1);
Cash and other liquid assets (up to $1,000 if taken instead of burial or real estate exemption): Code of Laws of South Carolina 15-41-30(5);
Health aids (unlimited amount): Code of Laws of South Carolina 15-41-30(9);
Implements, books, and tools of a trade (up to $750): Code of Laws of South Carolina 15-41-30(6);
Jewelry (up to $500): Code of Laws of South Carolina 15-41-30(4);
Motor vehicle (up to $1,200): Code of Laws of South Carolina 15-41-30(2);
Personal injury recoveries (unlimited amount): Code of Laws of South Carolina 15-41-30(11)(B);
Wrongful death recoveries (unlimited amount): Code of Laws of South Carolina 15-41-30(11)(B).

Real Estate: Real property used as a residence, including a co-op (up to $5,000): Code of Laws of South Carolina 15-41-30(1).

Wages: Earnings from personal service: Code of Laws of South Carolina 15-39-410.

SOUTH DAKOTA

South Dakota residents may **not** use the Federal Bankruptcy Exemptions, but may use the Federal Non-Bankruptcy exemptions listed on p. 238 and the following state exemptions.

Benefits: Aid to families with dependent children (unlimited amount): South Dakota Codified Laws 28-7-16;
Unemployment compensation (unlimited amount): South Dakota Codified Laws 61-6-28;
Workers compensation (unlimited amount): South Dakota Codified Laws 62-4-42.

Insurance: Annuity contract proceeds (up to $250 per month): South Dakota Codified Laws 58-12-6; 58-12-8;
Endowment or life insurance policy, proceeds, or cash value (up to $20,000): South Dakota Codified Laws 58-12-4:
Fraternal society benefits (unlimited amount): South Dakota Codified Laws 58-37-68;
Health benefits (up to $20,000): South Dakota Codified Laws 58-12-4;
Life insurance proceeds, if held by insurance company and if policy prohibits proceeds from being used to pay creditors: South Dakota Codified Laws 58-15-70;
Life insurance proceeds (up to $10,000 if beneficiary is spouse or child): South Dakota Codified Laws 43-45-6.

Miscellaneous: Property of a business partnership (unlimited amount): South Dakota Codified Laws 48-4-14.

Pensions: City employees (unlimited amount): South Dakota Codified Laws 9-16-47;
Public employees (unlimited amount): South Dakota Codified Laws 3-12-115.

Personal Property: Bible, books (up to $200), burial plot, church pew, clothing, food and fuel (amount to last 1 year); (unlimited amount unless noted): South Dakota Codified Laws 43-45-2;
Head of household exemptions: Any personal property (up to $4,000): South Dakota Codified Laws 43-45-4,5;
or: Books and musical instruments (up to $200): South Dakota Codified Laws 43-45-5.
Cows (2); lambs (all under 6 months); sheep with wool (25); swine (5); feed for 1 year: South Dakota Codified Laws 43-45-5;
Farm equipment and machinery (up to $1,250 total): South Dakota Codified Laws 43-45-5;
Horses, mules, or oxen: South Dakota Codified Laws 43-45-5;
Library and tools of a professional (up to $300): South Dakota Codified Laws 43-45-5;
Tools of a trade (up to $200): South Dakota Codified Laws 43-45-5;
Non-head of household exemption: Any personal property (up to $2,000): South Dakota Codified Laws 43-45-4.

Real Estate: Real property, including mobile home (unlimited value; up to 1 acre in town or up to 160 acres elsewhere); limited proceeds from sale are exempt for 1 year (up to $30,000; unlimited if over 70, or unmarried widow or widower: South Dakota Codified Laws 43-31-1; 43-31-2; 43-31-3; 43-31-4.

Wages: Wages earned up to 60 days prior to filing for bankruptcy (amount needed for support): South Dakota Codified Laws 15-20-12;
Wages of prisoners (unlimited amount): South Dakota Codified Laws 24-8-10.

TENNESSEE

Tennessee residents may **not** use the Federal Bankruptcy Exemptions, but may use the Federal Non-Bankruptcy exemptions listed on p. 238 and the following state exemptions.

Benefits: Aid to aged, blind, disabled, and families with dependent children (unlimited amount): Tennessee Code Annotated 71-2-216, 71-3-121, 71-4-117, 71-4-1112;
Crime victims compensation (up to $7,500 and up to $15,000 total of all personal injury, wrongful death, and crime victims compensation): Tennessee Code Annotated 26-2-111(2)(A), 29-13-111, 26-2-111(2)(C);
Local public assistance (unlimited amount): Tennessee Code Annotated 26-2-111(1)(A);
Social security (unlimited amount): Tennessee Code Annotated 26-2-111(1)(A);
Unemployment compensation (unlimited amount): Tennessee Code Annotated 26-2-111(1)(A);
Veterans benefits (unlimited amount): Tennessee Code Annotated 26-2-111(1)(B);
Workers compensation (unlimited amount): Tennessee Code Annotated 50-6-223.

Insurance: Accident, health or disability benefits (unlimited amount): Tennessee Code Annotated 26-2-110;
Annuity contract proceeds if payable to dependent: Tennessee Code Annotated 56-7-203;
Disability or illness benefits (unlimited amount): Tennessee Code Annotated 26-2-111(1)(C);
Fraternal society benefits (unlimited amount): Tennessee Code Annotated 56-25-1403;
Homeowners insurance proceeds (up to $5,000): Tennessee Code Annotated 26-2-304.

Miscellaneous: Alimony (up to $5,000 if owed for 30 days before filing for bankruptcy): Tennessee Code Annotated 26-2-111(1)(E);
Property of a business partnership (unlimited amount): Tennessee Code Annotated 61-1-124.

Pensions: Public employees (unlimited amount): Tennessee Code Annotated 8-36-111;
Retirement benefits (unlimited amount): Tennessee Code Annotated 26-2-111(1)(D);
State and local government employees (unlimited amount): Tennessee Code Annotated 26-2-104;
Teachers (unlimited amount): Tennessee Code Annotated 49-5-909.

Personal Property: Any personal property (up to $4,000): Tennessee Code Annotated 26-2-102;
Bible, clothing, pictures, portraits, schoolbooks, and storage containers (unlimited amount): Tennessee Code Annotated 26-2-103;
Burial plot (unlimited value, up to 1 acre): Tennessee Code Annotated 26-2-305, 46-2-102;
Health aids (unlimited amount): Tennessee Code Annotated 26-2-111(5);
Implements, books, and tools of a trade (up to $750): Tennessee Code Annotated 26-2-111(4);
Lost earnings payments: Tennessee Code Annotated 26-2-111(3);
Personal injury recoveries except for pain and suffering (up to $10,000 and up to $15,000 total of all personal injury, wrongful death, and crime victims compensation): Tennessee Code Annotated 26-2 111(2)(B), 26-2-111(2)(C);
Wrongful death recoveries (up to $10,000 and up to $15,000 total of all personal injury, wrongful death, and crime victims compensation): Tennessee Code Annotated 26-2 111(2)(B), (C).

Real Estate: Real property used as a residence (up to $5,000 and $7,500 for joint owners): Tennessee Code Annotated 26-2-301;
Real estate life estate (unlimited amount): Tennessee Code Annotated 26-2-302;
2-15 year lease (unlimited amount): Tennessee Code Annotated 26-2-303.

Wages: 75% of earned but unpaid wages, plus $2.50 per week per child (judge may allow more for low-income debtors): Tennessee Code Annotated 26-2-106, 26-2-107.

TEXAS

Texas residents **may use either** the Federal Bankruptcy Exemptions on p. 237 or the state exemptions listed below. If state exemptions are used, then the Federal Non-Bankruptcy exemptions on p. 238 may also be used.

Benefits: Aid to families with dependent children (unlimited amount): Texas Revised Civil Statutes Annotated, Human Resources 31.040;

Medical assistance (unlimited amount): Texas Revised Civil Statutes Annotated, Human Resources 32.036;

Unemployment compensation (unlimited amount): Texas Revised Civil Statutes Annotated 522lb-13;

Workers compensation (unlimited amount): Texas Revised Civil Statutes Annotated 8308-4.07.

Insurance: Fraternal society benefits (unlimited amount): Texas Revised Civil Statutes Annotated, Insurance 10.28;

Life, health, accident or annuity benefits, cash value, or proceeds (see limits under Personal Property): Texas Revised Civil Statutes Annotated, Insurance 21.22;

Life insurance if beneficiary is debtor or debtor's dependent (unlimited amount): Texas Revised Civil Statutes Annotated 42.002(a)(12);

Retired public school employees group insurance (unlimited amount): Texas Revised Civil Statutes Annotated, Insurance 3.50-4(11)(a);

Texas employee uniform group insurance (unlimited amount): Texas Revised Civil Statutes Annotated, Insurance 3.50-2(10)(a);

Texas state college or university employee benefits (unlimited amount): Texas Revised Civil Statutes Annotated, Insurance 3.50-3(9)(a).

Miscellaneous: Property of a business partnership (unlimited): Texas Revised Civil Statutes Annotated 6132b-25.

Pensions: County and district employees (unlimited): Texas Revised Civil Statutes Annotated, Government 811.005;

Firefighters: Texas Revised Civil Statutes Annotated 6243e(5), 6243e.1(12), 6243e.2(12);

Judges (unlimited amount): Texas Revised Civil Statutes Annotated, Government 811.005;

Municipal employees (unlimited amount): Texas Revised Civil Statutes Annotated 6243g and Government 811.005;

Police officers (unlimited amount): Texas Revised Civil Statutes Annotated 6243d-1(17), 6243j(20), 6243g-1(23B);

Retirement benefits (unlimited amount if tax-deferred): Texas Revised Civil Statutes Annotated, Property 42.0021;

State employees (unlimited amount): Texas Revised Civil Statutes Annotated, Government 811.005;

Teachers (unlimited amount): Texas Revised Civil Statutes Annotated, Government 811.005.

Personal Property: Athletic and sporting equipment, bicycles, boat, books, cattle (12), clothing, equipment, farming or ranching equipment, firearms (2), food, heirlooms, home furnishings, horses or donkeys (2 and saddle, blanket and bridle for both), jewelry (up to 25% of total exemption), livestock (60), motor vehicle, pets, and poultry (170), tools; (total of all personal property, life insurance cash value, and unpaid commissions up to $30,000 or up to $60,000 for head of family): Texas Revised Civil Statutes Annotated, Property 42.001, 42.002, 42.002(a)(4);

Burial plots (unlimited amount): Texas Revised Civil Statutes Annotated, Property 41.001;

Health aids (unlimited amount): Texas Revised Civil Statutes Annotated, Property 42.001 (b) (2).

Real Estate: Real property (unlimited value; up to 1 acre in town, village, city and 200 acres elsewhere; 100 acres limit if single); must file exemption with county; proceeds of sale are exempt for 6 months: Texas Revised Civil Statutes Annotated, Property 41.001, 41.002, 41.003.

Wages: Earned but unpaid wages (unlimited amount): Texas Revised Civil Statutes Annotated, Property 42.001(b)(1);

Unpaid commissions (up to 75%) (see limits under Personal Property): Texas Revised Civil Statutes Annotated Property 42.001(d).

UTAH

Utah residents may **not** use the Federal Bankruptcy Exemptions, but may use the Federal Non-Bankruptcy exemptions listed on p. 238 and the following state exemptions.

Benefits: Crime victims compensation (unlimited amount): Utah Code 63-63-21;
General assistance (unlimited amount): Utah Code 55-15-32;
Occupational disease disability benefits (unlimited amount): Utah Code 35-2-35;
Unemployment compensation (unlimited amount): Utah Code 35-4-18;
Veterans benefits (unlimited amount): Utah Code 78-23-5(1)(e);
Workers compensation (unlimited amount): Utah Code 35-1-80.

Insurance: Disability, illness, medical, or hospital benefits (unlimited amount): Utah Code 78-23-5(1)(c), (d);
Fraternal society benefits (unlimited amount): Utah Code 31A-9-603;
Life insurance policy (cash surrender value up to $1,500) (unlimited amount): Utah Code 78-23-7;
Life insurance proceeds if beneficiary is insured's spouse or dependent (amount needed for support): Utah Code 78-73-6(2).

Miscellaneous: Alimony or child support (amount needed for support): Utah Code 78-23-5(1)(f), (k); 78-23-6(1);
Property of a business partnership (unlimited amount): Utah Code 48-1-22.

Pensions: Any pension (amount needed for support): Utah Code 78-23-6(3);
Public employees (unlimited amount): Utah Code 49-1-609;
Retirement benefits (unlimited amount): Utah Code 78-23-5(1)(j).

Personal Property: Animals, books, and musical instruments (up to $500 total): Utah Code 78-23-8(1)(b);
Appliances and household furnishings (up to $500 total): Utah Code 78-23-8(1)(a);
Artwork depicting, or done by, family member (unlimited amount): Utah Code 78-23-5(1)(h);
Bed, bedding, carpets, washer and dryer (unlimited amount): Utah Code 78-23-5(1)(g);
Burial plot (unlimited amount): Utah Code 78-23-5(1)(a);
Clothing (unlimited amount, but not furs or jewelry): Utah Code 78-23-5(1)(g);
Equipment required for military use (unlimited amount): Utah Code 39-1-47;
Food and fuel (amount to last 3 months): Utah Code 78-23-5(1)(g);
Health aids (amount needed): Utah Code 78-23-5(1)(b);
Heirlooms or sentimental item (up to $500): Utah Code 78-23-8(1)(c);
Implements, books, and tools of a trade (up to $1,500 total): Utah Code 78-23-8(2);
Motor vehicle (up to $1,500): Utah Code 78-23-78(2);
Personal injury recoveries (unlimited amount): Utah Code 78-23-5(1)(i);
Proceeds for damaged exempt property (up to exemption amount): Utah Code 78-23-9;
Refrigerator, freezer, sewing machine, and stove (unlimited amount): Utah Code 78-23-5(1)(g);
Wrongful death recoveries (unlimited amount): Utah Code 78-23-5(1)(i).

Real Estate: Real property or mobile home used as a residence, or water rights (up to $8,000; plus additional $2,000 for spouse and $500 for each dependent); must file exemption with county: Utah Code 78-23-3.

Wages: 75% of earned but unpaid wages (judge may allow more for low-income debtors): Utah Code 7OC-7-103.

VERMONT

Vermont residents **may use either** the Federal Bankruptcy Exemptions on p. 237 or the state exemptions listed below. If state exemptions are used, then the Federal Non-Bankruptcy exemptions on p. 238 may also be used.

Benefits: Aid to aged, blind, disabled, and families with dependent children, general assistance (unlimited amount): Vermont Statutes Annotated 33-124;
Crime victims compensation (amount needed for support): Vermont Statutes Annotated 12-2740(19)(E);
Social security (amount needed for support): Vermont Statutes Annotated 12-2740(19)(A);
Unemployment compensation (unlimited amount): Vermont Statutes Annotated 21-1367;
Veterans benefits (amount needed for support): Vermont Statutes Annotated 12-2740(19)(B);
Workers compensation (unlimited amount): Vermont Statutes Annotated 21-681.

Insurance: Annuity contract benefits (up to $350 per month): Vermont Statutes Annotated 8-3709;
Disability or illness benefits (amount needed for support): Vermont Statutes Annotated 12-2740(19)(C);
Fraternal society benefits (unlimited amount): Vermont Statutes Annotated 8-4478;
Group life or health benefits (unlimited amount): Vermont Statutes Annotated 8-3708;
Health benefits (up to $200 per month): Vermont Statutes Annotated 8-4086;
Life insurance proceeds if beneficiary not the insured (unlimited amount): Vermont Statutes Annotated 8-3706;
Life insurance proceeds (unlimited amount): Vermont Statutes Annotated 12-2740(19)(H);
Life insurance proceeds if policy prohibits proceeds from being used to pay creditors (unlimited amount): Vermont Statutes Annotated 8-3705;
Supplemental disability benefits (unlimited amount): Vermont Statutes Annotated 8-3707;
Unmatured life insurance contract (unlimited amount): Vermont Statutes Annotated 12-2740(18).

Miscellaneous: Alimony or child support (amount needed for support): Vermont Statutes Annotated 12-2740(19)(D);
Any property (up to $400): Vermont Statutes Annotated 12-2740(7);
Property of a business partnership (unlimited amount): Vermont Statutes Annotated 11-1282.

Pensions: Any pensions (unlimited amount): Vermont Statutes Annotated 12-2740(19)(j);
Municipal employees (unlimited amount): Vermont Statutes Annotated 24-5066;
IRAs and Keoghs (up to $10,000): Vermont Statutes Annotated 12-2740(16);
State employees (unlimited amount): Vermont Statutes Annotated 3-476;
Teachers (unlimited amount): Vermont Statutes Annotated 16-1946.

Personal Property: Animals, appliances, books, clothing, crops, furnishings, goods, and musical instruments (up to $2,500 total): Vermont Statutes Annotated 12-2740(5);
Bank deposits (up to $700): Vermont Statutes Annotated 12-2740(i)(15);
Books and tools of a trade (up to $5,000 total): Vermont Statutes Annotated 12-2740(2);
Firewood (10 cords), or coal (5 tons), or heating oil (500 gallons), or bottled gas (500 gallons): Vermont Statutes Annotated 12-2740(9)-(10);
Farm crops and animals: bees (3 swarms), crops (up to $5,000), chickens (10), cow, goats (2), horses (2), sheep (10), yoke of oxen or steers, feed (amount to last through winter): Vermont Statutes Annotated 12-2740(6), (11)-(13);
Farm equipment: chains (2), halters (2), harnesses, plow and yoke: Vermont Statutes Annotated 12-2740(6), (14);
Freezer, heating unit, refrigerator, sewing machines, stove, and water heater (unlimited amount): Vermont Statutes Annotated 12-2740(8);
Jewelry (up to $500; unlimited amount for wedding ring): Vermont Statutes Annotated 12-2740(3), (4);
Health aids (unlimited amount): Vermont Statutes Annotated 12-2740(17);
Lost future earnings (unlimited amount): Vermont Statutes Annotated 12-2740(19)(i);
Motor vehicles (up to $2,500): Vermont Statutes Annotated 12-2740(1);
Personal injury recoveries (unlimited amount): Vermont Statutes Annotated 12-2740(19)(F);
Wrongful death recoveries (unlimited amount): Vermont Statutes Annotated 12-2740(19)(G).

Real Estate: Real property or mobile home (up to $30,000): Vermont Statutes Annotated 27-101.

Wages: 75% of earned but unpaid wages (judge may allow more for low-income debtors; unlimited amount if debtor received welfare within 2 months of filing for bankruptcy): Vermont Statutes Annotated 12-3170.

VIRGINIA

Virginia residents may **not** use the Federal Bankruptcy Exemptions, but may use the Federal Non-Bankruptcy exemptions listed on p. 238 and the following state exemptions.

Benefits: Aid to aged, blind, disabled, families with dependent child and general relief (unlimited amount): Code of Virginia 63.1-88;

Crime victims compensation (unlimited amount except not for debt for treatment of injury incurred during crime): Code of Virginia 19.2-368.12;

Unemployment compensation (unlimited amount): Code of Virginia 60.2-600;

Workers compensation (unlimited amount): Code of Virginia 65.2-531.

Insurance: Accident or sickness benefits (unlimited amount): Code of Virginia 38.2-3549;

Burial benefits (unlimited amount): Code of Virginia 38.2-4021;

Cooperative life insurance benefits (unlimited amount): Code of Virginia 38.2-3811;

Fraternal society benefits (unlimited amount): Code of Virginia 38.2-4118;

Government group life or accident insurance (unlimited amount): Code of Virginia 51.1-510;

Group life insurance policy or proceeds (unlimited amount): Code of Virginia 38.2-3339;

Sickness benefits (unlimited amount): Code of Virginia 38.2-3549.

Miscellaneous: Any property for disabled veterans homeowner (up to $2,000): Code of Virginia 34-4.1;

Property of a business partnership (unlimited amount): Code of Virginia 50-25.

Pensions: 75% of earned but unpaid pension payments (judge may allow more for low-income debtors): Code of Virginia 34-29;

City, town, and county employees (unlimited amount): Code of Virginia 51.1-802;

Retirement benefits (up to $17,500 per year): Code of Virginia 34-34;

Personal Property: *Note:* Debtor must be a householder to claim any personal property exemption in Virginia.

Any personal property (up to amount of unused real estate exemption): Code of Virginia 34-20;

Bible (unlimited amount): Code of Virginia 34-26(1);

Burial plot (unlimited amount): Code of Virginia 34-26(3);

Clothing (up to $1,000): Code of Virginia 34-26(4);

Crops (unlimited amount): Code of Virginia 8.01-489;

Family portraits and heirlooms (up to $5,000 total): Code of Virginia 34-26(2);

Health aids (unlimited amount): Code of Virginia 34-26(6);

Farm equipment: fertilizer (up to $1,000, horses, mules (2) with gear, pitchfork, plows (2), rake, tractor (up to $3,000), and wagon: Code of Virginia 34-27;

Household furnishings (up to $5,000): Code of Virginia 34-26(4)(a);

Motor vehicle (up to $2,000): Code of Virginia 34-26(8);

Personal injury recoveries or causes of action (unlimited amount): Code of Virginia 34-28.1;

Pets (unlimited amount): Code of Virginia 34-26(5);

Tools, books, and instruments of trade, including motor vehicles (up to $10,000): Code of Virginia 34-26;

Uniforms, arms, equipment required for military use: Code of Virginia 44-96;

Wedding and engagement rings (unlimited amount): Code of Virginia 34-26(1)(a).

Real Estate: Real property (up to $5,000 plus $500 per dependent); proceeds from the sale of exempt real estate are also exempt; must file homestead declaration before filing for bankruptcy: Code of Virginia 34-4, 34-6.

Wages: 75% of earned but unpaid wages (judge may allow more for low-income debtors): Code of Virginia 34-29.

WASHINGTON

Washington residents **may use either** the Federal Bankruptcy Exemptions on p. 237 or the state exemptions listed below. If state exemptions are used, then the Federal Non-Bankruptcy exemptions on p. 238 may also be used.

Benefits: Aid to aged, and families with dependent children (unlimited amount): Revised Code of Washington Annotated 74.08.210, 74.13.070;
    Crime victims compensation (unlimited amount): Revised Code of Washington Annotated 7.68.070, 51.32.040;
    General assistance (unlimited amount): Revised Code of Washington Annotated 74.04.280;
    Unemployment compensation (unlimited amount): Revised Code of Washington Annotated 50.40.020;
    Workers compensation (unlimited amount): Revised Code of Washington Annotated 51.32.040.

Insurance: Annuity contract proceeds (up to $250 per month): Revised Code of Washington Annotated 48.18.430;
    Disability proceeds or benefits (unlimited amount): Revised Code of Washington Annotated 48.18.400;
    Fraternal society benefits (unlimited amount): Revised Code of Washington Annotated 48.36A.180;
    Group life insurance policy or proceeds (unlimited amount): Revised Code of Washington Annotated 48.18.420;
    Insurance proceeds for destroyed exempt property (up to exemption amount): Revised Code of Washington Annotated 6.15.030;
    Life insurance proceeds if beneficiary is not the insured (unlimited amount): Revised Code of Washington Annotated 48.18.410.

Miscellaneous: Property of a business partnership: Revised Code of Washington Annotated 25.04.250.

Pensions: City employees (unlimited amount): Revised Code of Washington Annotated 41.28.200;
    IRAs (unlimited amount): Revised Code of Washington Annotated 6.15.020
    Public employees (unlimited amount): Revised Code of Washington Annotated 41.40.052;
    Retirement benefits (unlimited amount): Revised Code of Washington Annotated 6.15.020
    State patrol officers (unlimited amount): Revised Code of Washington Annotated 43.43.310;
    Volunteer firefighters (unlimited amount): Revised Code of Washington Annotated 41.24.240.

Personal Property: Any personal property (up to $1,000; only $100 may be cash, bank deposits, bonds, stocks or securities): Revised Code of Washington Annotated 6.15.010(3)(b);
    Appliances, furniture, home and yard equipment, and household goods (up to $2,700 total): Revised Code of Washington Annotated 6.15.010(3)(a); [Note: This exemption is for an unlimited value if for property located in Washington and if debtor is seeking to discharge debt for a state income tax assessed on retirement benefits received while a resident of Washington];
    Books (up to $1,500): Revised Code of Washington Annotated 6.15.010(2);
    Burial plots in non-profit cemetery association (unlimited amount): Revised Code of Washington Annotated 68.20.120;
    Clothing (unlimited amount, but only up to $1,000 of furs or jewelry): Revised Code of Washington Annotated 6.15.010(1);
    Farm equipment: equipment, seed, stock, tools, and vehicles (up to $5,000 total): Revised Code of Washington Annotated 6.15.010(4)(a);
    Food and fuel (amount needed): Revised Code of Washington Annotated 6.15.010(3)(a);
    Keepsakes and pictures (unlimited amount): Revised Code of Washington Annotated 6.15.010(2);
    Library, office equipment, office furniture, and supplies of attorney, clergy, physician, surgeon, or other professional (up to $5,000 total): Revised Code of Washington Annotated 6.15.010(4)(b);
    Motor vehicles (up to 2 and up to $2,500 total): Revised Code of Washington Annotated 6.15.010(3)(c);
    Tools of a trade (up to $5,000): Revised Code of Washington Annotated 6.15.010(4)(c).

Real Estate: Real property or mobile home (up to $30,000); must file exemption with county: Revised Code of Washington Annotated 6.13.010, 6.13.030; [Note: This exemption is for an unlimited value if for property located in Washington and if debtor is seeking to discharge debt for a state income tax assessed on retirement benefits received while a resident of Washington].

Wages: 75% of earned but unpaid wages (judge may allow more for low-income debtors): Revised Code of Washington Annotated 6.27.150.

WEST VIRGINIA

West Virginia residents may **not** use the Federal Bankruptcy Exemptions, but may use the Federal Non-Bankruptcy exemptions listed on p. 238 and the following state exemptions.

Benefits: Aid to aged, blind, disabled, families with dependent children, and general assistance (unlimited amount): West Virginia Code 9-5-1;
Crime victims compensation (unlimited amount): West Virginia Code 14-2A-24, 38-10-4(k)(1);
Social security (unlimited amount): West Virginia Code 38-10-4(j)(1);
Unemployment compensation (unlimited amount): West Virginia Code 38-10-4(j)(1);
Veterans benefits (unlimited amount): West Virginia Code 38-10-4(j)(2);
Workers compensation (unlimited amount): West Virginia Code 23-4-18.

Insurance: Fraternal society benefits (unlimited amount): West Virginia Code 33-23-21;
Group life insurance policy or proceeds (unlimited amount): West Virginia Code 33-6-28;
Health or disability benefits (unlimited amount): West Virginia Code 38-10-4(j)(3);
Life insurance proceeds (unlimited amount): West Virginia Code 38-10-4(k)(3);
Unmatured life insurance contract (unlimited amount; accrued dividend, interest or loan value up to $4000, if debtor is the insured or one debtor is dependent upon): West Virginia Code 38-10-4(g),(h).

Miscellaneous: Alimony and child support (amount needed for support): West Virginia Code 38-10-4(j)(4);
Any property (up to $400 plus any unused amount of real estate or burial exemption): West Virginia Code 38-10-4(e);
Property of a business partnership (unlimited amount): West Virginia Code 47-8A-25.

Pensions: Public employees (unlimited amount): West Virginia Code 5-10-46;
Retirement benefits (amount needed for support): West Virginia Code 38-10-4(j)(5);
Teachers (unlimited amount): West Virginia Code 18-7A-30.

Personal Property: Animals, appliances, books, clothing, crops, furnishings, household goods, and musical instruments (up to $200 per item and $1,000 total): West Virginia Code 38-10-4(c);
Burial plot (up to $7,500; if taken instead of real estate exemption): West Virginia Code 38-10-4(a);
Health aids (unlimited amount): West Virginia Code 38-10-4(i);
Implements, books, and tools of a trade (up to $750): West Virginia Code 38-10-4(f);
Jewelry (up to $500): West Virginia Code 38-10-4(d);
Lost future earnings payments (amount needed for support): West Virginia Code 38-10-4(k)(5);
Motor vehicle (up to $1,200): West Virginia Code 38-10-4(b);
Personal injury recoveries (up to $7,500, but not for pain and suffering): West Virginia Code 38-10-4(k)(4);
Wrongful death recoveries (amount needed for support): West Virginia Code 38-10-4(k)(2).

Real Estate: Real or personal property used as residence (up to $7,500): West Virginia Code 38-10-4(a).

Wages: 75% of earned but unpaid wages (judge may allow more for low-income debtor): West Virginia Code 38-5A-3.

WISCONSIN

Wisconsin residents **may use either** the Federal Bankruptcy Exemptions on p. 237 or the state exemptions listed below. If state exemptions are used, then the Federal Non-Bankruptcy exemptions on p. 238 may also be used.

Benefits: Aid to families with dependent children and any other social services payments (unlimited amount): Wisconsin Statutes Annotated 49.41;
Crime victims compensation (unlimited amount): Wisconsin Statutes Annotated 949.07;
Unemployment compensation (unlimited amount): Wisconsin Statutes Annotated 108.13;
Veterans benefits (unlimited amount): Wisconsin Statutes Annotated 45.35(8)(b);
Workers compensation (unlimited amount): Wisconsin Statutes Annotated 102.27.

Insurance: Federal disability insurance (unlimited amount): Wisconsin Statutes Annotated 815.18(3)(d);
Fraternal society benefits (unlimited amount): Wisconsin Statutes Annotated 614.96;
Insurance proceeds for exempt property destroyed within 2 years of filing for bankruptcy (up to amount of exemption): Wisconsin Statutes Annotated 18(3)(e);
Life insurance policy or proceeds if beneficiary is a married woman (up to $5,000): Wisconsin Statutes Annotated 766.09;
Life insurance proceeds if beneficiary was a dependent of the insured (amount needed for support): Wisconsin Statutes Annotated 815.18(3)(1)(a);
Life insurance proceeds if held in trust by insurer and if policy prohibits proceeds from being used to pay creditors): Wisconsin Statutes Annotated 632.42;
Unmatured life insurance contract (unlimited amount; accrued dividend, interest or loan value up to $4000, if debtor is the insured or one debtor is dependent upon)): Wisconsin Statutes Annotated 815.18(3)(f).

Miscellaneous: Alimony and child support (amount needed for support): Wisconsin Statutes Annotated 815.18(3)(c);
Property of a business partnership (unlimited amount): Wisconsin Statutes Annotated 178.21.

Pensions: Certain municipal employees (unlimited amount): Wisconsin Statutes Annotated 66.81;
Firefighters and police officers who worked in city with population over 100,000 (unlimited amount): Wisconsin Statutes Annotated 815.18(3)(e), (f);
Military pensions (unlimited amount): Wisconsin Statutes Annotated 815.18(3)(n);
Private or public retirement benefits (amount needed for support): Wisconsin Statutes Annotated 815.18(3)(j);
Public employees (unlimited amount): Wisconsin Statutes Annotated 40.08(1).

Personal Property: Animals, appliances, books, clothing, firearms, furnishings, household goods, jewelry, keepsakes, musical instruments, sporting goods, or any other personal property held for personal use (up to $5,000 total): Wisconsin Statutes Annotated 815.18(3)(d);
Bank accounts (up to $1,000): Wisconsin Statutes Annotated 815.18(3)(k);
Burial plot (unlimited amount): Wisconsin Statutes Annotated 815.18(3)(a);
Equipment, inventory, farm products, books and tools of a trade (up to $7,500 total): Wisconsin Statutes Annotated 815.18(3)(b);
Lease or interest in housing co-op (up to real estate exemption amount): Wisconsin Statutes Annotated 182.004(6);
Lost future earnings recoveries (amount needed for support): Wisconsin Statutes Annotated 815.18(3)(i)(d);
Motor vehicles (up to $1,200): Wisconsin Statutes Annotated 815.18(3)(g);
Personal injury recoveries (up to $25,000): Wisconsin Statutes Annotated 815.18(3)(i)(c);
Wrongful death recoveries (amount needed for support): Wisconsin Statutes Annotated 815.18(3)(i)(b).

Real Estate: Real property used, or intended to be used, as a residence (up to $40,000); proceeds from sale of exempt real estate is exempt for 2 years): Wisconsin Statutes Annotated 815.20.

Wages: 75% of earned but unpaid wages (judge may allow more for low-income debtors): Wisconsin Statutes Annotated 815.18(3)(h);
Wages used for the purchase of savings bonds (unlimited amount): Wisconsin Statutes Annotated 20.921(1)(e).

WYOMING

Wyoming residents may **not** use the Federal Bankruptcy Exemptions, but may use the Federal Non-Bankruptcy exemptions listed on p. 238 and the following state exemptions.

Benefits: Aid to families with dependent children and general assistance (unlimited amount): Wyoming Statutes Annotated 42-2-113;
    Crime victims compensation (unlimited amount): Wyoming Statutes Annotated 1-40-113;
    Unemployment compensation (unlimited amount): Wyoming Statutes Annotated 27-3-319;
    Workers compensation (unlimited amount): Wyoming Statutes Annotated 27-14-702.

Insurance: Annuity contract proceeds (up to $350 per month): Wyoming Statutes Annotated 26-15-132;
    Disability benefits if policy prohibits proceeds from being used to pay creditors (unlimited amount): Wyoming Statutes Annotated 26-15-130;
    Fraternal society benefits (unlimited amount): Wyoming Statutes Annotated 26-29-218;
    Group life or disability policy or proceeds (unlimited amount): Wyoming Statutes Annotated 26-15-131;
    Life insurance proceeds if held in trust by insurer and if policy prohibits proceeds from being used to pay creditors (unlimited amount): Wyoming Statutes Annotated 26-15-133.

Miscellaneous: Liquor and beer licenses (unlimited amount): Wyoming Statutes Annotated 12-4-604;
    Property of a business partnership (unlimited amount): Wyoming Statutes Annotated 17-13-502.

Pensions: Criminal investigators and highway patrol (unlimited amount): Wyoming Statutes Annotated 9-3-620;
    Firefighters, police officers (only payments being received): Wyoming Statutes Annotated 15-5-209;
    Game and fish wardens (unlimited amount): Wyoming Statutes Annotated 9-3-620;
    Private or public retirement accounts (unlimited amount): Wyoming Statutes Annotated 1-20-110;
    Public employees (unlimited amount): Wyoming Statutes Annotated 9-3-426.

Personal Property: Bedding, food, furniture, and household articles (up to $2000 per person in household): Wyoming Statutes Annotated 1-20-106(a)(iii);
    Bible, schoolbooks, and pictures (unlimited amount): Wyoming Statutes Annotated 1-20-106(a)(i);
    Burial plot (unlimited amount): Wyoming Statutes Annotated 1-20-106(a)(ii), 35-8-104;
    Clothing and wedding rings (up to $1,000): Wyoming Statutes Annotated 1-20-105;
    Library and equipment of a professional (up to $2000): Wyoming Statutes Annotated 1-20-106(b);
    Motor vehicle (up to $2,000): Wyoming Statutes Annotated 1-20-106(a)(iv);
    Pre-paid funeral contracts (unlimited amount): Wyoming Statutes Annotated 26-32-102;
    Tools, motor vehicle, implements, team, and stock-in-trade used in trade or business (up to $2,000): Wyoming Statutes Annotated 1-20-106(b).

Real Estate: Real property or house trailer used as a residence (up to $10,000; $20,000 for joint owners; only up to $6,000 for house trailer; up to $12,000 for joint owners of house trailer): Wyoming Statutes Annotated 1-20-101, 1-20-102, 1-20-104.

Wages: 75% of earned but unpaid wages (judge may allow more for low-income debtors): Wyoming Statutes Annotated 1-15-511;
    Wages of National Guard members (unlimited amount): Wyoming Statutes Annotated 19-2-501;
    Wages of inmates on work release (unlimited amount): Wyoming Statutes Annotated 7-16-308.

FEDERAL BANKRUPTCY EXEMPTIONS

Federal Bankruptcy Exemptions are only available to residents of the following states: Arkansas, Connecticut, District of Columbia, Hawaii, Massachusetts, Michigan, Minnesota, New Jersey, Mew Mexico, Pennsylvania, Rhode Island, South Carolina, Texas, Vermont, Washington, and Wisconsin. If the debtor elects to use the Federal Bankruptcy Exemptions listed here, they may not use either their own state exemptions or the Federal Non-Bankruptcy Exemptions listed on p. 238. The Federal Exemption amounts will be adjusted for inflation on April 1, 1998. Married couples filing jointly may double the exemption amounts listed.

Benefits: Crime victims compensation (unlimited amount): 11 United States Code § 522(d)(11)(A); Public assistance (unlimited amount): 11 United States Code § 522(d)(10)(A); Social security (unlimited amount): 11 United States Code § 522(d)(10)(A); Unemployment compensation (unlimited amount): 11 United States Code § 522(d)(10)(A); Veterans benefits (unlimited amount): 11 United States Code § 522(d)(10)(A).
Insurance: Disability or illness benefits (unlimited amount): 11 United States Code § 522(d)(10)(C); Life insurance proceeds (amount needed for support): 11 United States Code § 522(d)(11)(C); Life insurance policy loan value, dividends, or interest (up to $8,000): 11 United States Code § 522 (d)(8); Unmatured life insurance contract (unlimited amount, but not credit insurance policy): 11 United States Code § 522(d)(7).
Miscellaneous: Alimony and child support (amount needed for support): 11 United States Code § 522(10)(D); Any property (up to $7,500 of unused portion of real estate exemption): 11 United States Code § 522(d)(1), (5); Any property (up to $800): 11 United States Code § 522(d)(5).
Pensions: Retirement benefits (amount needed for support): 11 United States Code § 522(d)(10)(E).
Personal Property: Animals, appliances, books, clothing, crops, furnishings, household goods, and musical instruments (up to $400 per item and up to $8,000 total): 11 United States Code § 522(d)(3); Health aids (unlimited amount): 11 United States Code § 522(d)(9); Implements, books, and tools of a trade (up to $1,500): 11 United States Code § 522(d)(6); Jewelry (up to $1,000): 11 United States Code § 522(d)(4); Lost earnings payments (unlimited amount): 11 United States Code § 522(d)(11)(E); Motor vehicle (up to $2,400): 11 United States Code § 522(d)(2); Personal injury recoveries (up to $15,000, but not for pain and suffering or pecuniary loss): 11 United States Code § 522(d)(11)(D); Wrongful death recoveries (unlimited amount): 11 United States Code § 522(d)(11)(B).
Real Estate: Real property, co-op, or mobile home (up to $15,000): 11 United States Code § 522(d)(1).
Wages: None.

FEDERAL NON-BANKRUPTCY EXEMPTIONS

The following Federal Non-Bankruptcy Exemptions may only be used if the debtor elects to use their specific state exemptions. If the debtor elects to use the Federal Bankruptcy Exemptions on p. 237, they may not use the Federal Non-Bankruptcy Exemptions listed here.

Benefits: Government employee death and disability benefits (unlimited amount): 5 United States Code § 8130;
Harbor workers death and disability benefits (unlimited amount): 33 United States Code § 916;
Judges survivor benefits (unlimited amount): 28 United States Code § 376;
Judicial center directors survivor benefits (unlimited amount): 28 United States Code § 376;
Lighthouse workers survivor benefits (unlimited amount): 33 United States Code § 775;
Longshoremen death and disability benefits (unlimited amount): 33 United States Code § 916;
Military service survivor benefits (unlimited amount): 10 United States Code § 1450;
Supreme Court Chief Justice administrators survivor benefits (unlimited amount): 28 United States Code § 376;
U.S. court directors survivor benefits (unlimited amount): 28 United States Code § 376;
War hazard death or injury compensation (unlimited amount): 42 United States Code § 1717.

Insurance: Military group life insurance (unlimited amount):38 United States Code § 1977(g);
Railroad workers unemployment insurance (unlimited amount):45 United States Code § 352(e).

Miscellaneous: Klamath Indian tribe benefits (unlimited amount): 25 United States Code § 543, 545.

Pensions: CIA employees (unlimited amount): 50 United States Code § 403;
Civil service employees (unlimited amount): 5 United States Code § 8346;
Foreign service employees (unlimited amount): 22 United States Code § 4060;
Military honor roll pensions (unlimited amount): 38 United States Code § 562;
Military service employees (unlimited amount): 10 United States Code § 1440;
Railroad workers (unlimited amount): 45 United States Code § 231(m); 228(l);
Social security (unlimited amount): 42 United States Code § 407;
Veterans benefits (unlimited amount): 38 United States Code § 3101;
Veterans medal of honor benefits (unlimited amount): 38 United States Code § 1562.

Personal Property: Savings account deposits while on permanent military duty outside U.S. (unlimited amount): 10 United States Code § 1035;
Seamen's clothing (unlimited amount):46 United States Code § 11110.

Real Estate: None.

Wages: 75% of earned but unpaid wages (judge may allow more for low-income debtors)15 United States Code § 1673;
Wages of seamen while on a voyage (unlimited amount):46 United States Code § 11111.

Appendix C

Federal Bankruptcy Courts

Alabama

112th & Noble Streets
122 US Courthouse
Anniston AL 36201
Phone: 205-237-8397

1800 5th Avenue North
Room 120
Birmingham AL 35203
Phone: 205-731-1614

PO Box 1289
222 Federal Courthouse
Decatur AL 35602
Phone: 205-353-2817

201 Saint Louis Street
Mobile AL 36602
Phone: 205-441-5391

PO Box 1248
Suite 127
One Court Square
Montgomery AL 36102
Phone: 205-223-7348

1118 Greensboro Avenue
Tuscaloosa AL 35401
205-752-0426

Alaska

605 West 4th Avenue
Suite 138
Anchorage AK 99501
Phone: 907-271-2655

Arizona

US Courthouse
230 North First Avenue
Room 5000
Phoenix AZ 85025
Phone: 602-514-7321

110 South Church Avenue
Suite 8112
Tucson AZ 85701
Phone: 602-670-6304

325 West 19th Street
Yuma AZ 85364
Phone: 602-783-2288

Arkansas

PO Drawer 2381
600 West Capitol Avenue
Little Rock AR 72203
Phone: 501-324-6357

California

5301 US Courthouse
1130 O Street
Fresno CA 93721
Phone: 209-487-5217

255 East Temple
Los Angeles CA 90012
Phone: 213-894-3118

PO Box 5276
1130 12th Street
Modesto CA 95352
Phone: 209-521-5160

PO Box 2070
1300 Clay Street
Oakland CA 94604
Phone: 510-273-7212

8308 US Courthouse
650 Capitol Mall
Sacramento CA 95814
Phone: 916-498-5525

222 East Carrillo Street
Room 101
Santa Barbara CA 93101
Phone: 805-897-3879

699 North Arrowhead Avenue
Room 105
San Bernardino CA 92401
Phone: 909-383-5717

5-N-26 US Courthouse
940 Front Street
San Diego CA 92189
Phone: 619-557-5620

PO Box 7341
235 Pine Street
San Francisco CA 94120
Phone: 415-705-3200

280 South First Street
Room 3035
San Jose CA 95113
Phone: 408-291-7286

506 Federal Building
34 Civic Center Plaza
Santa Ana CA 92701
Phone: 714-836-2993

99 South East Street
Santa Rosa CA 95404
Phone: 707-525-8520

Colorado

US Customs House
721 19th Street
Denver CO 80202
Phone: 303-844-4045

Connecticut

US Courthouse
915 Lafayette Boulevard
Bridgeport CT 06604
Phone: 203-579-5808

712 US Courthouse
450 Main Street
Hartford CT 06103
Phone: 203-240-3675

Delaware

824 Market
Wilmington DE 19801
Phone: 302-573-6174

District of Columbia

US Courthouse
Room 4400
3rd & Constitution Avenues NW
Washington DC 20001
Phone: 202-273-0992

Florida

299 East Broward Boulevard
Room 206B
Ft Lauderdale FL 33301
305-356-7224

PO Box 559
311 West Monroe Street
US Post Office & Courthouse
Jacksonville FL 32201
Phone: 904-232-2827

51 SW First Avenue
Miami FL 33130
Phone: 305-536-5216

135 West Central Avenue
Room 950
Orlando FL 32801
Phone: 407-648-6364

220 West Garden Street
Room 700
Pensacola FL 32501
Phone: 904-435-8475

227 North Bronough Street
Room 3120
Tallahassee FL 32301
Phone: 904-942-8933

4921 Memorial Highway
Room 200
Tampa FL 33634
Phone: 813-225-7063

701 Clematis Street
Room 335
West Palm Beach FL 33401
Phone: 407-655-6774

Georgia

1340 R B Russell Building
75 Spring Street SW
Atlanta GA 30303
Phone: 404-331-6886

PO Box 2147
901 Front Avenue
One Arsenal Place
Room 310
Columbus GA 31902
Phone: 706-649-7837

Federal Building
126 Washington Street
Room 201 **Gainsville** GA 30501
Phone: 706-534-5954

PO Box 1957
Old Federal Building
Macon GA 31202
Phone: 912-752-3506

PO Box 939
Newnan GA 30264
Phone: 404-253-8847

PO Box 1186
Rome GA 30162
Phone: 706-291-5639

PO Box 8347
212 US Courthouse
Savannah GA 31412
Phone: 912-652-4100

Hawaii

Prince Kuhio Federal Building
Honolulu HI 96850
Phone: 808-541-1791

Idaho

550 West Fort Street
Box 042
Federal Building
Boise ID 83724
Phone: 208-334-1074

Illinois

US Courthouse
219 South Dearborn Street
Room 614
Chicago IL 60604
Phone: 312-435-5693

PO Box 657
301 Federal Building
Room 127
201 North Vermilion Street
Danville IL 61834
Phone: 217-431-4817

PO Box 309
750 Missouri Avenue
1st Floor
East Saint Louis IL 62202
Phone: 618-482-9365

156 Federal Building
100 NE Monroe Street
Peoria IL 61602
Phone: 309-671-7035

211 South Court Street
Rockford IL 61101
Phone: 815-987-4350

PO Box 2438
226 US Courthouse
600 East Monroe Street
Springfield IL 62705
Phone: 217-492-4551

Indiana

101 NW Martin Luther King Boulevard
Evansville IN 47708
Phone: 812-465-6440

1188 Federal Building
1300 South Harrison Street
Ft Wayne IN 46802
Phone: 219-420-5100

221 Federal Building
610 Connecticut Street
Gary IN 46402
Phone: 219-881-3335

123 US Courthouse
46 East Ohio Street
Indianapolis IN 46204
Phone: 317-226-6710

102 Federal Building
New Albany IN 47150
Phone: 812-465-6440

224 US Courthouse
204 South Main Street
South Bend IN 46601
Phone: 219-236-8247

203 Post Office Building
30 North 7th Street
Terre Haute IN 47808
Phone: 812-238-1550

Iowa

PO Box 74890
800 The Center
425 2nd Street SE
Cedar Rapids IA 52407
Phone: 319-362-9696

PO Box 9264
318 US Courthouse
Des Moines IA 50306
Phone: 515-284-6230

US Courthouse
320 6th Street
Sioux City IA 51101
Phone: 712-252-3757

Kansas

500 State Avenue
Kansas City KS 66101
Phone: 913-551-6732

240 US Courthouse
444 SE Quincy Street
Topeka KS 66683
Phone: 913-295-2750

167 US Courthouse
401 North Market Street
Wichita KS 67202
Phone: 316-269-6486

Kentucky

PO Box 1111
Merrill Lynch Plaza
Lexington KY 40588
Phone: 606-233-2608

551 G Snyder Courthouse and Customs House
601 West Broadway
Louisville KY 40202
Phone: 502-582-5140

Louisiana

PO Box 111
300 Jackson Street
Alexandria LA 71309
Phone: 318-473-7387

412 North 4th Street
Room 301
Baton Rouge LA 70802
Phone: 504-389-0211

Hale Boggs Federal Building
501 Magazine Street
Suite 701
New Orleans LA 70130
Phone: 504-589-6506

205 Federal Building
Corner of Union & Vine
Opelousas LA 70570
Phone: 318-942-2161

300 Fannin Street
Shreveport LA 71101
Phone: 318-676-4267

Maine

PO Box 1109
331 US Courthouse
202 Harlow Street
Bangor ME 04401
Phone: 207-945-0348

US Courthouse
537 Congress
Portland ME 04101
Phone: 207-780-3482

Maryland

US Courthouse
101 West Lombard Street
Room 919
Baltimore MD 21201
Phone: 410-962-2688

451 Hungerford Drive
Rockville MD 20850
Phone: 301-344-8018

Massachusetts

Tip O'Neill Federal Office Building
10 Causeway Street
Room 1101
Boston MA 02222
Phone: 617-565-6080

595 Main Street
Worcester MA 01601
Phone: 508-793-0518

Michigan

Federal Building
Bay City MI 48707
Phone: 517-892-1506

US Courthouse
231 West Lafayette
Room 1060
Detroit MI 48226
Phone: 313-226-7064

102A Federal Building
600 Church Street
Flint MI 48502
Phone: 313-766-5050

PO Box 3310
299 Federal Building
110 Michigan Street NW
Grand Rapids MI 49503
Phone: 616-456-2693

PO Box 909
314 Post Office Building
Marquette MI 49855
Phone: 906-226-2117

Minnesota

416 US Courthouse
515 West 1st Street
Duluth MN 55802
Phone: 218-727-6692

405 US Courthouse
118 South Mills Street
Fergus Falls MN 56537
Phone: 218-739-4671

600 Towle Building
330 Second Avenue South
Minneapolis MN 55401
Phone: 612-348-1855

200 US Courthouse
316 North Robert Street
Saint Paul MN 55101
Phone: 612-290-3184

Mississippi

PO Drawer 867
Arberdeen MS 39730
Phone: 601-369-2596

Biloxi Federal Building
725 Washington Loop
Room 117
Biloxi MS 39533
Phone: 601-432 5542

PO Drawer 2448
Jackson MS 39225
Phone: 601-965-5301

Missouri

US Courthouse
811 Grand Avenue
Room 913
Kansas City MO 64106
Phone: 816-426-3321

1 Metropolitan Square
211 North Broadway
7th Floor
Saint Louis MO 63102
Phone: 314-425-4222

Montana

PO Box 689
273 Federal Building
400 North Main Street
Butte MT 59701
Phone: 406-782-3354

Nebraska

PO Box 428
Downtown Station
215 North 17th Street
New Federal Building
Omaha NB 68101
Phone: 402-221-4687

460 Federal Building
100 Centennial Mall North
Lincoln NB 68508
Phone: 402-437-5100

Nevada

300 Las Vegas Boulevard South
Las Vegas NV 89101
Phone: 702-388-6257

4005 Federal Building & Courthouse
300 Booth Street
Reno NV 89509
Phone: 702-784-5559

New Hampshire

275 Chestnut Street
Room 404
Manchester NH 03101
Phone: 603-666-7532

New Jersey

15 North 7th Street
Camden NJ 08102
Phone: 609-757-5023

50 Walnut Street
Newark NJ 07102
Phone: 201-645-2630

US Post Office & Courthouse
402 East State Street
Trenton NJ 08608
Phone: 609-989-2198

New Mexico

421 Gold Avenue SW
3rd Floor
Albuquerque NM 87102
Phone: 505-766-2051

New York

PO Box 398
Courthouse
Albany NY 12201
Phone: 518-472-4226

75 Clinton Street
Brooklyn NY 11201
Phone: 718-330-2188

310 US Courthouse
68 Court Street
Buffalo NY 14202
Phone: 716-846-4130

601 Veterans Highway
Hauppauge NY 11788
Phone: 516-361-8601

1 Bowling Green
New York NY 10004
Phone: 212-668-2867

176 Church Street
Poughkeepsie NY 12601
Phone: 914-452-4200

100 State Street
Room 2120
Rochester NY 14614
Phone: 716-263-3148

Alexander Pirnie Federal Building
Room 230
Utica NY 13501
Phone: 315-793-8101

1635 Privado Road
Westbury NY 11590
Phone: 516-832-8801

101 East Post Road
White Plains NY 10601
Phone: 914-683-9591

North Carolina

401 West Trade Street
Charlotte NC 28202
Phone: 704-344-6103

PO Drawer 2807
1760 Parkwood Boulevard
Wilson NC 27894
Phone: 919-856-4752

PO Box 26100
202 South Elm Street
Greensboro NC 27420
Phone: 919-333-5647

North Dakota

PO Box 1110
655 1st Avenue
Fargo ND 58107
Phone: 701-239-5129

Ohio

455 Federal Building
2 South Main Street
Akron OH 44308
Phone: 216-375- 5840

124 US Courthouse
85 Marconi Boulevard
Columbus OH 43215
Phone: 614-469-6638

US Bankruptcy Court
121 Cleveland Avenue SW
Canton OH 44702
Phone: 216-455-2222

705 Federal Building
US Courthouse
200 West 2nd Street
Dayton OH 45402
Phone: 513-225-2516

US Courthouse
100 East 5th Street
Room 735
Cincinnati OH 45202
Phone: 513-684-2572

411 US Courthouse
1716 Spielbusch Avenue
Toledo OH 43624
Phone: 419-259-6440

US Courthouse
127 Public Square
Cleveland OH 44114
Phone: 216-522-4373

9 West Front
Youngstown OH 44501
Phone: 216-746-7027

Oklahoma

Post Office-Courthouse
215 D A McGee Avenue
Oklahoma City OK 73102
Phone: 405-231-5141

320 Grantson Building
111 West 5th Street
Tulsa OK 74103
Phone: 918-581-7181

PO Box 1347
US Post Office & Federal Building
Okmulgee OK 74447
Phone: 918-758-0126

Oregon

PO Box 1335
404 Federal Building
211 East 7th Street
Eugene OR 97440
Phone: 503-465-6448

1001 SW 5th Avenue
9th Floor
Portland OR 97204
Phone: 503-326-2231

Pennsylvania

PO Box 1755
314 US Courthouse
Erie PA 16507
Phone: 814-453-7580

1602 Federal Building
1000 Liberty Avenue
Pittsburgh PA 15222
Phone: 412-644-2700

PO Box 908
Federal Building
3rd & Walnut Streets
Harrisburg PA 17108
Phone: 717-782-2260

400 Washington Street
The Madison
Room 350
Reading PA 19601
Phone: 215-320-5255

3726 US Courthouse
601 Market Street
Philadelphia PA 19106
Phone: 215-597-1644

217 Federal Building
197 South Main Street
Wilkes-Barre PA 18701
Phone: 717-826-6450

Rhode Island

380 Westminster Mall
Federal Center
Providence RI 02903
Phone: 401-528-4477

South Carolina

PO Box 1448
1100 Laurel Street
Columbia SC 29202
Phone: 803-765-5436

South Dakota

PO Box 5060
104 Federal Building & US Courthouse
400 South Phillips Avenue
Sioux Falls SD 57117
Phone: 605-330-4541

Tennessee

31 East 11th Street
Chattanooga TN 37401
Phone: 615-752-5163

200 Jefferson Avenue
Room 413
Memphis TN 38103
Phone: 901-544-3202

PO Box 1527
Jackson TN 38302
Phone: 901-424-9751

207 Customs House
701 Broadway
Nashville TN 37203
Phone: 615-736-5590

Texas

624 South Polk Street
Amarillo TX 79101
Phone: 806-376-2302

816 Congress
First City Centre
Room 1420
Austin TX 78701
Phone: 512-482-5237

300 Willow Street
Suite 100
Beaumont TX 77701
Phone: 409-839-2617

615 Leopard Street
Suite 113
Corpus Christi TX 78476
Phone: 512-888-3487

14-A-7 US Courthouse
1100 Commerce Street
Dallas TX 75242
Phone: 214-767-0814

111 East Broadway
Room L100
Del Rio TX 78840
Phone: 512-775-2021

511 East San Antonio Street
El Paso TX 79901
Phone: 915-598-6769

501 West 16th Street
Room 310
Fort Worth TX 76102
Phone: 817-334-3802

Federal Building
515 Rusk Avenue
4th Floor
Houston TX 77002
Phone: 713-250-5150

102 Federal Building
1205 Texas Avenue
Lubbock TX 79401
Phone: 806-743-7336

316 US Courthouse
200 Wall Street
Midland TX 79701
Phone: 915-683-2001

PO Box 191
Pecos TX 79772
Phone: 915-445-4228

First Interstate Bank Building
660 North Central Expressway
Suite 300B
Plano TX 75074
Phone: 214-423-6605

PO Box 1439
Old Post Office Building
615 East Houston Street
Room 139
San Antonio TX 78295
Phone: 512-229-6720

200 East Ferguson Street
2nd Floor
Tyler TX 75702
Phone: 903-592-1212

US Courthouse
800 Franklin
Room 303
Waco TX 76701
Phone: 817-756-0307

Utah

350 South Main Street
Salt Lake City UT 84101
Phone: 801-524-5157

Vermont

PO Box 6648
67 Merchants Row
Rutland VT 05702
Phone: 802-747-7625

Virginia

408 Dominion Bank Building
206 North Washington Street
Alexandria VA 22314
Phone: 703-557-1716

PO Box 586
320 Federal Building
Harrisonburg VA 22801
Phone: 703-434-6747

PO Box 442
226 Federal Building
Lynchburg VA 24505
Phone: 804-845-8880

222 US Post Office Building
101 25th Floor
Newport News VA 23612
Phone: 804-595-9805

480 Courthouse
600 Gramby Street
Norfolk VA 23510
Phone: 804-441-6651

US Courthouse Annex Building
Richmond VA 23206
Phone: 804-771-2878

PO Box 2390
200 Old Federal Building
210 Church Avenue
Roanoke VA 24011
Phone: 703-857-2391

Washington

315 Park Place Building
1200 6th Avenue
Seattle WA 98101
Phone: 206-553-7545

PO Box 2164
904 West Riverside Avenue
Room 321
Spokane WA 92210
Phone: 509-353-2404

1717 Pacific Avenue
Room 2100
Tacoma WA 98402
Phone: 206-593-6310

West Virginia

PO Box 3924
500 Quarrier Street
Room 2201
Charleston WV 25339
Phone: 304-347-5337

PO Box 70
12th & Chapline Street
Wheeling WV 26003
Phone: 304-233-1655

Wisconsin

PO Box 5009
500 South Barstow Commons
Eau Claire WI 54702
Phone: 715-839-2985

PO Box 548
Room 340
120 North Henry
Madison WI 53701
Phone: 608-264-5178

216 Federal Building
517 East Wisconsin Avenue
Room 171
Milwaukee WI 53202
Phone: 414-297-3291

Wyoming

PO Box 1107
Cheyenne WY 82003
Phone: 307-772-2191

Glossary of Bankruptcy Legal Terms

Annuity: An insurance contract which pays the insured person during their life, rather than paying a beneficiary after the insured person's death. An annuity is a type of retirement plan.

Asset: Anything of value. May be *real estate* or *personal property*. Personal property can be *tangible* or *intangible property*.

Attachment: The seizure or repossession of property by a governmental agent. Generally, attachment is carried out by a county sheriff or the Internal Revenue Service.

Automatic stay: An court order from the bankruptcy court which goes into effect automatically upon filing for bankruptcy. It orders creditors to stop taking any further action to collect on any debts owed by the debtor filing for bankruptcy.

Bankruptcy Code: The U.S. Bankruptcy Code is the set of U.S. laws relating to bankruptcy. They are contained in Title 11 and Title 28 of the United States Code.

Bankruptcy Court Rules: In addition to the Bankruptcy Code, there are three further sets of rules which govern the procedures in Bankruptcy Courts: the Federal Rules of Bankruptcy Procedure; the Federal Rules of Civil Procedure; and Local Bankruptcy Court Rules. Local bankruptcy court rules may not conflict with any of the federal rules.

Bankruptcy Courts: The United States is divided into various bankruptcy court districts. All bankruptcy court districts are referenced by the name of the state (Federal Bankruptcy Court, Idaho District). Many districts are also referenced geographically, if there is more than one district within the state (ie. Southern District of Illinois).

Bankruptcy estate: All of the property, whether real estate or personal property, which is owned by a debtor who files for bankruptcy. Control over the bankruptcy estate is given to the court by filing for bankruptcy.

Bankruptcy petition preparer: A private non-lawyer paralegal who can assist persons in preparing the legal papers necessary for bankruptcy. They may not, however, provide any legal advice. They are now authorized and regulated by the Bankruptcy Code.

Bankruptcy trustee: A person who is appointed by the bankruptcy court to handle the *bankruptcy estate* of a debtor. The trustee will examine the papers, handle the *creditors meeting*, collect and sell any *non-exempt property*, and pay off the creditors.

Co-signor: A person who has also signed loan or contract with another and who is jointly liable on the loan or contract.

Codebtor: A person who is jointly liable on a particular debt, either because of co-signing on the debt, acting as a guarantor on the debt, or by virtue of being a spouse or partner of the debtor.

Common law property: Property in those states which follow common law property rules. In general, the ownership of common law property is determined by the name on the title document for the property. This is true for married couples also, with the exception of gifts or inheritances which are received jointly and thus held jointly. See also *community property*.

Community property: Property held by a husband and wife in those states which follow community property law rules (Arizona, California, Idaho, Louisiana, Nevada, New Mexico, Texas, Washington, Wisconsin). Generally, all property which either spouse receives during their marriage is owned jointly by both spouses and is referred to as *community property*. See also *common law property*.

Creditor: A creditor is a person or entity (corporation, partnership, etc.) who is owed a debt of some type. Creditors may be *secured creditors* who hold the title or a lien or some form of collateral for the debt. Creditors may also be *unsecured creditors* who have no security for the debt.

Creditors meeting: This meeting is held in all Chapter 7 bankruptcies approximately 1 month after filing. It is attended by the bankruptcy trustee and the debtor(s). It may also be attended by any of the creditors. At this meeting the bankruptcy papers will be examined, priority claims determined, and the property which is exempt will be resolved.

Debtor: A debtor is a person (or entity) who owes a debt of some kind. The persons or entities who file for bankruptcy are referred to as debtors in the court papers.

Debts: A debt is an obligation of some type which is owed to another person or entity. A debt may be secured if collateral of some type has been pledged or if a lien exists against some type of property. A debt may also be unsecured if there is no collateral securing the debt. Debts may also be further classified as contingent, unliquidated, or liquidated. See those definitions.

Disability benefits: Payments made to a person under a disability insurance plan because of injury, disability, or sickness.

Discharge: The total elimination of all dischargeable debts. This is the final result of a Chapter 7 bankruptcy.

Dischargeable debts: Those debts which may, by bankruptcy law, be discharged (eliminated) by a bankruptcy action. See also *non-dischargeable debts*.

Disputed debts: Those debts which a debtor claims are in error, either in part or in whole.

ERISA benefits: Payments made to a person under a pension or retirement plan which qualifies under the Federal Employees Retirement Income Security Act. IRA's, KEOGH's, and many other pensions are ERISA plans. Ask your retirement plan administrator.

Execution: The process of seizing and selling property under a court order or judgement for a money judgement against a person or entity.

Executory contract: A contract which is not fully completed, which has some obligation or action yet to be fulfilled.

Exempt property: Property which may not be seized, repossessed by a private creditor, or executed against by a government agent because of debts which the owner has incurred. Property may either be exempt based on state or federal law.

Family farm bankruptcy: A Chapter 12 bankruptcy. Similar to a Chapter 13 bankruptcy but which is only available to those debtors who fit the description of a "family farmer".

Fraternal society benefits: Group life or other insurance benefits which are maintained and paid to members by fraternal societies, such as the Elks, Masons, Moose, etc.

Group insurance: A single insurance policy under which a group of persons is covered. Often employee insurance plans are based on group insurance policies.

Guarantor: A person who has agreed to guarantee payment on a debt should the original debtor fail to keep up on the required payments.

Health aids: Items or material which a person uses to maintain their own health, such as a wheelchair.

Health benefits: Payments made to a person under a health insurance policy.

Homestead declaration: A document which is placed on county property records which asserts your homestead exemption. Filing such a declaration is a requirement in certain states in order to take advantage of your homestead exemption. Check your state's listing in Appendix B.

Homestead exemption: A state or federal exemption which protects a personal residence from being seized to pay for the owner's debts. Often is limited to only a certain dollar value.

Household goods: Non-disposable items which are used to maintain a household, such as dishes, utensils, pots and pans, lamps, radios, etc.

Insurance benefits: Payments made to a person under an insurance policy.

Intangible property: Property which has no actual existence, such as stocks, bonds, copyrights, trademarks, etc. These items may be represented by some type of document, but the property itself has no physical existence. See also *tangible property*.

Involuntary bankruptcy: A bankruptcy action which is instituted by creditors against a debtor who has defaulted on debt obligations.

Joint tenancy: Joint ownership of property in which the owners of the property hold equal undivided ownership interest in the property and which each owner has the right of survivorship (the survivor will automatically inherit the other's interest on death).

Judgement lien: A real estate lien which has been established by a court order or judgement. The lien is recorded on official records and generally must be satisfied before the property is sold.

Judgement: The final determination by a court of the matter before it.

Liability: A legal obligation or debt.

Lien: A legal claim against property for the payment of a debt.

Life insurance: A contract under which an insurance company agrees to pay a specified sum to a beneficiary upon the death of the insured person.

Liquidate: To sell a debtor's property and pay off any debts. To finally settle all debts.

Liquidation bankruptcy: A Chapter 7 bankruptcy. A bankruptcy in which all non-exempt property is sold to pay off all debts.

Lost future earnings: The amount of money awarded in a personal injury lawsuit to cover the amount of future income which the plaintiff is determined to have lost because of the injury.

Mailing label matrix: A particular column and row arrangement of mailing addresses. It is required by many bankruptcy courts in order to make duplicate mailing labels for notification of creditors and other parties to a bankruptcy.

Matured life insurance benefits: Life insurance benefits which are currently payable to a beneficiary (because the insured person has already died).

Motor vehicle: Any vehicle which is powered by a mechanical engine.

Necessities: Items which are necessary to sustain life. Generally, food, clothing, and medical care are considered necessities.

Non-dischargeable debts: Those debts which can not be eliminated in a bankruptcy proceeding. Certain taxes, student loans, alimony, child support, and other debts are non-dischargeable.

Non-purchase money debt: A debt which is incurred other than to purchase the collateral for the debt, such as a home equity loan.

Pain and suffering payments: The amount of money awarded in a personal injury lawsuit to cover the amount of pain and suffering which the plaintiff is determined to have suffered because of the injury.

Pension benefits: Benefits which a person receives or will receive upon retirement. Generally received from some type of pension fund.

Personal injury causes of action: The right to file a suit and claim a right to compensation for personal injuries which may have occurred.

Personal property: All property, either intangible or tangible, which is not real estate. See also *real estate*.

Possessory lien: A right to seize and sell property which attaches to the property by law, such as a moving company's right to sell property which it has moved and has not been paid for.

Possessory non-purchase money debt: A debt which is incurred other than to purchase the collateral for the debt, and for which the creditor obtains possession of the collateral, such as a loan by a pawnshop for a pawned item.

Priority claims: Those claims for unsecured debts which, by law, are to be paid off in a bankruptcy before any other unsecured debts are paid. The most common priority claim is for the payment of taxes.

Proof of Service: An official statement under oath that a person has delivered to (served) another a specific legal document.

Purchase money debt: A debt which is incurred to purchase the property which is the collateral for the debt.

Reaffirmation of a debt: An agreement by a debtor to pay off a debt, regardless of bankruptcy. Must be approved by both the creditor and the bankruptcy court. A reaffirmed debt is not eliminated by bankruptcy, even if the debt was dischargeable.

Real estate: All land and any items which are permanently attached to the land, such as buildings.

Redemption of property: In bankruptcy, a debtor may purchase personal property which is subject to a creditors lien by payment of the market value of the property.

Reorganization bankruptcy: A Chapter 11 bankruptcy under which a business attempts to reorganize its affairs in order to satisfy its debt obligations.

Repossession: The taking, by a creditor of a defaulted-upon loan, of the collateral for the loan.

Retirement benefits: Those benefits which are paid to a person by reason of their retirement from a job or by virtue of their employment for a certain number of years.

Secured debts: Debts for which the creditors have some form of security for their repayment, such as collateral or a lien.

Setoff: The application by a creditor of other assets of a debtor to lessen the amount of debt, such as the application of a debtor's bank account balance to a pay off a defaulted loan.

Tangible property: Property which has existence, which may be touched. See also *intangible property*.

Tenancy by the entireties: A form of joint ownership of property by wives and husbands only (only in certain states). Similar to *joint tenancy* with a right of survivorship, but for married couples only.

Tools: Those items which are necessary to perform a certain type of work. For bankruptcy, any items which are used in a trade or business may generally qualify as a tool, including computers, motor vehicles, etc.

Unexpired lease: A lease which is still in force.

Unsecured nonpriority debts: Those debts which have no collateral pledged and which are not priority debts by law.

Unsecured priority debts: See *priority claims*.

Voluntary bankruptcy: A bankruptcy which is voluntarily filed by the debtor in an effort to obtain relief from debts.

Wages: The amount of money paid on a regular basis for work.

Wrongful death benefits: The amount of money awarded in a wrongful death lawsuit to compensate the plaintiff for having to live without the deceased person.

Index

Nova Publishing Company

The Finest in Small Business and Consumer Legal Books

Incorporate Your Business: The National Corporation Kit (1st Edition)

ISBN 0935755098	*256 pp.*	*8 .5" X 11"*	*$18.95*
Forms on Disk (ASCII format)	*IBM or MAC*	*3.5" or 5.25"*	*$12.95*

Contains clear, straight-forward information to help you maximize your business profits by turning your business into a corporation. Includes all of the forms and instructions that you will need to incorporate in any state. Forms are also available on computer disk.

Debt Free: The National Bankruptcy Kit (1st Edition)

ISBN 0935755187	*256 pp.*	*8 .5" X 11"*	*$17.95*

Everything you will need to file for personal bankruptcy. Contains forms, questionnaires, worksheets, checklists and instructions--all in understandable plain English. Includes information to allow you to prevent creditors from harassing you, keep the maximum amount of your property, and obtain a Chapter 7 personal bankruptcy.

Simplified Small Business Accounting (1st Edition)

ISBN 0935755152	*256 pp.*	*8 .5" X 11"*	*$17.95*

Everything that a small business will need to set up their accounting and bookkeeping records. Contains all of the forms and instructions necessary. Ledgers, expense records, profit and loss statements, balance sheets, payroll records, inventory records, and many more--all in plain and understandable English.

The Complete Book of Small Business Legal Forms (1st Edition)

ISBN 0935755039	*248 pp.*	*8 .5" X 11"*	*$17.95*
Forms on Disk (ASCII format)	*IBM or MAC*	*3.5" or 5.25"*	*$12.95*

A comprehensive business reference containing over 125 legal documents and instructions for use in small businesses. Includes contracts, leases, deeds, partnerships, collections documents, promissory notes, and many more. Forms are also available on computer disk.

The Complete Book of Personal Legal Forms (1st Edition)

ISBN 0935755101	*248 pp.*	*8 .5" X 11"*	*$16.95*
Forms on Disk (ASCII format)	*IBM or MAC*	*3.5" or 5.25"*	*$12.95*

A complete family legal reference containing over 100 plain-language legal forms and clear instructions for their use. Includes contracts, leases, marital agreements, wills, trusts, bills of sale, powers of attorney, and many others. Forms are also available on computer disk.

Prepare Your Own Will: The National Will Kit (4th Edition)

ISBN 0935755128	*256 pp.*	*8 .5" X 11"*	*$15.95*
W/Forms on Disk (ASCII format) ISBN 0935755241	*3.5" IBM*		*$27.95*

The most highly-recommended book available on preparing a will without a lawyer. Includes everything you will need to prepare your own will, living will, and medical power-of-attorney. Easy to use and understandable. This book is also available with all forms on computer disk.

Divorce Yourself: The National No-Fault Divorce Kit (3rd Edition)

ISBN 0935755136	*320 pp.*	*8 .5" X 11"*	*$24.95*
W/Forms on Disk (ASCII format) ISBN 093575525X	*3.5" IBM*		*$34.95*

The most critically-acclaimed divorce guide available. Contains all of the legal forms and instructions necessary to obtain a no-fault divorce in any state without a lawyer. Includes clear and understandable instructions. This book is also available with all forms on computer disk.

♦ Ordering Information ♦

♦ **by Phone:** (800)462-6420 (MasterCard and Visa)
♦ **by FAX:** (301)459-2118 (MasterCard and Visa)
♦ **by Mail:** Nova Publishing Company
    1103 West College Street
    Carbondale IL 62901
    Phone: (800)748-1175

♦ **Library and book trade orders:**
National Book Network
4720 Boston Way
Lanham MD 20706
Phone: (800)462-6420 *or*
Baker and Taylor/Ingram/Quality/Unique

Please include shipping and handling of $3.50 for first book or disk and $.75 for each additional book or disk.
Forms on Disk must be ordered by mail from Nova Publishing Co. Please indicate IBM or MAC and disk size.
Forms on Disk are in ASCII format and may be used with any computer word-processing program.